MY FAVOURITE DICTATORS

BY CHRIS MIKUL

ILLUSTRATIONS BY GLENN SMITH

A HEADPRESS BOOK
First published by Headpress in 2019
headoffice@headpress.com

MY FAVOURITE DICTATORS
The Strange Lives of Tyrants

Cover & book design : MARK CRITCHELL
: mark.critchell@googlemail.com

10 9 8 7 6 5 4 3 ~~2~~ ~~1~~

A CIP catalogue record for this book is available from the British Library

ISBN 978-1-909394-70-4 (paperback)
ISBN 978-1-909394-71-1 (ebook)
NO-ISBN (hardback)

HEADPRESS. POP AND UNPOP CULTURE.

CONTENTS

INTRODUCTION

he gold-plated statue of Saparmurat Niyazov, arms raised to the sky and a billowing flag behind him, was 39 feet (12 metres) tall. It stood atop a huge, rocket-like structure with three arched legs at its base, in the centre of Ashgabat, the capital of Turkmenistan. By night the statue was floodlit, by day it revolved imperceptibly so that it always faced the sun.

The statue was the most visible symbol of the rule of Niyazov, dictator of the oil-rich, former Soviet republic from the early 1990s to his death in 2006. Originally appointed the republic's leader by Mikhail Gorbachev in 1985, he jettisoned communism as soon as the country gained independence, embraced nationalism and adopted the title of Turkmenbashi — 'Father of all Turkmen'. There followed a flood of edicts as Niyazov reshaped the tiny country in his image. He renamed the months of January and April after himself and his mother. He banned car radios, smoking, lip-syncing to songs, opera, circuses and beards on young men. He had ten thousand statues of himself erected around the country, explaining "I'm personally against seeing my pictures and statues in the streets, but it's what the people want." And he poured all his wisdom into a quasi-religious book, the *Ruhnama* ('Book of the Spirit'). Everyone in the country was expected to study the book — Niyazov declared that reading it three times would guarantee you a place in heaven — and questions about it were asked during driving tests. Even more worryingly, when Niyazov developed a hatred of doctors towards the end of his rule and dismissed thousands of them, the *Ruhmana* supplanted medical textbooks throughout the country.

In his youth, Niyazov studied to be an electrical engineer. Had he remained an electrical engineer, he may very well have led a totally unremarkable life. But becoming a dictator does peculiar things to people.

We have the word 'dictator' from the ancient Romans. It originally signified a magistrate who, during a time of crisis and for a limited time (no more than six months), was given absolute authority over his fellow magistrates to lay down the law. So, if there was some terrible portent like a comet in the sky, a dictator would order the appropriate religious rituals; and during a period of civil unrest, he would do what was necessary to reimpose order. The term fell into disuse for around a century, but was revived by the general Lucius Cornelius Sulla when he and his army seized control of Rome in 82 BC. Sulla's aim was to enact laws that would restore the powers of the Senate, but there would be no time limit to his dictatorship. He immediately set about settling scores with his enemies, ordering thousands of noblemen and their relatives to be 'proscribed', which meant that anyone who murdered them would receive a reward, and so, as Plutarch put it, "filled the city with deaths without number or limit". Some of these victims were genuine political enemies, but most were killed for their property, which enriched Sulla and his cronies. With this mixture of bloodthirstiness and avarice, Sulla can be said to have set the template for all the dictators who would follow him — with one exception. Once he had put his laws in place, he resigned his dictatorship and restored normal government. That's a move few if any of his successors would make.

Every dictatorship is an elaborate social experiment in which an individual is given almost limitless power, and the results are almost invariably dire. Of course, Lord Acton's dictum that 'absolute power corrupts absolutely' is one of the hoariest of political clichés, but the power wielded by

dictators differs significantly from that traditionally wielded by emperors, monarchs or popes. While they may spend some of their time shuffling the elite members of society about, depending on who is in or out of favour, emperors, monarchs and popes have always been primarily concerned with maintaining the status quo within their own constituencies. Dictators have no such constraints. (The exception to this rule, at least among the dictators gathered within this volume, is Kim Jong-il, who attained power by presenting himself as the man best equipped to maintain the extraordinarily repressive system put in place in North Korea by his father, Kim Il-sung.) The most dangerous dictators are the visionaries, those who would tear up the status quo and replace it with another of their own making. Saparmurat Niyazov was such a visionary, and he had thousands of people who didn't buy into his vision imprisoned or exiled. But Turkmenistan is a relatively small country with a population of around five million, so there was a limit to the human havoc he could wreak. Other dictators have had far broader canvases to work on, and the result has been death and devastation on a scale that is difficult to process.

How should we react when confronted by this? Should we clap our hands to our mouths in horror? Should we turn on the human race itself, appalled by what poor stuff we can be? Should we look into ourselves and contemplate how we might act under a totalitarian regime? Yes, we should do all that, for the rich crop of dictators thrown up during the benighted twentieth century were collectively, by virtually any means you wish to measure it, among the worst criminals in history. But that doesn't mean we shouldn't also laugh at them.

Laugh bitterly, perhaps, but laugh all the same, for the most potent weapon we have against dictators is laughter. And usefully, many dictators collude in this process by being as ridiculous as possible.

This is no great insight of mine, of course. Dictators have always been prime targets for satire, from Charlie Chaplin's *The Great Dictator*, a poetic take, to Mel Brooks and the 'Springtime for Hitler' sequence in *The Producers*, a throwback to burlesque. Dictators almost beg to be sent up, and, amazingly, even Hitler understood this. In *Hitler: Ascent 1889-1939*, Volker Ullrich recounts how the Führer once did an impression of Mussolini, his political idol who, nevertheless, spurned him. "His chin thrust forward, his legs spread and his right hand on his hip, Hitler bellowed Italian or Italian-sounding words like giovinezza, patria, victoria, macaroni, belleza, bel canto and basta". Albert Speer said it was "indeed very funny".

When considering the myriad absurd pretensions of dictators, it's difficult to know where to begin. Their ostentatious costumes, from elaborate uniforms to the utterly bizarre creations worn by late-period Gaddafi, are too well known for comment, so let's start with literature, for many dictators have considered themselves to be great writers. Lenin paved the way here, his voluminous, belligerent and insult-laden writings being his chief weapon in the years leading up to the Russian Revolution. Following his example, no communist dictator during the twentieth century could consider himself truly legitimate until a multi-volume edition of his collected works was taking up a great deal of space on his country's bookshelves. (Whether he had actually written all the words in those books was by the by). But some dictators have felt the need to expand beyond dry political theory. In his final years, Saddam Hussein wrote several peculiar historical novels beginning with *Zabiba and the King*, and became so consumed by the idea of being a writer that, by the end, he seemed to have forgotten how to be a dictator. Gaddafi published two collections of 'stories', which range from odd allegories and fables to deranged rants. Mao, on the other hand, displayed some genuine literary talent. Some of the early articles and reports he wrote are much livelier and more vivid than the usual communist fare, while he had an unerring knack for coming up with catchy slogans (although he lifted some of them, including 'Let a thousand flowers bloom', from classical Chinese works). Mao also wrote poetry throughout his life. During the years when virtually every left-wing intellectual in the West was starry-eyed about him (don't get me started on the French), there were claims that he was actually a fine poet. That's going way too far, but his poetry, while often bombastic, does have some merit. The best writer among this sorry lot was, perhaps surprisingly, Mussolini, who was bombast incarnate. He wrote pungent journalism in his early years, published a vivid World War I diary recounting his experiences as a soldier, and even penned a novel, *The Cardinal's Mistress*, which is quite interesting and oddly prophetic. (More about this in the chapter on Mussolini.)

Dictators have, thankfully, usually stayed away from creating art (Hitler's early efforts aside), but are renowned for promoting the worst that art has to offer. Think Stalin's beloved 'socialist realism', the awful, clichéd and stodgy 'Aryan' art favoured by the Nazis, and the frighteningly cheery propaganda paintings of North Korea. Genuine art, art as a form of self-expression by an artist, is usually one of the first things to be supressed once a dictatorship takes over.

Sometimes it seems that there's no form of human expression that a dictator can't lay a dead hand on. Even interior decoration isn't safe, as demonstrated by Peter York's marvellous coffee table book *Dictators' Homes*. Dictators often come from humble beginnings, and once they have attained power, their ideas about appropriate spaces to live in — and more importantly be seen in — usually hark back to a very old-fashioned and stereotyped vision of opulence.

Dictators tend to go for neo-classical features and Louis XIV-style furnishings. Gilt abounds, as do marble floors, wood-panelled walls, chandeliers, oil paintings, tapestries and statues, while solid-gold taps in bathrooms seem almost obligatory. The results, as seen in the photos in York's book, are interiors that manage to look both lavish and cheap, while there is barely a single room that looks comfortable.

The truly successful dictators are those who manage to organise all aspects of their societies so that they reinforce their regime's ideology. Art, architecture, language, costume, design, movement and, of course, the entire apparatus of mass communication are all bent to the ruling party's ideology. The culmination of this is the mass event so beloved of totalitarian rulers, the meticulously choreographed rallies and military parades where a city is transformed into a film set with the dictator in the role of director.

I don't think it's a coincidence that so many dictators have been ardent fans of cinema, although their tastes, admittedly, varied widely. Hitler loved Fritz Lang's grandiose *Metropolis*, along with Hollywood productions such as *King Kong* (reputedly his all-time favourite film) and *Snow White and the Seven Dwarves*. (Even more puzzlingly, he is supposed to have enjoyed the films of the Marx Brothers.) Stalin employed his own projectionist, one Alexander Ganshin, who managed to hold down his job for eighteen years (perhaps a record among Stalin's inner circle). Mussolini is said to have had his own print of *Extase*, the 1933 film famous for Hedy Lamarr's nude swim. Mao became a great fan of Bruce Lee films in his later years, and Enver Hoxha adored the British comedian Norman Wisdom to such an extent that Wisdom's films were virtually the only Western productions Albanians were allowed to see during his rule. But it was Kim Jong-il who took cinephilia to its greatest heights. He amassed the largest collection of movies from all over the world ever put together by an individual, fancied himself a cinematic genius, oversaw the production of dozens of films, and wrote a textbook for directors.

I have so far been dwelling on the similarities between dictators, and it's tempting to think we can put them all in a box and say they are fundamentally the same in terms of psychology. And yet, while they share many characteristics (I think we can take overweening egotism and a lack of empathy for other human beings bordering on psychopathy as givens), the fact is that there are a great many differences between them. Take their sex lives, which are invariably a subject of some fascination. Dictators are, almost by definition, individuals who can have virtually anything they want, and people are naturally curious to know whether their appetites and excesses extend to sex. In some cases, they do. Mussolini's powers of seduction over women were an integral part of his public image, Mao's appetite for very young girls only increased the longer he lived, and Gaddafi (easily the worst in this department, as you will see) spent most of his waking hours raping anyone with a pulse. On the other hand, Stalin was content with having two wives and two or three mistresses, Marcos's acquisition of a sole mistress ended in farce, and Ceauşescu seems to have never been unfaithful to his wife Elena (although that may have been because he was frightened of her). As for Hitler, despite determined attempts to assign various sexual proclivities and perversions to him over the years, the man appears to have been essentially asexual.

The dictators considered in this book also attained power in markedly different ways. Gaddafi was certainly the most precocious, having set his sights on absolute power as a schoolboy and attaining it in his twenties. Ceauşescu, on the other hand, spent decades being (in Yevgeny Zamyatin's phrase) "a diligent and trustworthy functionary" within the Romanian Communist Party before taking the ultimate prize. Marcos entered politics via his father, who was also a politician (albeit an exceptionally ruthless one). For African dictators, the fastest path to power has usually been to rise through the ranks of the army, then mount a coup. This was the route that Gaddafi, Idi Amin and Bokassa all took. François Duvalier, AKA Papa Doc, initially wanted to be a doctor and ethnographer — ambitions that he realised — before becoming, almost by accident, a government minister while in his forties, and it was this that set him on the path to his particularly brutal dictatorship.

The only conclusion I can draw from this is that dictators are created as much by circumstance as by their own ambitions. Under different circumstances, many of the men we know today as inhuman monsters may have lived completely mundane, now forgotten lives.

My interest in dictators goes back a long way, back to my childhood in fact. I was born in Sydney in 1961 and grew up in one of its quiet, sun-drenched suburbs, seemingly a long way from the baleful influence of any dictator. But the bookshelves in my house contained books like William L. Shirer's *The Rise and Fall of the Third Reich*; Robert Payne's biography of Stalin; Eugen Kogon's history of Nazi concentration camps, *The Theory and Practice of Hell*; and other works on World War II and the Cold War. From the time I could read I was looking through these books, trying to figure out what they were all about, wondering who these strange, larger-than-life beings Hitler and Stalin were.

The books had been bought by my father, Jaroslav Mikuliča, who had been born in Czechoslovakia in 1927. He had lived through the war, then the early years of Communist rule, before managing to get out in the early 1950s and come to Australia as a refugee, where he did what they often did at the time and shortened his name. He was a man of very few words, and said virtually nothing about his experiences during the war, barring a single story about once seeing a crashed German plane with the pilot dead in the cockpit. Then, one day in around 1973, my mother came into the living room where I was sitting and said that Dad and just told her he had been a prisoner in Dachau. I can't say that I was as surprised about this as much as she was. My father had always said that the tattooed number on his arm had been given to him by the Russians when they made him work down the mines after the war, but I was familiar enough with the war by then to know that didn't sound right. He never mentioned it again.

Thanks to those books of my father's I had become obsessed with World War II. I eagerly watched films like *The Dam Busters* and *The Wooden Horse*, read books about escapes from prison camps, and made Airfix models of planes like the Spitfire and the Lancaster, the Stuka dive bomber and the Messerschmitt 109. I watched the magnificent documentary series *The World at War* entranced, and my best friend John and I even shot a Super 8 film version of it in my backyard. We recreated the burning opening credits, and John played Hitler.

Like many idealistic young people, I went through a period of being attracted to Marxism and communism while I was at school, although thankfully it didn't last long. (Reading Albert Camus's *The Rebel* was enough to bring it to an abrupt end.) But, although I had realised that communism was a dead end, I remained fascinated by communist countries. World War II was history, but the world of communism was still very much alive, and I had a direct connection as all my father's relatives lived in Czechoslovakia. I began to pick up dusty booklets and pamphlets by Lenin and Stalin that I found in left-wing bookshops, oddly fascinated by their turgid prose. For a while, I even kept a copy of Mao's Little Red Book in the pocket of my school blazer, and would occasionally produce it and read its inanities out to my schoolmates.

I've always been fascinated — and inspired — by eccentrics, those rare individuals who thumb their noses at conformity and live their lives as they please. On one level, many dictators have behaved so peculiarly and outrageously that there are similarities between the two breeds, but there are fundamental differences. True eccentrics are almost always fundamentally benevolent individuals, and they have generally exhibited signs of eccentricity from an early age. Dictators, of course, are rarely benevolent, and it's doubtful that their eccentric traits would have emerged had they not attained such absurd levels of power. I suppose you could also argue that, if eccentrics are people who reject the rules and conventions of their societies, and dictators are the ones who set them, a dictator can never truly be an eccentric. (I think I have to make an exception for Saparmurat Niyazov though.)

Now, finally, you may be wondering why Hitler and Stalin aren't in this book. Is it because they were two of the greatest mass murderers of the twentieth century? No — Mao was responsible for more deaths than Hitler and Stalin combined, and he's in here. Is it because they were responsible for blighting my father's early years? No — that would make me even more eager to get stuck into them. No, it's because they were both, at the end of the day, very dull men, and they're not among my favourites.

CHAPTER 1

BENITO MUSSOLINI

BENITO MUSSOLINI

Attained power in 1925
Murdered and strung up beside his mistress in 1945

as there ever a greater posturer than Mussolini? In collective memory he stands on a balcony addressing a crowd below, hands on hips, head thrown back, lips pursed and massive chin thrust forward, posturing away. Or there he is shoulder-to-shoulder with his friend Adolf Hitler, resplendent in their uniforms as massed ranks of goose-stepping soldiers pass by, totalitarian twins intent on dragging the West down to a new age of barbarism.

Yet it would be wrong to draw too close a comparison between Mussolini and Hitler. Mussolini was never driven, as Hitler was, by a grand ideology that pretended to be both a religion and a science. While he started out as a socialist firebrand, he was essentially a pragmatist who could have ended up anywhere on the ideological map, and his invention of Fascism was almost accidental. Mussolini really only believed in himself, so his entire political career was also little more than a series of elaborate postures.

enito Mussolini was born in Predappio, a town in the Italian province of Forli, in the Romagna region, on 29 July 1883. His mother, Rosa, was a schoolteacher; his father Alessandro, a blacksmith and ardent socialist who named his son after the Mexican revolutionary Benito Juarez. The young Mussolini had a hot temper and, aged ten, was expelled from one school after stabbing another boy in the buttock. He lost his virginity early to a prostitute who, he wrote,

"sweated from every pore". While still a schoolboy he started to dress in black to distinguish himself from other boys, and when he wasn't fighting or fornicating, he might be heard reciting poetry or playing the violin.

In the end Mussolini did well enough at school, and was briefly a schoolmaster. He acquired his first mistress, a soldier's wife whom he once stabbed in the leg during a quarrel. When the scandal of this affair led to the school not renewing his contract, he moved to Switzerland in 1902, worked there as a labourer and sometimes slept rough. Having inherited his father's political beliefs, he wrote inflammatory articles for socialist newspapers and devoured the works of Marx, Kropotkin and other philosophers of the left (while also imbibing a healthy dose of elitism from Nietzsche). His clothes may have been shabby, he shaved rarely and bathed less, but he was already a magnetic speaker and his passion for the cause was obvious. The Swiss authorities imprisoned him twice for inciting disorder, burnishing his socialist credentials. Back in Italy in 1904, he was referred to in a Roman newspaper as the *grande duce* of the socialists in his area, possibly the first time the word *duce* (leader) was applied to him.

He returned to Forli and in 1909 moved into a small apartment with Rachele Guidi, the daughter of his father's mistress. They first met when Rachele was a pupil in Mussolini's mother's classroom, and he, a replacement teacher, rapped her over the fingers with a ruler. Mussolini encountered her again a few years later and asked her to marry him, but at first she put him off. He grew more insistent, and a meeting took place at Rachele's mother's house where she told him that if he did not stop pestering her daughter she would notify the authorities. Mussolini left the room, then returned with a revolver and told her it had six bullets in it. "If Rachele turns me down, there will be one bullet for her and five for me."

Rachele agreed to his proposal immediately.

Rachele was a no-nonsense peasant and would remain so in the turbulent decades that followed. The following year she gave birth to Edda, the first of the five children they would have (they eventually married in 1915). Mussolini's fame among Italian socialists continued to grow, although some were put off by his insistence on "the iron necessity of violence". He churned out articles attacking capitalism, militarism, nationalism and Christianity, edited a socialist newspaper called *La Lotta di Classe* ('The Class Struggle'), and found the time to pen a lurid anti-clerical novel set in the seventeenth century, *The Cardinal's Mistress*, which was serialised in the newspaper *Il Popolo* (whose editor had suggested he write it). It tells the story of Cardinal Emanuel Madruzzo, ruler of the principality of Trent, and his much younger mistress, Claudia Particella. The Cardinal wants his niece, Filberta, to marry Claudia's brother, but she is in love with another man and refuses. Banished to a nunnery, she dies of tuberculosis. The people of Trent are outraged when they hear of this, and turn on Claudia and the Cardinal.

Mussolini's only attempt at fiction is a fairly turgid affair with some decidedly gruesome touches, but it does have some autobiographical interest, and it's also strangely prophetic. While he had set out to write an anti-clerical work, Mussolini clearly based the character of the Cardinal on himself, and he's remarkably uncritical about the fact that the cleric has a mistress. Mussolini would, of course, go on to have numerous mistresses, the most famous of whom was Claretta Petacci. In the novel, people are angry because they believe that Claudia has used her relationship with the Cardinal to further the interests of her family. Decades later, Claretta would be accused of the same crime thanks to her relationship with Mussolini. At one point, a character in the novel warns Claudia she should leave Trent for her own safety, but she refuses. He goes on to paint a picture of what will happen to her if she doesn't.

> *"Ah, you do not listen to me, shameless courtesan, harlot. Well, I shall come to get you in this same castle. I shall let the common brutes of the market place satiate their idle lusts on your sinful body. You shall be the mockery of the unreasoning mob. Your corpse will not have the rites of Christian burial... And when the hour of your agony comes, when, trampled on, transfixed and rent by the blows of the mob, you shall implore aid and succor with the eyes which now so disdainfully regard me, I shall be the evil demon of that supreme hour...."*

This is eerily prescient of the fate that would befall Claretta Petacci — and Mussolini himself.

ussolini was making a name for himself with his journalism, but he remained a big socialist fish in the small pond of the Romagna. When the government of Giovanni Giolotti announced its intention of invading Libya in 1911, he saw an opportunity to raise his profile. Adopting the usual socialist anti-war line, he called for a general strike, and incited rioting workers to tear up the train tracks in Forli, earning himself five months in prison. After his release he moved with his family to Milan to take up the editorship of the national socialist daily newspaper *Avanti!* Meanwhile, he travelled around the country giving speeches and honing his public speaking skills.

When war broke out in 1914, Mussolini initially took an anti-militaristic stance and demanded that Italy remain neutral. But he had been wavering about this for a while, just as he would waver about all sorts of issues for the rest of his political career. Eventually, swayed by Marx's observation that wars were always followed by social revolutions, he changed his tune and became just as fanatically certain that Italy should join the war on the side of England, France and Russia. Expelled from the Socialist Party, he started a new newspaper, *Il Popolo di'Italia*, which would eventually become the chief mouthpiece of Fascism. When Italy did enter the war in 1915, he served creditably in the army, taking part in front-line fighting, and was badly wounded when a grenade exploded beside him (he had just enough time to check that his testicles were still present and correct before he fainted).

Mussolini had ceased to be a socialist, but it was not yet clear what he *was*, to himself or anyone else. When the war ended, Italy was left with massive debts, high unemployment and political chaos as the Christian Democrats and the Socialists battled it out with the better-organised Communists. Mussolini began to talk of his country needing a dictator to clear up the mess — "A man who has when needed the delicate touch of an artist and the heavy hand of a warrior. A man who is sensitive and full of willpower. A man who knows and loves the people, and who can direct and bend them with violence if necessary." The inference, of course, was that he was just such a man.

On 23 March 1919, Mussolini and a group of followers met in Milan and formed an organisation called the *Fascio de Combattimento*. (*Fascio* derived from the *fasces*, a bundle of rods tightly bound around an axe, which symbolised a magistrate's power in ancient Rome.) Among its policies were a tax on war profits, the abolition of the Stock Exchange and the confiscation of Church property. Mussolini was interested in action more than policies, though. His Fascists wore black shirts, a fashion previously associated with anarchists, and also worn during the war by elite Italian soldiers known as the Arditi, many of whom now joined the new movement. They were responsible for introducing many of its military-style rituals, symbols and songs. (In some ways, all Mussolini had to do was sit back and watch Fascism spontaneously develop around him.) Fascist squads took to the streets to attack the Communists and Socialists, and thousands were killed over the next few weeks, with most elements of Italian society looking on with quiet approval. In elections in May 1921, Mussolini and thirty-four other Fascists were elected to the Chamber of Deputies.

Emboldened by their success, Mussolini and his closest associates planned their next move, a march on Rome to seize power. On 28 October, four columns of Fascist squads set off from different parts of the country, all heading for the capital. The Prime Minister, Luigi Facta, announced that he would declare martial law, but King Victor Emmanuel III (a secret admirer of Mussolini) wouldn't sign the decree. While all this was happening, Mussolini was in Milan, attending the theatre and putting on a great show of indifference. According to some accounts, he was worried about the consequences of what he had set in train, but then, before most of the Fascists got anywhere near Rome, a message came through from the King, asking him to form a new government.

Having attained power more easily than he could have imagined, Mussolini actually had little in the way of a political agenda, being driven by a sense of his own destiny more than anything else, and at first concentrated on bread-and-butter politics — balancing the government's books and getting Italians back to work. With the latter, he was determined to set a personal example. Fascist propaganda portrayed him as the hardest working man in the country, and he was often photographed working in the fields or at a blacksmith's forge, bare-chested and sweaty. When not

working hard he was playing hard — he was a keen amateur aviator, fencer, swimmer, skier and horse rider (who, according to one newspaper, could leap onto his horse like "a born cowboy"). Most Italians were entranced by their strange, hyperactive new leader, who continued to dress shabbily and refused to accept payment for being head of the government, living instead on his earnings from writing newspaper articles. His efforts were clearly bringing some improvements to the economy, although it is not true, as is often stated, that he got the trains running on time. (They may have improved during his rule, but this was due to changes planned before he came to power.)

As part of Mussolini's vision for reviving the glories of ancient Rome, the regime embarked on an ambitious building program. This entailed both restoring ancient buildings and sites, such as the Colosseum, and erecting new buildings in a grand and antiseptic 'Fascist' style (best seen today in the district known as EUR in the south of Rome, which was planned to be the site for an international exhibition marking the twentieth anniversary of the March on Rome in 1942). While much of this may have looked good on the surface (if you like Fascist architecture, that is) the building work was often shoddy. Despite Fascist claims to have revolutionised Italian society, it was still riddled with graft and corruption. Wages were generally low and unemployment high throughout the 1920s and '30s, and in regional areas the peasants remained illiterate and largely oblivious to Fascist rule.

Little of this was apparent to foreign observers, whose first impressions of the Duce were generally favourable. Sir Ronald Graham, the British ambassador to Italy, called him "a strange man and has lately caused some comment by driving about through Rome in his two-seater with a well-grown lion cub sitting beside him", but noted that "the Italians seem to like this sort of thing". Even when, as part of ongoing disputes with Greece, Italy briefly invaded Corfu, the international response was muted, with Graham writing that the act demonstrated Mussolini's limitless 'energy'.

Meanwhile, Fascism was slowly but inexorably imposing itself on all aspects of Italian society. Its opponents were beaten up, forced to drink castor oil or, as in the case of the prominent Socialist Matteotti, killed (although Mussolini probably didn't order this). Press freedom was curtailed, unions were banned, a Fascist militia was formed, parliament was stripped of its powers and eventually elections ceased. A secret police force was established called the OVRA (the name was chosen, not because the letters stood for anything, but because it sounded scary). It seems that most Italians accepted this ebbing away of democracy as the price that had to be paid for the country to be transformed, and many around the world agreed.

And yet, for all the parades and symbols and the Duce's bombastic rhetoric, Fascism never penetrated much below the surface. The ties that bound Italian society continued to be family and Catholicism. Most industrialists and businessmen carried on as they had done before the advent of Fascism, most ordinary Italians only paid lip service to it, and most peasants didn't give a damn either way. This was partly to do with the Italian national character, and partly due to Mussolini's own character, for the curious truth is that the Duce was never really much good at dictating. From the moment he became head of government he exhibited a most cavalier attitude to running his country. He was certainly a hard worker in his own way, spending long hours behind the huge desk in his enormous office in the Palazzo Venezia, going through newspapers and reports, acquainting himself with every problem in Italy that needed fixing. But he refused to delegate work to others, which meant that little was ever done about them. Unlike Hitler and any number of other

dictators, he was not a personally cruel man, so he lacked the ability to instil the sort of terror in his underlings that would have resulted in a top-down imposition of genuinely totalitarian rule.

ussolini is now so closely identified with Hitler that it's hard to comprehend just how admired he became during the 1920s, when he was often called the greatest statesman of his era. Visiting Rome in 1927, Winston Churchill declared, "If I were an Italian I would don the Fascist black shirt." The previously virulently anti-clerical Mussolini, in his usual pragmatic way, also made peace with the Vatican, signing the Lateran Pacts of 1929 which declared it an independent state, leading Pope Pius XI to describe him as "the man whom providence has sent us". The cult of Mussolini was fostered by hagiographical biographies and news stories. Millions of photographs of him in various poses were in circulation, with one journalist suggesting he must be the most photographed person in the world. He also spent an inordinate amount of time travelling around the country, showing himself off and enjoying the adulation of the crowds.

Mussolini continued to be an enthusiastic seducer of women after coming to power, and a sexual encounter with him was like life as defined by Thomas Hobbes: "Nasty, brutish and short". He didn't much care about the age or looks of his women, but liked them to smell strongly of sweat (he hated perfume), and his favourite place for lovemaking was the floor. Once the encounter was over — usually after a minute or two — he could be surprisingly tender, and many women came back for more. His wife Rachele knew about his infidelities, but turned a blind eye to them as long as he looked after her and the children. While Fascist propaganda painted him as the ideal family man, everyone in Italy had heard rumours of his priapic adventures, and his perceived supreme virility was undoubtedly an important part of his image. So many women sent letters or made phone calls to the Palazzo Venezia, more or less openly requesting a sexual liaison with him, that a small office was opened to sift through the requests and select the most promising. Successful candidates were often invited to Mussolini's office where sex would take place under his desk, or on the long stone seats under the bay windows — equipped with thick cushions for the purpose. The women would usually be in and out the door within half an hour. And this was just his daytime schedule. In later years, when his libido had subsided somewhat, Mussolini reminisced to his mistress Claretta Petacci, "There was a time when I had fourteen women on the go and would see three or four of them every evening, one after the other — at 8 p.m. I'd have Rismondo, then Sarfatti, then Magda. On one occasion I rounded off the evening at one in the morning with an insatiable Brazilian woman who'd have finished me off if a huge storm hadn't damaged the walls."

One of his earliest mistresses, and the one who gave him the most trouble, was Ida Dalser, whom he appears to have met around 1910. In 1915, she gave birth to their child, Benito Albino Mussolini. Dalser stalked Mussolini for years, claiming that he had married her, and often caused public scenes. She was put under police surveillance and eventually placed in a mental hospital where she died in 1935. Mussolini's biographers had always considered Dalser deluded, but in 2005 a journalist found a document that proved he *had* married her, in 1914, making her his first wife. After coming to power, he had attempted to have all evidence of their marriage destroyed, and nearly succeeded. Benito Albino's fate was no better than his mother's. Forcibly removed from her by Fascist agents, then told she was dead, he was placed with another family, but continued to tell people he was Mussolini's son. He also ended up in an asylum, and died in 1942.

Mussolini's favourite mistress was Claretta Petacci, whom he met in 1932 when he was being driven through Ostia in his Alfa Romeo and noticed her waving at him enthusiastically.

Claretta, who at the age of fourteen had plastered the walls of her bedroom with photos of the Duce, was frivolous and rather dim, but she was utterly devoted to him. She kept copious diaries, which have survived, in which she obsessively recorded the Duce's conversations with her, including his accounts of innumerable other lovers. While not entirely reliable, they are a treasure trove of information about his private life and sexual bravado. "You should be scared by my lovemaking," he told her once. "It's like a cyclone, it uproots everything in its path. You should tremble. If I could have done, today I would have entered you on a horse."

The foreign observer with the keenest interest in the development of Fascism was Adolf Hitler. He had borrowed many elements of Fascist ritual and rhetoric for his National Socialist movement, had long called for an alliance between Germany and Italy, and had unbounded admiration for Mussolini personally. Mussolini, initially, did not return this admiration at all. (When Hitler requested a signed photograph of him in 1927, he refused to send one.) After their first meeting, in Italy in 1934, Mussolini described Hitler as looking like "a plumber in a mackintosh". His eyes had glazed over as Hitler expounded on his racial views endlessly, especially when he started going on about how much Negro blood the Italians had in them. Mussolini had always been scathing about such views, calling the concept of a Master Race "arrant nonsense, stupid and idiotic", and after the meeting was over summed up Hitler as "a silly little clown". But there was a turning point in the relationship between the two dictators after Italy invaded Ethiopia in 1935.

If Mussolini was going to revive the glories of ancient Rome, Italy needed an empire. It already had colonies in Libya,

Eritrea and Somaliland, but Ethiopia (then Abyssinia), the only African country not under European rule, was a bigger prize, and would also give a younger generation of Fascists a chance to experience all the wonderful benefits of war. Italian casualties during the invasion, at around a thousand, were reckoned minimal, but the Ethiopians, who were bombed and gassed mercilessly, suffered terribly. While the Italian people had never given any indication that they wanted Ethiopia, they were quite pleased to get it, and the deification of the Duce reached new heights, with one journalist writing that "Mussolini's smile is like a flash of the Sun god, expected and craved because it brings health and life." The invasion, however, irreparably damaged the dictator's international reputation, his image transformed overnight from gifted statesman to murderous thug.

Germany was the only major power which did not criticise Mussolini's Ethiopian venture, and the Duce was coming round to the idea that the fate of Fascist Italy was tied to Nazi Germany, rather than to Britain and France. This became even more apparent when Italy sent troops to support Franco's forces in the Spanish Civil War. Mussolini visited Germany for the first time in September 1937, and Hitler made sure he got the full Nazi extravaganza. He was treated to banquets, visits to factories and endless military parades, and in Berlin addressed an enthusiastic crowd of over 800,000. Mussolini went home with his head swimming with Nazism, and immediately ordered the Italian army to adopt the ludicrous and difficult goose-step. He made a fateful speech in which he referred to "a Rome-Berlin axis around which all European states that desire peace can revolve," and described Hitler as "one of the few geniuses who make history". All of this was deeply disturbing to most ordinary Italians, who wanted nothing to do with the Third Reich.

Far worse than making Italian soldiers goose-step, Mussolini also adopted a policy of anti-Semitism. Prior to this, he had not been anti-Semitic, or rather, his views were no more anti-Semitic than was, sadly, the norm for most Europeans in the first decades of the twentieth century. One of his most important mistresses was a Jewish socialite, journalist and art critic, Margherita Sarfatti, who had been instrumental in the development of Fascist ideology, and has been called 'the Jewish mother of Fascism'. Mussolini had dismissed anti-Semitism as 'the German vice', and had earlier allowed thousands of Jews fleeing Nazi persecution to settle in Italy. However, while he privately continued to rubbish Hitler's racial ideas, he now contributed to a document called 'The Manifesto of Racial Scientists' which stated the Italians were Aryans after all, and enacted anti-Semitic laws. Fortunately, as with much Fascist legislation, the laws were only half-heartedly enforced, but many Italian Jews still lost their jobs or property, or were expelled from the country.

In March 1938, without bothering to tell Mussolini he was about to do it, Hitler invaded Austria. That there should be no political union or 'Anschluss' between Germany and Austria had long been a cornerstone of Fascist foreign policy, and Mussolini, who had no choice but to accept Hitler's action, looked foolish trying to deny it. Two months later Hitler paid his second visit to Italy. The Fascists did their best to put on a show of military might and pro-German enthusiasm, and although most shopkeepers stubbornly refused to display a photo of Hitler in their window, they did a reasonable job of it. Hitler wasn't too happy about protocol demanding that he stay in the King's palace, though, for he and Victor Emmanuel III had taken an instant dislike to each other. The King told Mussolini bitchily that on his first night there Hitler had asked for a woman (it later emerged that he only wanted her to turn over his bed) and suggested that the Führer shot up drugs. Mussolini noticed that Hitler was wearing rouge on his cheeks to disguise his pallor.

Hitler had another nasty surprise for Mussolini when he invaded Czechoslovakia in March 1939, again without giving him prior warning. The Duce was furious, but he was now committed to his 'Axis' with Germany. Hitler's move emboldened Mussolini to invade Albania, something he had been contemplating, and dithering about, for a long time. He also redoubled his efforts at making Italians more Fascist. An earlier ban on handshakes in favour of the 'Roman salute' was to be strictly enforced, more officials were put into uniform, and Fascist ministers were ordered to take part in sport and exercise as an inspiration for the people. "The Italians must learn," he declared, "to grow less likable and to become hard, implacable and hateful."

As keen as Mussolini was to go to war, he knew that Italy's armed forces would need at least three years to prepare for it. He was also anxious that plans for his pet project, the international exhibition to take place in 1942, would not be interrupted. When the Germans assured him they would abide by this timetable, Mussolini was reassured enough to sign the so-called 'Pact of Steel', which committed Italy to standing by Germany if it went to war.

Hitler, of course, wasn't going to wait three years, and it soon became apparent that the invasion of Poland was imminent. The Italian Foreign Minister and Mussolini's son-in-law, Count Galleazo Ciano, had previously been all for close ties with Germany, but now he told Mussolini that the "Germans are traitors and we must not have any scruples about ditching them". (Ciano was married to Mussolini's eldest daughter, Edda, and was at this point being groomed as his successor, despite the fact that he was a feckless playboy who spent much of his time on the golf course.) Mussolini wavered between berating the Germans and wanting to honour his agreement with them. Eventually he was prevailed upon to write a letter to Hitler, saying that he would support him politically, but military support would depend on Italy receiving a vast amount of equipment and materials. Hitler wrote back to say political support would do.

Mussolini initially remained neutral after Poland was invaded. He knew how incensed most Italians were about the brutal subjugation of another Catholic country, while both the King and the new Pope, Pius XII, were dead against joining Germany. But neutrality had been a dirty word to Mussolini since the First World War. "To make a people great it is necessary to send them into battle," he told Ciano, "even if you have to kick them in the pants." As further German successes, including an easy invasion of Norway, made a German victory seem more certain, the mood in Italy changed. Mussolini couldn't bear the thought of missing out on the spoils of an Axis victory, and many senior Fascists, as well as the King, had to agree. Still, it wasn't until 10 June, with France and Belgium clearly about to fall, that Mussolini stepped onto the balcony of the Palazzo Venezia and announced that Italy had declared war on Britain and France.

So, Mussolini had his war, but he expected it to be a short one. "I only need a few thousand dead so that I can sit at the peace conference as a man who has fought," he told the army chief of staff, General Badoglio. He repaired to his office and waited for a few Italian military victories, but they would never come. The great irony of Italy's going to war was that it instantly exposed as delusions Fascism's claims to have modernised Italy's moribund economy. The armed forces were in a more dreadful state than anyone had imagined, much of their already paltry resources having been squandered in the Ethiopian invasion and the Spanish Civil War. Mussolini had boasted of having seven army divisions to send into battle; in reality he had about one. There was little co-ordination between the military and industry, and production of arms and equipment remained at absurdly low levels — throughout the war years, Italy struggled to produce a single serviceable tank.

Mussolini was happy to leave the day-to-day running of the war to his military chiefs. During the first few months, unbelievably, he spent much of his time translating a nineteenth century Italian novel into German, while afternoons were often spent in the arms of Claretta Petacci. While the Italian public had been mostly kept in the dark about Mussolini's previous mistresses, they knew all about

Claretta, chiefly because of the incredibly grasping nature of the extended Petacci family, who exploited her association with the Duce for all it was worth.

Two weeks after Italy entered the war, Mussolini ordered his troops to invade Greece — pointedly, without telling Hitler. (He confided to Ciano that he was tired of Hitler invading countries without telling him, and this was to get back at him.) The Italians expected an easy victory, but the Greeks soon had them scurrying back to Albania. Italian troops fared no better against the British in Libya, and were soon forced out of Somaliland and Ethiopia. These defeats sapped any morale the Italian people may have had for the war. They were also incensed by the way the German troops treated their supposed Italian allies as inferiors, often leaving them in the lurch when things went wrong on the battlefield, while the many thousands of Italians sent to work in Germany were treated appallingly. (Incredibly, about thirty thousand of them died there.)

As Italy's war effort stumbled from one disaster to the next, Mussolini's physical state deteriorated. The stomach pains he had suffered from an ulcer since the mid-20s grew worse, and he was reduced to a virtually liquid diet of mainly milk. He lost a great deal of weight — the famed massive chin disappeared — and he looked far older than his years. Indeed, he looked so bad that some suspected he was in the terminal stage of syphilis. He had always been prone to mood swings, but these grew increasingly violent, and he barely slept. Perhaps most worrying for his followers, his once considerable charisma had seemingly evaporated away to nothing.

By July 1943, with an Allied invasion of the Italian mainland imminent, it was clear to all but the most blinkered Fascists that Mussolini needed to go. Rome was swirling with plots and rumours of plots. Many, including his wife Rachele, warned Mussolini about them, but he refused to take them

seriously. His only response was to reshuffle his ministries.

Mussolini was persuaded to hold a meeting of the Fascist Grand Council, the first since the beginning of the war. During the long and rowdy meeting, which began on 24 June, the Minister for Justice, Count Dino Grandi, read a resolution which called for Mussolini to relinquish his power to the King. Around 2 a.m., after hours more squabbling, Mussolini decided to put the resolution to the vote. Nineteen of the twenty-eight council members voted for it. Among them was Count Ciano, no longer foreign minister or Mussolini's heir apparent, who had recently been telling people he hoped that Britain would be victorious over Germany (after all, he reasoned, the British loved golf just as much as he did).

Next morning, Mussolini went to his office as usual. At 5 p.m., he went to meet the King. He was still unconcerned, and told the King the vote was not binding. The King disagreed and informed him that he would be replaced by General Badoglio. Mussolini took the news quietly, muttering repeatedly "Then it's all over." As he left the King's residence, a captain of the *carabinieri* approached, told Mussolini that he had been sent to protect him, and persuaded him to get into an ambulance.

He spent the night at a *carabinieri* barracks — only now was it dawning on him that he had been arrested. When the King announced on the radio that he had accepted the Duce's resignation, jubilant crowds rushed through the streets of Rome, tearing down Fascist symbols and destroying statues of Mussolini. But with German troops stationed in their country in a de facto occupation, the war was not yet over for the Italians.

Mussolini was taken to the small island of Ponza. Admiral Franco Maugeri, who escorted him there, said he looked "like a corpse". During his time there he occupied himself reading a life of Christ, making notes in it about the parallels between Christ's tragic fate and his own. After ten days he was moved to another island, Maddalena, where he was cheered by a birthday present from Hitler — a complete set of Nietzsche's works in twenty-four volumes, which he began to read avidly from the beginning. The government, fearing that he might be rescued by the Germans from Maddalena, moved him once more, back to the mainland, and a hotel high on the slopes of the Gran Sasso in the Abruzzi region.

Hitler had of course been infuriated by the news of Mussolini's arrest. The following day, he handpicked a Waffen SS officer, Otto Skorzeny, to lead a rescue mission. At first, the Germans had no idea where Mussolini was being kept (Himmler consulted an astrologer who was unable to help), but Skorzeny eventually got wind that he was on Maddalena. A rescue operation was planned, but the day before it was to happen, Mussolini was moved to San Grasso. Snatching him from such an inaccessible place presented a considerable challenge. Skorzeny contemplated a ground or parachute attack, but learning that there was a small airfield near the hotel where Mussolini was being held, decided on using gliders. Taking an Italian officer, General Soleti, with them to smooth things out, Skorzeny and his men flew in gliders to Gran Sasso on 12 September. Seeing that the airfield they had been told about was more of a hillside, they had no alternative but to land on the rough ground in front of the hotel. Mussolini, in his room, saw them approaching. As the first of the gliders crashed messily onto the ground, pandemonium erupted among the Italian troops guarding the hotel. "Don't shoot!' he told then as he saw the Italian general among the attackers. Skorzeny, emerging from another glider, saw Mussolini staring at him through a first floor window. Forcing his way into the hotel, he managed to get to Mussolini's room, where he saluted him and said he had been sent by the Führer. Mussolini hugged him and said, "I knew that my friend Adolf Hitler would not desert me."

A few days later Mussolini was flown to Munich for a meeting with Hitler, who was shocked by his appearance and mood of hopelessness. When Mussolini suggested that it might be best if he retired from politics to prevent an Italian civil war, Hitler would have none of it. Germany, he said, would occupy north-eastern Italy, and there would be a new Fascist republican government led by Mussolini. And on one point he was adamant — the traitors in the Fascist Grand Council who had betrayed him, including his son-in-law Ciano (who was then in custody in Germany) must be tried and executed. Mussolini listened to it all resignedly. He later claimed that he had accepted Hitler's demands because he feared what Germany would do to Italy if he didn't.

The Germans decided that the new government would be based at Salò, a town on the shores of Lake Garda (Rome was thought too vulnerable to Allied attack). Mussolini was installed in a villa some distance from the town, and was eventually joined there by Rachele and most of his family, while Claretta Petacci was housed in another villa closer to the lake. (Rachele was incensed when she found out about this, and one day went over to give her husband's mistress a piece of her mind, a tirade that caused Claretta to faint twice.) The trial of the traitors took place in Verona in January 1944. Edda had pleaded with her father to spare Ciano's life, but he had remained implacable. (Rachele, on the other hand, had always hated Ciano and was all for his execution.) After the tribunal had proved, to its satisfaction, that a conspiracy to depose Mussolini had existed, Ciano and four others were sentenced to death. They were taken at dawn to a fort outside Verona, tied to chairs so that their backs were to their executioners, and shot. At the last moment Ciano managed to loosen his bonds and turned to face his killers.

ussolini had German guards around him at the villa and whenever he left it, and was in no doubt that his was a puppet government, so it's not surprising he took little interest in it. He did make a few noises about wishing to return to his socialist roots, and introducing the foundations of a welfare state, but if the Salò Republic is characterised by anything, it's the fact that for the first time Fascist officials were systematic in enforcing the anti-Semitic laws. During its brief existence, some seven-and-a-half-thousand Jews were deported to face almost certain death. Instead of day-to-day politics, Mussolini seemed to be fixated on consolidating his place in history. He wrote numerous newspaper articles, and spent much of his time reading and talking politics and philosophy. When asked by an associate how he would evaluate himself, he replied, "I am not a statesman. I am more like a mad poet."

In private, Mussolini did not bother to hide the contempt he now had for the Germans, but his mutual admiration society with Hitler was still going strong. He went to Berlin in July to visit the Führer, and found him ashen-faced and clutching one arm to his side — Von Stauffenberg's attempt to assassinate him with a bomb had taken place just hours before. Mussolini agreed with Hitler that providence had saved him. When it was time for them to part at the end of this visit, Hitler became so emotional, holding Mussolini's hands and staring into his eyes, that others present were embarrassed. "You are the finest, indeed perhaps the only,

friend I have in the world," he told Mussolini.

In the early months of 1944, with the Allies making advances into Italian territory and fierce fighting between partisan brigades and the German and Fascist forces, Mussolini had to concede that whoever won the war, Italy had lost it. In April, he decided to move his government to Milan for the endgame. Many of his followers urged him to escape to another country such as Spain or Switzerland, but he was adamant that he would remain in Italy. In a last desperate attempt to salvage something from the situation, a meeting was organised at the Archbishop of Milan's house with two representatives from the National Liberation Committee, General Cadorna and a lawyer named Marazza, to discuss the terms of a Fascist surrender. Marazza told them from the start that the only surrender they would countenance was an unconditional one. When one of Mussolini's more fanatical subordinates, who was also present, said that surrender would be a betrayal of their German allies, Cadorna coolly told Mussolini that the German forces in Italy had been negotiating their own surrender with the National Liberation Committee. Although Mussolini had certainly heard whispers about this, he professed to be incensed and terminated the negotiations.

For some time, Mussolini and other leading Fascists had been talking about making a heroic last stand in the Valtellina, a valley in the Lombardy region near the Swiss border. He had ordered that munitions and food supplies be sent there in readiness (though whether they were is another matter — he never bothered to check). With the situation in Milan deteriorating rapidly, Mussolini declared that now was the time to head there. A convoy of around thirty vehicles was hastily assembled, including two lorries carrying German soldiers. Among the other passengers were Claretta Petacci, her brother Marcello, and Marcello's wife and children.

A few hours later the convoy arrived in Como, where Mussolini was supposed to be met by one of his ministers,

Pavorini, with three thousand Fascist fighters. There was no sign of them, though, and he became distraught when a lorry carrying two cases of official documents he had collected for his defence at a war crimes trial also failed to appear. He wrote a last letter to Rachele, telling her, "You know that you have been for me the only woman I have really loved", and advising her to flee to Switzerland. Then he ordered the convoy to drive north along the shore of Lake Como to Menaggio, where Pavorini caught up with him on the morning of 27 April. Instead of bringing 3,000 Fascist fighters, he had rustled up a grand total of twelve.

Some of Mussolini's followers now suspected that he was planning to flee to Switzerland. In fact, he probably didn't know what to do — it was the culmination of a life of indecisiveness. At this point, a convoy of retreating German soldiers arrived in Menaggio, and its commanding officer agreed to let Mussolini and the others join them. The convoy continued north, but was soon stopped by a roadblock placed there by partisans from the 52nd Garibaldi Brigade the night before. There was a brief exchange of shots, during which one partisan was killed, then a truce was called. While the German commander was negotiating at the partisans' headquarters, some of the Italians approached a local priest who had come to see what was going on, and asked for his protection. They told him Mussolini had been with them at Menaggio, but they didn't know where he was now.

The partisan commander, Count Bellini, agreed to let the Germans pass, but the Italians would have to remain behind (the partisans had by now recognised some of the Fascist ministers among them). One of the Germans suggested to Mussolini that he don a German greatcoat and helmet and hide in one of their lorries. He was reluctant to do this, but eventually Claretta and some of the others managed to persuade him. The German lorries were ordered to the

BENITO MUSSOLINI

26

nearby village of Dongo, where they were to be searched. The Italians left behind scattered, but were soon rounded up by the partisans.

In Dongo, a partisan named Giuseppe Negri, searching one of the lorries, saw a figure seated in the shadows at the back who appeared to be asleep, a machine gun between his knees. The other German soldiers said he was drunk. Negri nodded, then rushed over to one of the partisan leaders, Urbano Lazzaro, and said in the local dialect, "We've got Big-Head!" Lazzaro didn't believe him. Boarding the truck, he went to the hunched figure and asked if he was Italian. When Mussolini raised his head and said he was, Lazarro recognised him immediately, and exclaimed involuntarily "Excellency!"

Mussolini was taken to the Dongo barracks, where he chatted to his guards almost cheerfully. Informed of his capture, the Committee of National Liberation in Milan ordered him to be taken somewhere safe. To his surprise, Bellini allowed him to be reunited with Claretta, and they spent the night at the house of a peasant couple, who let them sleep in a double bed in an upstairs room.

In the early hours of that morning, several members of the National Liberation Committee met in Milan and ordered, without proper authority, that Mussolini be summarily executed. Walter Audisio, a committee member who went by the name Count Volario, left for Como, accompanied by a dozen partisans armed with machine guns. In Como, he found the local partisans reluctant to give up their prize. In Dongo, Bellini was also reluctant, and refused to tell Audisio where Mussolini was being held, but he found out anyway. Arriving at the peasants' house at around 4 p.m., he told Mussolini that he had come to rescue him. He and Claretta were escorted from the house and bundled into

Audisio's car, Claretta in her high heels, struggling with two bags and two coats. The car was driven to a nearby villa where Mussolini and Claretta were ordered out of the car. Audisio said a few quiet words to them, then pointed his machine gun at them. As Claretta, hysterical, threw her arms around her lover, Audisio squeezed the trigger, but the gun jammed. Taking a machine gun from another partisan, he shot both of them. Mussolini's last words are supposed to have been "Shoot me in the chest."

That, at least, is more or less the official version of their deaths. There are other versions — that they died earlier, or separately, or somewhere else. In any case, they were dead by the late afternoon of 28 April, and an hour or so later fifteen of the Fascists who had been travelling with Mussolini were also executed. All the bodies were loaded onto a removal van which was driven to Milan, and some time before dawn they were dumped in the Piazzale Loreto. A couple of youths who happened to be passing recognised Mussolini and kicked him repeatedly in the face, making a terrible mess of it.

As the sun came up, a crowd gathered who jeered at the corpses, spat at them, beat them with their fists and perhaps urinated on them. Someone called for them to be strung up. Ropes were tied around the feet of Mussolini, Claretta Petacci and five others, and soon they were dangling from the awning of an Esso petrol station. Claretta's dark skirt fell down over her face, and a man walked up and poked her body with a stick.

CHAPTER 2

ENVER HOXHA

ENVER HOXHA

Attained power in 1944
Died from heart failure in 1985

nver Hoxha wasn't your run-of-the-mill communist dictator. He was a good-looking man with a ready smile, always keen to put his arm around you and wish you well. He was never less than impeccably dressed, in his early years favouring stylish military uniforms, later tastefully-cut beige suits and, occasionally, a jaunty beret. He was urbane, fluent in French and extremely well-read, having a private library of over twenty thousand volumes. He liked to quote Shakespeare, Goethe and Moliere. And he had a sense of humour too, adoring the films of the British comedian Norman Wisdom.

He was also every bit as murderous as Stalin, and if his victims were numbered in the thousands rather than the millions, it was only because Albania, which he succeeded in isolating from the rest of the world for decades, is such a small country.

oxha (pronounced 'Hodja'), was the son of Halil and Gjylo Hoxha, and was born in the town Gjirokastër, southern Albania, on 16 October 1908. When he was young, his father, a cloth merchant and devout Muslim who was at one point an imam, left to try his luck in America, taking his eldest son with him. During the five years he was away, Enver was left in the care of his uncle, Halil Hoxha, who was involved in local government. He became Enver's true father figure, and it may have been his influence that started him thinking about a career in politics.

Little else is known about his childhood, which seems to have been thoroughly ordinary. As a teenager, he attended a French school in Gjirokastër, then in 1927 moved to another one in the more affluent town of Korça, which he attended for three years. A few records survive that show he was an indifferent student. Later, many of his fellow students — and indeed virtually all of his friends during these years — would fall foul of the Hoxha regime and wind up in prison or executed.

Although he had so far failed to distinguish himself in away way, Hoxha had a benefactor in a family friend, Eqrem Libohova, who was foreign minister in the government of Albania's engagingly named monarch, King Zog. Albania, which had declared its independence from the Ottoman Empire in 1912, remained an impoverished and backward country. It did not yet have a university, but Libohova secured Hoxha a scholarship to continue his studies in France. He went to Montpellier, ostensibly to study botany, but later admitted he had no interest in the subject, and wiled away much of his time in cafés. After making virtually no progress in three years, his scholarship was cancelled. He was supposed to return to Albania and repay the money, but instead went to Paris. He was penniless, but a student friend invited him to stay in a hostel.

In his voluminous memoirs, Hoxha wrote that he had by now become a confirmed communist. He claimed to have made contact with the French Communist Party, and written articles attacking the Kingdom of Albania for its newspaper, *L'Humanite*. Yet people who knew him at the time — at least the ones who weren't later shot — couldn't recall him having any particular interest in communism, or anything else for that matter, and none of the articles he supposedly wrote have ever come to light. Nevertheless, he certainly moved in bohemian circles in Paris, which included prominent communists, while also mixing with expatriate Albanians opposed to the monarchy.

After eleven months in Paris, Hoxha moved to Brussels to take up a position in the Albanian consulate arranged by Libohova. He left under a cloud a year later after consulate funds which he was in charge of went missing. He returned to Albania in 1936 and, once again with his benefactor's help, found work as a substitute teacher, first in Tirana, then at his old school in Korça, where he taught French and Moral Education. In the same year, he was a member of a delegation that brought the bodies of two Albanian patriots killed in 1916 back to their home town of Gjirokastër. Hoxha, representing the young people of Albania, gave a well-received speech from the town hall steps which was reported in a national newspaper. But if he now had definite political ambitions, he was still keeping them a secret from most people. When Italy invaded Albania in April 1939 and the communists of Korça organised a defence force, he declined to take part.

After the Italian invasion, the French school in Korça became an Italian one, and Hoxha was dismissed. He went to Tirana where he and a business partner opened a tobacco shop.

Hoxha's relationship with communism had always been ambiguous. He had mixed with the communists in Korça, and was a friend of their leader, Koço Tashko, but the extent of his involvement with them is unknown. He is said to have sold left-wing publications in his tobacco shop, and that it became a meeting place for communists, but the friends who visited him there later said they still had no idea that he was a communist. He seems to have flirted with the ideology for years without ever making a commitment. But when the various Albanian communist groups came together to found the Communist Party of Albania in November 1942, Hoxha was elected to its Central Committee.

The meeting came in the wake of Hitler's invasion of the Soviet Union, when Moscow ordered communists across Europe to organise themselves into an effective resistance movement. Relations between the three main Albanian groups — those based in Korça and Shkodra and the Youth Group — were as fractious as they tend to be among small political groups supposedly fighting for the same cause. The Yugoslav communist leader Marshal Tito was particularly insistent that the Albanians get their act together, and sent an envoy to the meeting to make sure it went as planned.

Hoxha wasn't even supposed to be at the meeting — he was brought along at the last moment by Koço Tashko, who thought that the Korça delegation needed a Muslim member. (While over half the Albanian population are Muslim, all the other delegates were Orthodox Christians.) Most of the Albanian communists were blue-collar workers, but Hoxha was an intellectual (well, he had been a school teacher) and a sophisticate (he had been to Paris!). He dressed smartly, spoke very well in public, and at thirty-three was still relatively young. He had also recently acquired some street cred — after striking an Italian *caribinieri* officer at an anti-Fascist demonstration, he had been forced to close the tobacco shop and go into hiding. It seems that it was Tito's envoy, Miladin Popović, who recognised Hoxha's leadership potential and became his backer. Of course, in Hoxha's later accounts of the meeting, he claimed that he was the one who had organised it, and made a stirring speech calling for a communist party to be formed.

Hoxha was initially only one of seven Central Committee

members — he would not be elected first secretary until a party conference the following year. But from the beginning he demonstrated an unexpected ruthlessness that far outstripped his party colleagues, ordering the executions of innumerable 'collaborators', but also party members he saw as rivals. Meanwhile, the Albanian communists, based in the highlands, were mounting a fierce insurgency against the Italians, and after the fall of Mussolini, the Germans. They also spent a fair amount of time fighting various Albanian nationalist groups who were theoretically their allies. Hoxha realised, though, that the nationalists were his real rivals for power.

By the middle of 1944, the National Liberation Army under the command of General Hoxha controlled over half of Albania. On 28 November, the anniversary of Albanian independence, Hoxha and his forces made a triumphant entrance into the capital, Tirana. A grand celebratory ball was held that evening in the Hotel Dajti, built by the Italians during the occupation in approved Fascist style, and it was here that Hoxha appeared in public for the first time with his fiancée, the former communist activist Nexhmije Xhuglini.

As a dictator in the Stalinist mould, Hoxha hit the ground running. Just a month after arriving in Tirana, he held his first show trial, the so-called 'Special Trial', where sixty former politicians, including some prime ministers, were accused of treason. Seventeen were sentenced to death and most of the others were given long prison sentences. Bahri Omari, a former nationalist politician and government minister who was also Hoxha's brother-in-law, was among those who faced a firing squad. He had been tremendously kind and helpful to Hoxha over the years, even putting him and Nexhmije up in his house for extended periods during the war, but that didn't save him. Indeed, so many of Hoxha's former friends would be executed or locked away during the next few years (including his closest childhood friend, Enver Zazani, shot in 1947) that it's hard not to believe this was a deliberate policy, designed to show that in the new Albania, no dissent of any kind from anyone would be tolerated. Another pet project of Hoxha's was eliminating all the other communists who had been at the 1941 meeting where the party was founded. He wanted no-one around who could contradict his story — that he was the father of communism in Albania.

Hoxha's political organisation, the Democratic Front, was the only one allowed to contest the election held in 1945, and won over 93 per cent of the vote. (Those foolhardy enough to vote for a nebulous opposition, identified only as the 'reactionaries' on ballot papers, were later rounded up and many were killed.) Hoxha became prime minister, foreign minister and commander-in-chief of the people's army. Koçi Xoxe, a former tinsmith and communist fighter with no formal education, became deputy prime minister and minister of the interior, and immediately busied himself setting up a security agency, the Sigurimi.

As the incessant purging of political opponents continued, Hoxha set about reorganising the country on Marxist-Leninist lines, seizing businesses, seizing businessmen, booting landowners off their land, collectivising agriculture and banning private property (it would eventually become illegal for a peasant to own so much as a chicken). He also embarked on the difficult task of dragging the traditionally isolated and backward Albania into the twentieth century, and undoubtedly did much good here. He put an end to the notorious *Gjakmarrja*, or blood feuds, which decimated entire communities and were sanctioned by a set of orally-transmitted Medieval laws called the Kanun of Lekë

Dukagjini. Albanian women also benefitted from Hoxha's reforms, having previously had almost no rights whatsoever. (One of the edicts of the Kanun was that when a pregnant woman was murdered, her belly would be cut open. If the foetus was a boy, the murderer had to pay twice as much compensation to the victim's family than if it was a girl.) Many new doctors were trained, and the country's high rate of malaria was slashed when its swamplands were drained. Most impressively, Hoxha introduced an education program that dramatically reduced Albania's appalling rates of illiteracy. If he was progressive in some ways, though, Hoxha also turned his back on many aspects of the twentieth century. Only party officials were allowed to have cars and refrigerators.

Hoxha initially had an excellent relationship with Tito, and Albania came close to unification with Yugoslavia. The plan was cancelled after Stalin fell out with Tito in 1948, and Hoxha learned that the Yugoslavs wanted to replace him with Koçi Xoxe. The interior minister was dragged from his house, which was next to Hoxha's, and executed, while other government members who had been pro-Yugoslav were arrested. (On the bright side, some who had been locked up for being anti-Yugoslav were released.) Spurned by Tito, Hoxha turned to Stalin, who had always been his political role model. Stalin couldn't really care less about Albania and its fewer than 1.5 million people, but reciprocated Hoxha's advances by sending massive amounts of aid to it.

The 'Stalinification' of Albania continued apace, with the Sigurimi growing into a fearsomely effective and all-pervasive instrument of control. It was popularly believed that one in four people were Sigurimi informers, and the slightest word that could be interpreted as criticism of the regime would see a person imprisoned, tortured and often killed. And the personality cult of Hoxha, the 'Supreme Comrade' and 'Sole Force', to give just two of his many epithets, blossomed.

Statues of him, some of them enormous, were erected all over the country. His portrait looked out from posters, murals, the front pages of every newspaper. No book on any subject could be written without quotations from his many works. Popular songs celebrated the exploits of Hoxha and his wife, the austere Nexhmije, when they were partisans together.

hen Stalin died in 1953, Hoxha plunged Albania into mourning. The *entire population* was gathered into a huge square in Tirana, where they had to kneel in front of a gigantic bronze stature of Uncle Joe and recite a syrupy 2,000-word oath of gratitude to him. Hoxha wasn't impressed when, shortly afterwards, Khrushchev denounced Stalin and his crimes and began to dismantle some of his apparatus of terror, but his relations with the new Soviet leader were initially good. Then Tito got in the way. The Yugoslav strongman had declared his independence from the Soviet Union in 1948, but Khrushchev was trying to coax him back into the fold. It was too much for Hoxha, whose hatred for Tito was boundless, and he and Khrushchev clashed bitterly over the issue. Hoxha feared (with good reason, as it turned out) that the Soviets were planning to overthrow him. When he visited Moscow in 1960 for a meeting of Communist representatives from eighty-one countries, he made sure to eat only meals prepared by his own staff.

It was clearly time for a new dictator-to-dictator relationship, and the lovelorn Albanian now fell into the welcoming arms of Mao Zedong. So close did the pair become ideologically that in 1967 Hoxha emulated Mao's worst idea of all — the Cultural Revolution. Young people were encouraged to denounce their parents for their ideological failings, and intellectuals were forced to deliver 'self-criticisms', then packed off to labour camps. All foreign travel was forbidden. Finally, with the declaration that

'The religion of Albania is Albanianism', God was banned. Mosques and churches were torn down or converted for other purposes (one cathedral was used for volleyball matches), and hundreds of imams and priests were shot. Even names with religious connotations were banned.

Hoxha's visit to Moscow in 1960 proved to be the last time he set foot outside Albania, and he became obsessed with keeping his country pure and free of contamination from the rest of the world. TV and radio broadcasts from Italy and Yugoslavia were jammed. Almost all fiction from the West was banned, apart from a handful of unlikely authors who were allowed because Hoxha liked them, including the Victorian humorist and author of *Three Men in a Boat*, Jerome K. Jerome, and the British popular novelist A.J. Cronin. Even more bizarrely, virtually the only Western films allowed to be screened were those of the aforementioned Norman Wisdom, the star of *Just My Luck*, *On the Beat* and a host of other knockabout comedies. Hoxha apparently saw him as a symbol of the working class man up against authority, and Wisdom became a cult figure in Albania, where he was known as 'Mr Pitkin'. How Hoxha acquired such Anglophile cultural tastes remains a mystery.

Just as Albania was isolated from the rest of the world, Hoxha spent most of his time isolated from Albania. He and the other members of the Politburo, along with their families, lived in 'the Bllok', a tightly-secured enclave in Tirana. The Bllok had its own shops, stocked with Western goods ordinary Albanians could only dream about. The leaders and their wives socialised with each other, and their families intermarried to such an extent that it became a standing joke in the country. It was all very jolly on the surface, but the marriages were mostly tactical, designed to shore up positions in the hierarchy, and the friendships were illusory. Everyone knew they were under close surveillance by the Sigurimi, and any twist or turn in government policy dictated by Hoxha could result in their downfall.

A great deal of government business was done in a large house in the Bllok known as the 'Party House', which also served as a sort of club which the leaders were expected to frequent every night. It had a cinema and a billiards room, billiards being one of Hoxha's few interests. (He was said to be unbeatable at it.) His only other interest was reading, with most of the books in his vast library being imported from France, one of the few countries with which he maintained friendly relations. Many were political works, but there was a great deal of fiction as well, with Hoxha's tastes running to Agatha Christie mysteries and vampire stories. He was also a compulsive writer, producing seventy-one books by the end of his life. They were published in huge

print runs by the Institute of Marxist-Leninist Studies, where Nexhmije was the director, and were compulsory reading in Albania. They were also translated into many other languages, so people in other countries had the opportunity to not bother reading them.

Hoxha had always been paranoid about foreign invasion (street signs were prohibited lest they prove useful to an invading army), and his paranoia only increased after the Soviet invasion of Czechoslovakia in 1968. He desperately needed some method of repelling would-be attackers. Huge numbers of tanks would have been good, but Albania didn't have the money to buy them, let alone the resources to make them. Then he came up with a brilliant idea — cement tanks! Well, actually dome-shaped cement bunkers or 'pill-boxes', with the interiors modelled on a tank, and slits at the front through which the soldiers inside could fire on the enemy. Some 750,000 of these were built, taking up an astonishing 10 per cent of Albania's arable land and reducing the country's ability to grow its own food. If an invasion came, Albanian soldiers were to remain in these bunkers, surviving on grass if need be, until overwhelmed. As it happened, the bunkers did have one use — young Albanians who still lived at home found them excellent places to have sex in.

Hoxha's health began to decline in the early '70s — he suffered from diabetes, and had a heart attack in 1973 that left him incapacitated for months. His place at official functions was often taken by a double, a former dentist, Petar Shapallo, who had been taken hostage by the Sigurimi and lived in the Hoxhas' home. Nexhmije, always a power behind the throne, was increasingly making the decisions (it was apparently at her instigation that beards were banned in Albania, because foreigners might try to hide behind them). By this time, Hoxha's relationship with his last international friend, Mao, had soured — he had been disgusted by Mao's decision to meet Nixon in 1972. The final break with China came in 1978, leaving the Republic of Albania as isolated from the communist world as it had always been from the capitalist one.

The '70s saw another major purge, this time focused on the armed forces. Several senior military figures including the defence minister were executed, and hundreds of officers and soldiers imprisoned. Sometimes their sons were arrested too, while other family members were sent into internal exile. Whether anybody had actually been involved in planning a coup, as was alleged, is unknown.

The most dramatic downfall of anyone during the Hoxha regime was that of Mehmet Shehu, who had commanded the partisan forces that liberated Tirana in 1944. He had been the prime minister of Albania for twenty-seven years, and was one of Hoxha's closest friends, as well as his heir apparent. In other words, he was a marked man.

In August 1981, one of Shehu's three sons, Skënder, told his father he wanted to marry a pretty young girl named Silva Turdiu. Her father was a respected university professor, and Silva was a member of Albania's national volleyball team. But the Turdius were a tainted family, with both of Silva's parents having relatives who had opposed the regime. Shehu was concerned enough about this to request a security file on them, but satisfied himself that there would be no serious objection to the marriage, and told his son he could announce the engagement. His mistake was not running the decision by Hoxha, who was on holiday with Nexhmije. He later said he hadn't wanted to disturb them.

All seemed well at first. Returning from their holiday,

Hoxha and Nexhmije went to the Shehus' house in the Bllok to congratulate them on the engagement. Hoxha told Silva, who was there, that her father was a respectable man, and he was thrilled about the marriage; Nexhmije told her she had been to school with her mother, and to send her regards. But shortly after their visit, someone told Nexhmije that people had been talking about the engagement, and she also asked for the file on the family. She didn't like what she read, and neither did Hoxha. What probably angered them the most was the fact that Silva's mother was related to a well-known Albanian dissident named Arshi Pipa. After a period of imprisonment during the '50s, Pipa had moved to the United States where he became a university professor and kept up his criticism of Hoxha's rule in books and articles. In 1973, he published a satirical poem in which he referred to the dictator's alleged homosexuality. ("Glory to your ass, oh dandy, / This is what explains it all.") That Hoxha was a closet homosexual had been rumoured in Albania ever since his time in Paris.

Shehu called the engagement off eight days later, after a long meeting with Hoxha. Over the next few weeks, he saw signs that he was being frozen out. Hoxha had ceased to confide in him, he disappeared from TV news reports, and he noticed an uncommon lack of deference among his subordinates. Yet, when he attended Hoxha's birthday celebrations on 16 October, everything seemed normal. The dictator greeted Shehu with a hug, they sat together during the formalities, and during the speeches acknowledged their long friendship and wished each other a long life.

It was all very different at the Communist Party's Eighth Congress just two months later, with one delegate after another standing up to denounce Shehu in the most virulent terms. Hoxha hadn't spoken when the first day's proceedings adjourned, but as he left, said to Shehu, "Reflect on the criticism." Shehu went home and shot himself in his bedroom.

His suicide note read in part:

> *Yes, Comrade Enver, I am always ready to give my life for the party. And this is exactly what I'm doing now. I'm giving my life for the party, so that I, your closest friend in times of trouble and success, as you yourself rightly called me, can use this as a last resort to give you yourself, my friend, my teacher and my dear brother, an opportunity to learn the truth.*

Shehu's suicide note is eerily similar to many letters written to Hoxha by people prior to their executions. They invariably affirmed their dedication to communism and their devotion to Hoxha personally, while suggesting that other, unnamed individuals had poisoned his mind against them. Perhaps they really believed Hoxha wasn't to blame for their fate. Perhaps they thought that writing in these terms would lead to more lenient treatment for their families. There is something truly Kafkaesque about such letters (when you remember that, at the end of *The Trial*, Josef K goes willingly to his death).

Shortly after Shehu's suicide, Hoxha's daughter-in-law Liljana was staying in his villa in Pogradec. One evening, passing the living room, she saw Hoxha and Nexhmije watching a video of Shehu's widow, Fiqirete, being interrogated and tortured.

Thanks to Hoxha's economic policies, by the early 1980s Albania was the poorest country in Europe, and the third-poorest in the world. The average income was just $15 per month, and many in the countryside lived close to starvation. In Tirana, large families were crammed into tiny flats in huge, hideous concrete blocks with walls devoid of

that luxury, plaster. While most Eastern Bloc countries made at least an attempt to keep their people pacified by producing facsimiles of Western goods, shoddy though they might have

been, no such effort was made in Albania. Meanwhile, the huge, pyramid-shaped Enver Hoxha Museum was being constructed at vast expense in the capital, with three floors of Carrara marble devoted to exhibitions about the life and achievements of the 'Supreme Comrade'. His shoes, and the tailored suits he had worn in Paris, were there in glass cases to be admired.

Shehu's suicide was followed by further purges. Referring to the birthday party that lulled Shehu into a false sense of security, Hoxha's biographer Blendi Fevziu notes, "In the space of just a few months, 12 people who were warmly embraced by Hoxha that day were given extreme punishments: four were executed, one committed suicide and the remaining seven would serve long prison terms."

Hoxha withdrew from public life in his last years. He saw few people other than his immediate family, including his sons Ilir and Sokal, and daughter Pranvera (none of whom had the slightest interest in entering politics). He had no old friends to talk to anymore — they had all been liquidated. He spent most of his time working on his memoirs — thirteen volumes in all — in which he fashioned a thoroughly self-serving version of his past. By the end he was wheelchair-bound, sometimes disoriented, almost blind and barely able to speak, yet his grip on power was as tight as ever. He made his final public appearance in November 1984, on the 40th anniversary of his coming to power. With his frail body carefully propped up he gave a short speech, which he mimed to a recording, extolling the brilliant transformation Albania had undergone under communist rule.

On April 9 1985, he lurched out of his sickbed, took a couple of steps, then fell heavily to the floor in a coma. He died three days later.

ENVER HOXHA

Enver Hoxha wrote more about himself than any other dictator, but he remains one of the most unfathomable.

He liked to present himself as a great thinker, a visionary, a theorist of socialism *par excellence*. It's no surprise then that he was thoroughly pissed off by Tito's gibe about him: "Poor Mr Hoxha. He doesn't know anything about Marxism beyond its name." But Tito, who practised a far more flexible form of communism, was undoubtedly right. Hoxha inflicted on the unfortunate Albanian people a mindless, by-the-numbers version of Stalinism, equal parts rigid social repression and state control of every aspect of the economy, leavened towards the end with some Maoist craziness. Compared to Hoxha, the wooden-headed Nicolae Ceauşescu was a fountain of ideas.

Most communist leaders begin as youthful firebrands, but not so Hoxha. As a student in Paris, he was known as an insouciant character, a well-dressed dandy who wasn't passionate about anything apart from being the centre of attention. And perhaps that's the key to him. It took him a long time to commit to communism, and when he finally did, I think it was because he saw the potential it held for *him*. He seems to have sensed early on how the war would go, that the Allies would win, and that the communists, far better organised and determined than the nationalists, would come out on top when it was over.

Having attained power, he was indifferent to the material rewards that usually went with it. On a visit to Tito in 1948, he was taken aback by the luxury of the Yugoslav leader's lifestyle, and later made fun of it. Hoxha's home at the time was a fairly modest house in the Bllok, formerly owned by a civil engineer. In 1973, he had a far larger (though still non-descript) residence built nearby. It was filled with imported furniture, carpets and appliances (the Albanian equivalents would have been simply too embarrassing), but nothing was particularly stylish or expensive.

Rather than wealth, it was power that motivated Hoxha. The same goes for every dictator, of course, and yet the way he maintained his power over four decades had a single-mindedness, even a sort of purity about it, that was really quite remarkable. He seems to have looked at everyone he ever met through the prism of his own survival. He made sure to surround himself with people who were no better educated than he was — not a single member of Albania's elite had a university degree. He would have people arrested on the slighted pretext, and often for no apparent reason. Many were people who had liked him, sometimes loved him. This seems to me to go beyond political expediency, and enter the realms of psychopathology.

If anyone ever deserved the soubriquet 'smiling assassin' it was Enver Hoxha. Yet there was an even more unusual aspect to him. Occasionally, people who had spent decades in prisons or labour camps would have a chance encounter with Hoxha after their release. They would be petrified, of course, but he would approach them like a long lost friend, pat them on the back, ask them how they were. As the old joke goes, "Love your enemies — it'll confuse the heck out of them."

After Hoxha's death, nothing much changed in Albania for a while. There had been no organised opposition at all during his rule, so there was nothing to immediately take his place. In the elections held in 1987 under Hoxha's successor, Ramiz Alia, all but one of the country's 1,830,653 registered voters chose the ruling party. But in 1992, with the economy still floundering and thousands of Albanians attempting to flee to Italy, the Albanian Democratic Party triumphed over the remnants of Hoxha's Communists.

The statues of Hoxha were torn down, the Sigurimi were disbanded, Nexhmije Hoxha was arrested and the Enver Hoxha Museum became a disco. Albanians embraced capitalism with the eagerness of lost and dehydrated wanderers coming upon a river, but sadly they mostly embraced it in the form of pyramid schemes run by foreigners that managed to bankrupt many of them and almost the country as well.

While the Albanian economy has improved in recent years, the country remains one of the poorest in Europe. People now live in the concrete bunkers which still dot the land, while blood feuds have reportedly made a return.

CHAPTER 3

MAO ZEDONG

MAO ZEDONG

Attained power in 1949
Died of motor neurone disease in 1976

Mao Zedong was born in an isolated valley called Shaoshan in Hunan province, China, on 26 December 1893. His father, Mao Yichang, was a pig farmer and grain merchant who made enough money to have the thatched roof of the family home replaced with a tile one, a sure sign of status. He thought the best place for the young Mao was out in the fields working, but his son preferred reading, and the two often clashed. Mao's favourite books, which he read at night by the light of an oil lamp, were ancient Chinese novels about bandits and rebels that he took to be true. In later years, this avid reader would become both the world's all-time best-selling author, and the man responsible for burning more books than any other individual in history.

Mao hated his father but adored his mother Wen Qimei, from whom he inherited his round face and full lips. She was a Buddhist so Mao was also a Buddhist in his earliest years. He was a good student with an excellent memory that allowed him to rote learn long passages from Confucius, but he was as quarrelsome and rebellious with his various tutors as he was with his father. When he was fourteen, in an attempt to make him settle down, Mao's father arranged a marriage between him and a girl six years older. Mao wanted nothing to do with her, though, and she died a year later.

When he was sixteen, Mao left the farm for good. He went to the provincial capital of Changsha, attended several schools, and became an ardent republican, cutting off his 'queue' or pigtail, the symbol of the Manchu Dynasty. He also became a physical culture enthusiast and toughened himself by swimming in icy waters, sleeping in the open and dancing naked in the snow. Another favourite pastime was to stand in the face of strong winds and shout his defiant poetry.

To fight with Heaven is infinite pleasure!
To fight with earth is infinite pleasure!
To fight with men is infinite pleasure!

fter the fall of the Manchu dynasty in 1911, power in China was divided between the Nationalist government of Sun Yat-sen; various competing warlords; and foreign powers such as Britain, France and Japan which controlled whole territories, known as concessions. It was a time of unprecedented freedom, with people allowed to travel around the country without restrictions, and to espouse radical ideas. Mao and his friends took advantage of this, with Mao delighting in being the most radical of all. He argued that China should turn its back on centuries of culture and history and start afresh, even if such a transition resulted in violent conflict.

Mao enrolled at a teacher training college when he was nineteen, and supplemented his education with intense periods of reading in public libraries. After graduating from college in 1918, he obtained a few teaching positions and dabbled in journalism. Then came a fortuitous meeting with Professor Chen Duxiu, who was busy establishing (with Soviet funding) a Chinese Communist Party. He asked Mao to set up a bookshop, and in 1921, he was one of thirteen Communists from across the country who gathered in Shanghai for the First Congress of the Communist Party of China.

Mao was appointed party secretary in Hunan province, a well-paid position that allowed him to move into a house with his second wife, Yang Kaihui. He set about organising unions, strikes and night schools. According to Marxist ideology, it was the urban workers who would bring about the revolution, but these were a tiny minority in China. 80 per cent of the population were peasants, and Mao realised any revolution was going to depend on them. The idea was opposed by Stalin and most of the Chinese Communists. Mao ignored them all and started recruiting peasants.

During the early 1920s, the Soviets had instructed the Chinese Communists to join forces with the Nationalists, their stated aim being to throw out the foreign occupiers. Sun Yat-sen was keen to accept Soviet funds and happy enough with the arrangement, but most Chinese Communists hated it. Mao, being a pragmatist, was one of the few who didn't. His policy of mobilising the peasantry now began to take off. Peasant activists ransacked the houses of landlords, paraded them through the streets wearing dunce's caps, and beat some of them to death. Mao, who had always relished the idea of chaos, was hugely impressed. He began to be noticed by the Soviets.

In 1927, after the death of Sun Yat-sen, General Chiang Kai-shek became leader of the Nationalists. Chiang despised the Communists and ordered a brutal crackdown on them. Tens of thousands were massacred, and Mao was put on a wanted list. He took refuge in the Jinggang Mountains, a remote area on the border of Hunan province, and managed to take some six-hundred men with him, mostly deserters from the Nationalist army. Stalin had ordered the Communists to form their own army, and although Mao had no experience as a military leader, he agreed wholeheartedly with the policy. The Jinggang Mountains

were outlaw territory, and Mao, no doubt recalling the books he had loved as a child, told his followers they would live like outlaws too, looting the houses of the rich (although 'rich' had a fairly elastic definition), but they were forbidden from taking so much as a needle from a peasant. They were to move through the people, Mao said, like fish through water.

Mao studied Sun Tzu's classic *The Art of War*, learning the importance of exploiting the enemy's weaknesses, and of giving ground in the face of superior forces. He had some early military successes, including the taking of a provincial capital, which again impressed Moscow. Captured Nationalist soldiers were given a quick dose of propaganda and invited to join the Reds. If they refused they were released — minus their weapons. Many joined.

Learning that Chang Kai-shek was preparing a major assault, Mao abandoned the Jinggang Mountains. His army, numbering around 15,000, headed for Fujian province and captured the small but prosperous city of Tingzhou. Here they acquired uniforms for the first time. Mao next mounted an assault on the city of Changsha which failed. An unintended victim of this was his wife, Yang Kaihui, who had been living on the outskirts of the city with their three children. Mao had left them there when he took off for the mountains, and had since taken a third wife, a committed young Communist named He Zizhen. Yang Kaihui was dragged to a court and ordered to denounce Mao. When she refused, she was executed.

Chiang Kai-shek led a huge force of 300,000 men against the Communists in July 1931 and came close to defeating them. But then Japan invaded the Chinese territory of Manchuria. Facing this new threat, Chiang was forced to withdraw his army. In its absence, Mao set up the first Red state, known as the Chinese Soviet Republic, which covered several provinces and had a population of ten million. Mao was declared head of state and acquired the title of 'chairman' for the first time. His triumph was short-lived, for a month after the Red state was founded, Zhou Enlai arrived from Shanghai to be its party chief. Zhou had a direct line to Moscow, and Mao found himself outranked.

Mao had been operating as a law unto himself for the last four years, robbing landlords and recruiting peasants, but he had made no real effort to reorganise them along communist lines. Zhou, in comparison, was the bureaucrat from hell, and set about making Mao's fledging state into a model for the Red China of the future. A huge temple outside the Red state's capital, Ruijin, became the headquarters of fifteen government departments. Under the system Zhou implemented, people were enmeshed in the party from the age of six, when they joined the Children's Corps, after which they passed through the Youth Brigade and were finally inducted into the army. Everyone was expected to work seven days a week, with their only hours of leisure spent at interminable party meetings.

Prior to the coming of the Communists, the region's peasants were poor but generally had a few possessions in addition to farming tools and cooking utensils, and women usually owned at least one piece of jewellery. Now, hit with high taxes, they were forced to sell anything they owned with any value. They were forbidden to leave their villages without a pass, and normal social relations were all but curtailed. Mao had long believed that women were as capable of hard physical labour as men, and as most of the Red state's able-bodied men under the age of fifty were occupied with army duties, women were left to do the farm work. This may not seem that harsh until you remember they all had crippled feet from the centuries-old Chinese tradition of foot binding.

Being outranked by Zhou Enlai was bad enough, but Mao also lost his command of the army. He took himself off to a Buddhist temple where he sulked and schemed for a while. Zhou Enlai eventually relented and put him back in charge of about two-thirds of the army, and he took the opportunity to capture the coastal city of Zhangzhou, which made headlines around the world. When the Nationalists mounted another major offensive, however, and Mao refused to fight them, believing (probably correctly) that he had no chance against their superior forces, he was dismissed again.

Time was running out for the Red state. By early 1934, Chiang Kai-shek had a million troops closing on Ruijin from all sides, and the Reds knew they needed another stronghold. As they prepared to evacuate, they did some housekeeping, and on Zhou Enlai's orders thousands who were deemed to be 'unreliable' were executed and buried in pits. This was the Chinese Communists' first great purge.

Over 80,000 set off on the 'Long March', which would become the foundation legend of the Chinese Communists. In just over a year they covered six thousand miles while facing harassment from Chiang's forces which included aerial bombing. Dressed in light cotton uniforms and usually shoeless they crossed snow-covered mountains (which inspired Mao to poetry) and spent six days wading through waist-deep grass and poisonous mud in the dreaded 'grasslands' on the China-Tibet border.

Their goal was Schizuan province, which was occupied by the Red military commander Zhang Guotao and his force of 80,000 men, and close enough to Russian-controlled territory for Soviet military assistance to get through. In January 1935, as they approached Schizuan, Mao's troops clashed with the Nationalists in the battle of Tucheng, and four thousand were killed or wounded — their worst defeat in the Long March (although Mao declared the battle a victory). Four months later, they began another push towards Schizuan, but to reach it they would have to cross the raging Dadu River via a suspension bridge of iron chains covered with planks of wood. According to the official version, Mao and his men arrived to find many of the bridge's planks removed, and a Nationalist force on the other side waiting for them. As the Reds began to cross it, the Nationalists sprayed them with machine gun fire and set fire to the bridge, forcing them to crawl over bare chains that glowed red hot. However, while there was some sort of battle at the bridge, it seems that the story was wildly exaggerated, and the Reds may have suffered only three casualties.

After meeting up with Zhang Guotao's army in the Tibetan

highlands, Mao was confirmed as party leader and Zhang as army chief. Mao and his remaining men then pushed on to Shaanxi province, where he sent an envoy to Moscow with news of his arrival. Only 8,000 of the original marchers made it to the north-western town of Yan'an where Mao, his tactics vindicated and his authority upheld, set up a new Red capital.

As the legend of the Long March spread, thousands flocked to Yan'an to join the Red Army. The first foreign journalists also arrived to interview Mao, who certainly didn't look the part of a military commander. Now in his mid-forties, he was a tall, stooped, sloppily dressed figure with long, glossy black hair. He lived in a cave where he spent much of his time writing, smoked constantly and ate the same peasant food he always had. He was almost permanently constipated, and when he did manage a bowel movement it was a cause for rejoicing among his men.

His most important visitor during these years was the American journalist Edgar Snow, who conducted extensive interviews with him. Mao gave a sanitised account of the early years of the Chinese Communist Party which Snow accepted without question, and his 1937 book *Red Star Over China*, with its admiring portrait of Mao, would colour accounts of the Chinese revolution in the West for decades.

The atmosphere at Yan'an was upbeat, and there were even weekly square dances initiated by another visiting American journalist, Agnes Smedley. Mao was no dancer, but after his initial reluctance he realised what an excellent way it was to pick up young women, something with which he was increasingly preoccupied. He also took a new wife in Yan'an, an ambitious and devious actress from Shanghai named Jiang Qing. Lacking revolutionary credentials, she seemed a poor choice of companion to Mao's colleagues, especially compared to Mao's existing wife, He Zizhen, one of the few women to endure the Long March. (Mao had sent her to

Russia for medical treatment, and she died there in 1948.) He threatened to resign and return to his home village unless his new marriage was approved. The Central Committee eventually gave in, but only on the condition that Jiang Qing stay away from politics. Decades later, this injunction would be ignored — with dire consequences.

Mao had cannily declared war on Japan during the Long March, drawing many Nationalists to his cause. Then, in January 1937, Stalin ordered the Communists and Nationalists to put aside their differences and unite to fight Japan. The Japanese had set up the puppet state of Manchuria in the north of China, but the Chinese government had not yet declared war on them. That changed in June, when thousands of Japanese soldiers poured south. They invaded Shanghai, almost levelling it in the process, and perpetrated the infamous Rape of Nanjing, when drunken Japanese soldiers ran amok in the city for six weeks, killing some 200,000 soldiers and civilians.

Over the next few years, Mao was happy to accept massive military aid from the Soviets, but he was always wary of pitting his forces against the Japanese. For him, Chiang and the Nationalists were his real enemy, and he was quite happy to see the Japanese overrunning Nationalist-held territory, while concentrating on expanding his own.

Volunteers continued to pour into Yan'an. Many were idealistic young men inspired by the vision of social equality offered by communism, but it didn't take them long to see there was little equality in Yan'an, where leaders enjoyed significantly higher standards of living than the rest. When newcomers began to openly criticise this state of affairs, Mao ordered a crackdown, going so far as to make satire and irony criminal offences. He went further in 1943, launching a new and far-reaching campaign. Most of the young volunteers had come from territories controlled by the Nationalists, and Mao now declared that many of them were spies. Thousands were thrown into hastily-constructed prisons, tortured, and forced to confess and denounce others at mass rallies. Everyone had to write 'thought examinations', where they recorded their every thought or utterance against the party, and to compile reports of what they had heard others say. After two years of this, during which the campaign was extended to Red territories across China, Mao declared a general amnesty, his goals achieved. His rank and file were so terrorised that dissent had become virtually unthinkable.

The beginnings of Mao's personality cult can also be traced to this period. The first Mao badges were produced, along with portraits of him which party members were expected to buy and hang in their homes.

ao had predicted a long war against Japan, perhaps decades long, but said that Japan would eventually over-extend itself and succumb to China's overwhelming population. Japan's entry into World War II changed everything. As the odds turned against the Japanese, the Americans, thinking they might need to invade Japan via China, tried to organise a truce between the Communists and the Nationalists. Then the atom bomb ended the war more quickly than anyone had expected.

But there would no peace for the long-suffering Chinese, who had endured a state of war since the Japanese invasion in 1931. Instead, Mao and Chiang prepared for a final showdown that would be as ferocious as anything that had gone before. That Mao eventually prevailed, despite the Communists having virtually no popular support at the beginning, can be attributed to a number of factors. These included Soviet military assistance, and the fact that Mao was for the most part fighting a guerrilla war against Chiang's conventional one. Mao's cultivation of the peasants was also crucial, with land reforms put in place in Red-controlled territory to keep them onside. Finally, the Reds were simply more ruthless than the Nationalists, engaging in tactics that left entire regions devastated. In the most famous instance, they laid siege to the city of Changsha for five months, during which some 160,000 of its inhabitants starved to death. For his part Chiang, while he began with vastly superior forces, made serious strategic mistakes. During the four years of civil war, the Nationalist government also showed itself to be hopelessly corrupt, thus losing a great deal of popular support.

The Reds had gained control of Manchuria, China's industrial heartland, by the end of 1948, and in April 1949 began moving towards Chiang's capital, Nanjing. Chiang and his remaining followers fled to Taiwan. On 1 October, Mao stood on top of Beijing's Gate of Heavenly Peace and announced to cheering crowds that "The central government of the People's Republic of China is established." As he always did after a momentous event, Mao composed a poem. It begins:

Over Chungshan swept a storm, headlong,
Our mighty army, a million strong, has crossed the Great River,
The City, a tiger crouching, a dragon curling, outshines its ancient glories;
In heroic triumph heaven and earth have been overturned.

ao now had the lives of 550 million people — a quarter of the earth's population — to play with. What was he going to do with them? At this point, it's unlikely that even his closest followers really knew.

Women were the initial winners in the Chinese Revolution. Female slavery and foot binding were banned, and for the first time women were given the right to divorce and own property. The so-called 'landlords', unsurprisingly, were the immediate losers. The campaign against them, which had continued in Communist-controlled areas during the civil war, was now stepped up. Units of party members, known as cadres, were despatched to the countryside to incite the peasants to stage uprisings, and some two million landlords were shot, beaten to death or buried alive. (In fact, few of them were really landlords; they were just people marginally better off than others in their village.) Cities were cleared of petty criminals, beggars and prostitutes, who were sent to re-education camps or to the countryside to work. Communist functionaries took over the running of all institutions and the media, but there was initially little attempt to reorganise the economy.

The most profound change was a suspension of the rule of law, with courts replaced by party committees. From now on people would be governed by edicts and 'campaigns' initiated by the Central Committee (which meant, for the next twenty-seven years, initiated by Mao). The first of these, which began in 1950, was the campaign against 'counter-revolutionaries', who might be former Nationalists, criminals, or anyone who had expressed criticism of the new regime. Mao announced that one death for every thousand people would be appropriate, but the death rates in some regions were higher as people took advantage of the campaign to eliminate their enemies. After two or three years of this, and with the economy in a steep decline, most of the population were reduced to a state of poverty, a fact which the party celebrated. ('To be Poor is Glorious' was the slogan.)

Most dictators, from Hitler and Stalin down, have chosen to liquidate their enemies out of the public eye, usually behind the walls of prisons or concentration camps. But not Mao. He wanted ordinary people — even children — to denounce their fellow citizens. The accused would be paraded through the streets bearing placards on which their supposed crimes were written, then publicly executed. This was a policy he had initiated with his campaign against the landlords in the 1920s, and it served two purposes — to instil fear throughout the population, and to make ordinary people complicit. And it was this, rather than any variant of Marxist ideology, that became the essence of Maoism.

It was to China's history, and the reigns of the various emperors, that Mao increasingly turned for inspiration. His favourite emperors, like the eleventh century Emperor Zhou, were the ones considered by the Chinese to be the most tyrannical and brutal. They may have had to sacrifice many lives, Mao argued, but they got the job done.

From the moment he assumed control of China, Mao wanted to turn the country into a global power. The Korean War, which began in June 1950 when North Korean dictator Kim Il-sung's forces invaded the South, offered an opportunity to further this goal. Mao offered to commit a large number of troops to the conflict, and in return Stalin (who didn't want Russia to be directly involved) agreed to provide military assistance and help China set up an arms industry. After a year of fighting, North Korea had been so devastated by U.S. bombing that Kim was desperate for the war to end, but Mao demurred — he wanted his troops (who had already suffered massive casualties) to keep killing Americans for a while.

When the war finally ended a year and a half later, Mao was determined to keep receiving Soviet industrial and military aid (he particularly wanted to get his hands on some atom bombs). All he could offer in return was China's only exportable commodity — food. From this point on, vast quantities of grain, cooking oil, eggs, pork and other foodstuffs were shipped off to Russia each year. At the same time, Mao provided food aid to other Eastern Bloc countries, no strings attached (this was basically to generate goodwill — part of Mao's long-term plan to become leader of the Communist world). Inevitably, this policy saw the already lamentably poor diet of China's peasants reduced to subsistence level.

ao's official residence in Beijing was in a Ming dynasty pavilion called the Chrysanthemum Fragrance Study which was adjacent to the Forbidden City, the traditional home of the emperors. His bedroom, the size of a ballroom, featured a massive bed and mountains of books. In some ways he continued to live simply, eating peasant food (although of the finest quality — his rice had to be husked in a very particular way) and remaining indifferent to the trappings of wealth that most dictators loved so much, and he only ever dressed properly when making one of his extremely rare public appearances. His teeth, blackened by smoking, were covered in a greenish film, but he refused to brush them or have dental work. Yet, if he lacked some of the usual trappings of power, he was as free from daily cares as the most pampered of emperors. When Mao sat down in his private cinema to watch an American movie, there was a soldier ready to loosen his belt for him.

In the early 1950s, an American-trained doctor, Li Zhisui, was appointed to be Mao's personal physician, and held the post until Mao's death. His account of these years, *The Private Life of Chairman Mao*, provides a remarkable picture of life in Mao's inner circle.

Dr Li soon found himself invited to one of Mao's dances. After the revolution, ballroom dancing had been banned in China as a symbol of Western decadence, but Mao continued to hold the weekly dances which had begun in Yan'an. At these affairs he and a few other male officials were vastly outnumbered by hordes of nubile young girls supplied by the Cultural Work Troupe of the Central Garrison Corps. Whether the music playing was Western swing or Chinese opera, Mao would dance in the same slow shuffle while girls fought for the honour of being his partner. That they were not just there for dancing eventually became clear to Dr Li. Later, the dances became twice weekly, and Mao had another one of his huge, purpose-built beds installed in a room adjoining the ballroom. Into this Mao would periodically retire during the evening, accompanied by one or more of the girls. A few of the party hierarchy were appalled by such goings on, but most looked the other way.

Dr Li found that Mao's appetite for sex was insatiable, and the older he got the more insatiable he became. Like his hero, Emperor Zhou, who had thousands of concubines, Mao shared the Daoist belief that the more young sex partners a man had, the longer he would live. As Mao believed China's destiny was inextricably linked with his own, it was virtually his duty to sleep with these girls. Mao's sexual interests did not end with women either. Soldiers appointed to his personal guard found, to their dismay, that one of the duties expected of them was to send the Great Helmsman off to sleep with a relaxing groin massage.

ao had hit on communism as the best recipe for returning China to its former greatness, but he despaired about the pace of change. He was highly critical of the way the Soviet Union had turned into a rigid, bureaucratic society. He thought the ideal state for any society was constant flux and change.

Always quick with slogans, he coined a new one in 1957: 'Let a hundred flowers bloom, let a hundred schools contend.' During the Hundred Flowers Campaign which followed, people were encouraged to criticise the party so that it might be reformed. Reluctant to speak at first, they gradually found their voices. Soon some were going so far as to call for the overthrow of the party.

Whether Mao had genuinely wanted to hear a diversity of opinion, then saw it go too far, or whether the whole thing was a ruse from the start to flush out the party's enemies, the result was the same. In the crackdown that followed, hundreds of thousands of people who had spoken out were accused of being 'Rightists' and sent to remote country areas to live and work with the peasants. This was always Mao's favourite way of dealing with intellectuals, for whom he had nothing but contempt. No-one was so clever, he thought, that years of back-breaking work in mines or paddy fields wouldn't do them a power of good.

Mao only ever made two trips out of China — both to the Soviet Union — and he had little idea about life in the West. His knowledge of economics never much exceeded that of the average peasant, but he still chafed at the slowness of economic progress. In May 1958, he announced a grand new campaign, the 'Great Leap Forward', which would see China catch up with Great Britain industrially in just fifteen years. To achieve this, the pace of collectivisation was dramatically increased. Millions of reluctant peasant farmers were forced to amalgamate their tiny plots of land into large communes. They lost their property, were forced to eat in communal dining rooms where the quickest got the most food, and men and women were confined to separate barracks. Much of the agricultural output produced by the communes was seized by the state and exported, leaving farmers and their families with just enough to feed themselves — if they were lucky.

At the same time, a series of vast irrigation projects commenced. These appealed to Mao because they required almost no investment, just peasant slave labour. Around a million peasants were set to work building dams and reservoirs which were poorly planned, often never completed, and resulted in more than a few environmental catastrophes. In 1975, a system of reservoirs in Henan province built during this period disintegrated in a storm, and up to 240,000 people were drowned.

Mao knew that one of the main measures of a country's economic strength was steel production. As China had few steel mills, someone — their name, sadly, seems to have gone unrecorded — suggested that people build small furnaces in their backyards. Mao seized on this idea with typical excitement, and overnight, backyard furnaces sprang up over China. Faced with a shortage of iron ore, and with quotas to fill, people resorted to feeding the furnaces scrap metal, then their farming tools and household pots and pans, while all available wood was used to fuel the fires. The metal produced was impure and useless.

The more one considers the Great Leap Forward, the more apparent it becomes that there was an element of — I can't put it any other way — childishness to it. It was as if China had been put into the hands of a group of not-terribly-bright ten-year-olds. Huge projects were launched with little or no scientific input or, indeed, no serious attempt to engage with reality at all. As part of the push to increase agricultural production, a number of new farming methods were introduced, including 'close-cropping' (planting seeds closer together). From generations of experience, peasant farmers knew these methods wouldn't work, but cadres forced them to adopt them. Mao had the curious conviction that people and nature were entirely separate, and the latter could be tamed with brute force. This was the reasoning behind the grand irrigation projects, but the most absurd expression of it was the war he declared on pests in 1958, specifically sparrows, rats, flies and mosquitos. Sparrows were singled out because they ate grain and were therefore enemies of the people. A veritable army of men and women across the country went to war against sparrows, shooting them, destroying their nests, and making such a racket by screaming and banging pots that the birds were too frightened to land and eventually fell to earth exhausted. The campaign was such a success that sparrows virtually disappeared from China, along with a great many other birds. Alas, all the insects that those birds would have eaten then descended on crops, destroying many of them.

With the peasants disgruntled and millions of people wasting their time melting down saucepans or scaring sparrows, agricultural production plummeted. Provincial officials who had been given impossibly high production targets to meet resorted to falsifying their figures. Mao was delighted when he read all the reports of bumper harvests that were coming in, wondering aloud what the Chinese people would do with all this extra food. Then he took the opportunity to raise food exports.

As the first reports of mass starvation in the provinces filtered through to Beijing in 1959, Mao did what he usually did when his schemes went awry — he tried to blame his subordinates. When problems with the communes were being discussed during a meeting of party leaders in April, Mao said airily, "That was somebody else's idea, not mine. I had a look at it but I didn't understand it. I just had a faint impression that communes are good." But instead of easing the pace of change, Mao began a purge of hundreds of thousands of 'Rightists' within the party who were deemed to be insufficiently enthusiastic about the Great Leap. As the situation deteriorated, peasants were reduced to eating leather belts, tree bark, leaves, straw and mud. In the worst-hit regions, some resorted to cannibalism. When word of the famine began to reach the outside world, the Chinese government blamed it on natural disasters.

By the time the Great Leap Forward had shuddered to a

halt in 1962, up to 40 per cent of the houses in China had been demolished, many to make way for grand projects that were never built, others so that their mud bricks and straw could be used as fertiliser. Thousands of factories stood idle, their machinery so poorly maintained it had ceased to function, their furnaces unlit due to shortages of coal. Vast tracts of China's arable land lay fallow, and at least forty-five million people had starved to death. It was the worst famine in China's history, and the worst caused by human actions of all time.

And China is still littered with lumps of useless metal.

The appalling death toll of the Great Leap Forward didn't faze Mao in the least. The fact is that he had no problem with death, and even welcomed it (for others, of course). At the height of the Cold War, he was heard to say several times that he welcomed the dropping of an atom bomb on China. "The death of ten or twenty million people is nothing to be afraid of," he told the Indian prime minister, Nehru. As the Great Leap was getting under way, he warned his insiders half of China's population might have to die before his grand project was completed. "Deaths have benefits," he remarked a month later. "They can fertilise the ground."

Mao may have been insouciant, but the Great Leap Forward was a disaster on such an epic scale that other party leaders finally stood up to him. At the Party Congress in January 1962, the country's president, Liu Shaoqi, abandoned the keynote speech he was supposed to give. Having recently visited his home province where he saw the horrendous conditions there, Liu revealed the scope of the Great Leap's failure and held Mao firmly responsible. The seven thousand delegates could hardly believe their ears, and Mao was forced to stand up and indulge in self-criticism — something most of his subordinates had done hundreds of times, but a novel experience for him. After he flounced off to Shanghai in a rage, Lui and the other party leaders set about dismantling the apparatus of the Great Leap, cutting food aid to other countries, cancelling industrial projects, and easing up on collective farming.

Mao sought consolation in the arms of his young girls, so that three or four of them could often be found in his bed. (It must be said that, according to their testimony, even into his seventies he put on an impressive performance.) At some point he had contracted an infection called *trichomunas vaginalis* which, as is usual with men, caused no symptoms in Mao, but violent discomfort to the many young women he infected with it. As it wasn't hurting him, Mao saw no reason to take drugs to treat it. Mao never bathed or showered, receiving only a nightly rubdown with a hot towel, and Dr Li begged him to at least wash his genitals, but Mao refused this too, saying, "I wash myself inside the bodies of my women."

The day-to-day running of China had passed into the hands of men like Liu Shoaqi and Deng Xiaoping. Both veterans of the Long March, they had been Mao's comrades for years, but he had come to see them and other high-ranking officials as betrayers of the revolution. Mao began to gather around him a small group of people he thought he could trust. These included his wife, Jiang Qing, and another Long March veteran, Lin Biao, who expressed fanatical devotion to Mao. Lin was made Minister of Defence and set about fostering a Maoist personality cult among the army. He edited a selection of excerpts from the Chairman's writings, the ubiquitous, plastic-bound 'Little Red Book', and every soldier was expected to carry it at all times and recite its timeless wisdom.

In approaching a problem a Marxist should see the whole

as well as the parts. A frog in a well says, "The sky is no bigger than the mouth of the well." That is untrue, for the sky is not just the size of the mouth of the well. If it said, "A part of the sky is the size of the well," that would be true, for it tallies with the facts.

Mao was plotting far more than the downfall of the party leaders who had humiliated him. He wanted a whole new revolution that would turn the country upside down — and it would begin with an attack on culture itself.

Mao's attitude to culture was deeply ambivalent. He loved traditional Chinese opera, and had devoured books from a young age, but thought 'the masses' had no need for such things, saying that the more books people read the more stupid they became. To achieve his cultural revolution, he turned to the most malleable elements in society, the young. In June 1966, the word went out in state media that students should denounce their teachers for their 'bourgeois' ideas, and the students responded with enthusiasm. Over the next few weeks, teachers in schools and universities in Beijing and other cities were beaten, stomped on, doused with boiling water, and had their heads shaved (the 'yin and yang' cut, where one side of the head was shaved, was very popular). The young revolutionaries, dubbed 'Red Guards', wore green army uniforms, red armbands and belts with brass buckles (good for beating people with), and invariably clutched a copy of the Little Red Book. On 16 August 1966, wearing the same army uniform, Mao stood on the rostrum of Tiananmen Gate and addressed over a million Red Guards. He had declared war on the 'Four Olds' — old ideas, culture, customs and habits.

Millions of Red Guards, allowed to travel free on trains and provided with food and accommodation, spread out from Beijing across the country. They had carte blanche to invade homes and interrogate, beat up and kill anyone whose ideas they deemed old, or Western, or anti-Mao. They slashed paintings, smashed phonograph records, stomped on musical instruments, burned books. Never before had a state sanctioned such teenage kicks. Many people, fearing an imminent visit by the Red Guards, took it upon themselves to destroy every cultural artefact they owned.

The Red Guards were let loose on the very fabric of China's millennia-old society. They destroyed buildings, temples, antiquities, monuments, scrolls, statues, libraries. The home of Confucius, which housed a museum, was trashed. A huge amount of China's heritage disappeared almost overnight. The Red Guards also targeted anything that could be considered 'bourgeois', ransacking barbershops and florists, and attacking women wearing fashionable dresses or shoes with high heels. They tore down signs, giving streets, shops and organisations new, revolutionary names. Cemeteries were laid waste. The police were ordered not to intervene as they went about their business.

Mao had appointed his wife Jiang Qing to the Cultural Revolution Group, which had overall control of the campaign. As their marriage had cooled and Mao had occupied himself with legions of young girls, she had become an increasingly isolated and paranoid figure, a hypochondriac who couldn't stand bright lights or the colours pink and brown (she insisted that everything in her house be painted green, even the furniture). Now, allowed to participate in politics for the first time, Madame Mao threw herself into her new job with gusto. With her background as an actress, she was put in charge of cultural affairs and banned traditional Chinese opera (despite the fact that she was as much a fan of it as Mao).

To take its place, eight officially sanctioned works were created — five operas, two ballets and a symphony — which extolled Mao and the Red Guards. The printing of virtually all books apart from Mao's ceased. By the end of the decade, an astonishing one billion copies of the Little Red Book had been printed, causing a paper shortage.

While the prevailing image of the Cultural Revolution is of Mao-intoxicated students causing havoc, people of all ages and backgrounds took part in it. As with the other counter-revolutionary campaigns and purges that had swept the country since the revolution, people took the opportunity to settle scores with those they didn't like. This was taken to a new level in the town of Wuxuan, in Guangxi province, where the locals began to eat people they had designated as 'class enemies'. They were sliced and diced with enthusiasm (sometimes while they were still alive), their hearts and livers going to the dining tables of the town's leaders, while ordinary people had to make do gnawing on arms and legs. Several teachers were made into tasty casseroles by their students. One of the leaders responsible for all this later defended his actions, saying, "Cannibalism? It was the landlord's flesh! The spy's flesh!"

As the nation convulsed, Mao turned his attention to his real enemies — the ones at the top. Deng Xiaoping was purged; Liu Shaoqi, once seen as his successor, was beaten in the street, subjected to endless denunciations, and thrown into a prison cell where he died.

Having triggered his revolution, Mao kept changing his mind about how it should proceed, and his pronouncements did not always match the Cultural Revolution Group's directives. With the party line constantly shifting, someone hailed a revolutionary hero one day might find themselves denounced as a rightest or capitalist-roader the next. No party member was safe, and this had unintended consequences. As many provincial leaders and cadres were denounced and purged, and no immediate replacements arrived, people in remote areas found to their surprise that they had more freedom than they had enjoyed for years. They seized the opportunity to abandon collectivisation and go back to the

old ways. Farmers started growing their own crops again, black markets were established, and small businesses and factories sprang up.

With the whole fabric of Communist China unravelling, Mao realised he had to change course. And as always, he laid the blame for failure on others. In August 1967, he called a meeting of Red Guard leaders and told them that they had let him down. They were arrested, and the Red Guards were abolished. In the following months, some two million of them were shipped off to the countryside in what is said to be the largest forced migration in history. Deprived of an education, despised by the rest of the population, they were mostly starved or worked to death. A few remnants still wander the country, like ghosts.

Mao turned to the army, led by his staunch supporter (and now designated successor) Lin Biao, as the best hope for continuing the revolution. Around a million party officials were sacked and replaced by army personnel, while Lin and his generals moved quickly to impose control over the country and restore collectivisation. At the same time a grand new purge began. The records of all party members, going back as far as the 1930s, were meticulously examined for any indication that they had ever harboured anti-party thoughts.

Mao had intended the Cultural Revolution to sweep away the last vestiges of the old China and enshrine 'Mao Zedong Thought' as its national ideology. In this, he was partly successful, at least in the short term. After the Red Guards had done their bit, there were virtually no plays or movies for people to see, no music to listen to, no books to read apart from a little red one. People were so worried about saying something to strangers that could get them denounced that they rarely strayed from the topic of Mao and his infinite wisdom. Over a billion portraits of him were printed and distributed. People competed to get the most desirable Mao badges, and peppered their conversation with his quotes. Stories even went around, and were printed in newspapers, that reciting an apt quote at the appropriate time could result in a miracle. The cult of Mao was in full bloom.

Mao had recreated China in his own image, and yet even now he wasn't happy. The very success of the army in restoring order — and the power it now wielded — unnerved him. As paranoid as ever, he was worried about the ambitions of Lin Biao.

Lin had been a supporter of Mao since the 1920s, and had become one of the Communists' most successful army commanders, but he was a very strange man indeed. He

was a hypochondriac like Madame Mao, and had even more phobias than she did, the chief ones being air and water. He didn't like people walking too quickly past him lest they created a breeze, he couldn't stand the sight of the sea, and the only way he would consume water was to eat soggy steamed buns. He was no fool though, and was soon aware of Mao's moves to undermine him.

Lin's son, Liguo, whose nickname was Tiger, was an army officer, but he was an admirer of Western culture and despised Mao. He began to plot an assassination attempt with some of his friends, with his father's consent, but events moved too quickly for them. In August 1971, Lin learned that Mao was about to have him purged and they prepared to flee to Russia in Lin's plane. Tiger made the mistake of telling his sister, who was a fanatical Mao supporter, and she told their bodyguards about it. Arriving at the airport, Lin, his wife and Tiger realised they were being pursued. They boarded the plane and ordered it to take off, despite the fact that it had insufficient fuel to reach Russia. The plane exploded when they attempted to land in Mongolia, and everyone on board was killed.

Mao was aghast when told about the assassination plot. Many people had known about it, but no-one had informed. He fell ill and took to his bed where he remained for two months. He was now seventy-seven and his age was finally catching up with him.

The Cultural Revolution was almost Mao's last gasp, but he had one more surprise to spring. He wanted to make friends with America.

Mao had always had an awkward relationship with the Soviet Union. Although he had grudging respect for Stalin as an authoritarian, he came to despise Khrushchev, and had virtually no relationship with

Brezhnev. In the meantime, he had developed something of a fascination with the U.S. In the 1960s Mao used to confuse the hell out of visitors from Eastern Bloc countries by telling them that the Soviet Union was as big a threat to China as the U.S. Meanwhile America, mired in the Vietnam War, had much to gain by improving relations with China.

China sent an invitation for Nixon to visit in January 1971, but Nixon and his secretary of state Henry Kissinger were wary of moving too quickly. Then Mao had a stroke of genius. In March, the American and Chinese table tennis teams competed in the world championships in Japan, and Mao took the unprecedented step of inviting the American team to China. They were given a rousing reception, and so-called 'ping-pong diplomacy' was on the front pages of newspapers across the world. Nixon realised what a publicity coup a meeting with Mao could be.

Kissinger went to China for a secret meeting with Zhou Enlai to pave the way. He offered the Chinese a whole host of concessions — withdrawing American troops from Indochina and South Korea, sharing intelligence reports on Russia, and abandoning support for Taiwan — while asking for nothing in return. (A few months later, with American consent, China replaced Taiwan on the U.N. Security Council.) Kissinger didn't even ask that China tone down its anti-American rhetoric.

When the two leaders finally met in February 1972, Mao played Nixon like a violin. Both Nixon and Kissinger went out of their way to flatter Mao, and Nixon even recited some of the Chairman's poetry. The favour wasn't returned, and all Mao would offer was some grudging praise for Nixon's *Six Crises*, saying it "wasn't a bad book". He flatly refused to discuss any weighty political issues, referring them to Zhou Enlai. In the end, America gained little from the whole exercise. But Nixon, who had been rabidly anti-Communist for his whole career, had succeeded in turning Mao into a world statesmen.

Mao was a very sick man by this time. He had contracted motor neurone disease, which was (and remains) incurable, may also have been suffering from Parkinson's disease, and his lungs were shot from years of smoking. China was in a state of limbo in Mao's last years. His 'confidential secretary', Zhang Yufeng, a former train conductor and dancing partner, gained immense power because she was the only one who could understand his slurred speech. Unable to face the fact of his own mortality, Mao dithered about who would succeed him

Despite the best efforts of Dr Li and his team, Mao died in September 1972. They braced themselves for the inevitable accusations that his death had been caused by their negligence — if they hadn't in fact murdered him. What they weren't ready for was the Politburo's order that Mao's body be permanently preserved, as Lenin's had been. Having no idea how to do this, Dr Li and his colleagues frantically consulted medical literature. There followed a farcical and grotesque scene as he and the other doctors pumped so much preservative into Mao's body that his head became as round as a ball.

In the aftermath of Mao's death, Jiang Qing and her cohorts (the so-called 'Gang of Four') were arrested and took most of the blame for events for which Mao had, frankly, sole responsibility. Deng Xiaoping, rehabilitated, declared Mao to be 30 per cent bad and 70 per cent good, and began to steer China towards capitalism.

hanks to the Chinese government's iron grip on the media, few Chinese today are aware of the full horrors of the Mao era. His round, avuncular face is once again seen everywhere, and his words are quoted to any effect. People avidly collect Mao badges and dine in Cultural Revolution

themed restaurants. For many, Mao is a god to pray to.

The frequently indulgent view of Mao outside China is more difficult to understand. He attracts nothing like the opprobrium heaped on Hitler or Stalin. People who should know better still quote his sayings such as 'Let a million flowers bloom' or 'Women hold up half the sky', as if he was someone actually open to a free exchange of ideas — and a feminist to boot.

For Mao apologists, his excesses are often excused because of the enormity of the task he had set himself: the transformation of a poor, agrarian, superstitious society beset by warlords into a unified, prosperous, industrialised world power. This would be an easier argument to make if all of Mao's major initiatives — his early purges, farm collectivisation, the Great Leap Forward and the Cultural Revolution — had not all sent China's economy careering backwards. It seems to me that China was industrialised in spite of Mao, not because of him.

For all his vaunted concern for the masses, there is abundant evidence that Mao lacked any regard for people as individuals. Dr Li tells the story of Mao's reaction when, during a theatrical performance he was attending, a child acrobat slipped and was seriously injured. The rest of the audience were aghast, but Mao kept chatting away as if nothing had happened. His oft-expressed lack of concern if such-and-such a course of action might result in millions of deaths have been cited as proof that he was a monster or psychopath whose chief motivation was to destroy things and kill people. While I'm afraid I can't mount a really spirited argument against that notion, I think Mao's fundamental flaw was impatience.

Based on precious little empirical evidence but a whole lot of leaden Marxist-Leninist theory, Mao was convinced he had come up with the infallible blueprint for a perfect China, and he was in a hurry to see it. Of course, impatience in revolutionaries is not unusual. Lenin was just as impatient to see in Russia the revolution that Marx had prophesied the proletariat would bring about, even though Russia barely had a proletariat. But in Mao, impatience became something like frenzy. Even Stalin warned him that he was moving too fast with collectivisation, but of course Mao ignored that slacker. He truly believed that the people of China, properly mobilised and sufficiently steeped in 'Mao Zedong Thought', would be able to overcome any obstacles, even nature itself. When his plans inevitably resulted in chaos and disaster on a grand scale, he blamed others, and he never learned from his mistakes. Mao's entire rule was one ill-thought-out, decades-long experiment, and some seventy million people were swept into its vortex and destroyed.

Still, he wrote some okay poetry.

CHAPTER 4

FRANÇOIS DUVALIER

FRANÇOIS DUVALIER

Elected president of Haiti in 1957
Declared himself president-for-life in 1964
Died in his bed in 1971

It is difficult to think of another group of people so royally screwed by their leaders, over such a long period of time, as the benighted inhabitants of Haiti. For a nation which emerged in 1804, after the only successful slave revolt in history, as the world's first independent black republic, this is a terrible irony. Prior to the revolt one of the most fertile countries in the Caribbean, producing vast quantities of sugar, coffee and other exports for its French colonial masters, Haiti soon became known for its production of dictators. Between 1843 and 1915, there were no less than twenty-two of them, mostly military men who barely had time to proclaim themselves emperor, king or president before the next coup or uprising swept them away. This apparent instability disguised the fact that most of these rulers upheld the privileges of a small, predominately mulatto (half-caste) elite who ruthlessly exploited the black peasant majority, at first through maintaining slavery in all but name, and later by taxing their meagre produce. This political exploitation was accompanied by a slow but inexorable process of environmental devastation. The plantations were split up into smaller and smaller holdings, suitable only for subsistence farming; roads fell into disrepair, isolating the country, where 80 per cent of the population lived, from the cities; and the once densely-forested mountains were stripped of trees by peasants desperate for charcoal.

In a land of such widespread poverty and entrenched corruption, it took a man of exceptional qualities to make things even worse.

rançois Duvalier, or 'Papa Doc' as he was later universally known, was born in the Haitian capital of Port-au-Prince on 14 April 1907. His father, Duval Duvalier, was a teacher; his mother, Uritia Abraham, worked in a bakery. When François was fourteen, Uritia had a mental breakdown and spent the rest of her life in an asylum. He was forbidden to talk about her, and was afterwards brought up by an aunt.

Duvalier grew up a few blocks away from the gleaming white National Palace, at a time when the turnover of presidents was particularly high. This political turmoil was being watched closely by the U.S., which had both economic and strategic interests in the country. The Americans were particularly worried by increasing German influence in the region, and looking for an excuse to intervene. In 1915, the latest president, Guillaume Sam, who had been in office for just four months, was dragged by his opponents from the French legation where he had taken refuge and hacked to pieces in the street. A few hours later, U.S. Marines landed and took control of Port-au-Prince. They remained there for nineteen years.

The young Duvalier was an introverted, bespectacled, softly spoken (when he spoke at all) and studious boy who was, even then, something of a mystery to those around him. From an early age he was keenly aware of the inequities of Haiti's broken society, and as a teenager became interested in nationalist politics. He studied medicine, graduating in 1934, the same year that the Americans departed from Haiti. He also joined a literary circle called 'Les Griots' who celebrated the nation's African heritage — a philosophy known as *noirisme* — and saw voodoo as the ultimate expression of Haitian culture.

During the long centuries of slavery, the slaves of Haiti had been subjected to a regime of almost unbelievable brutality. They worked punishingly long hours, nearly naked and in chains under the blazing sun, were poorly fed and, if they appeared to be slacking, were subjected to gruesome punishments that included being whipped, flayed or beaten with nail-studded paddles, having boiling cane sugar poured on them, having limbs hacked off with machetes, and being buried alive. Amidst this hell, the only solace for the slaves was religion. As it was the practice of French slave owners to work their slaves to death within five or six years, then import some fresh ones, a constant stream of new arrivals from Africa brought with them the traditional religious beliefs of their homelands (chiefly Dahomey and the Congo). By the middle of the eighteenth century, these had cohered into a system of belief in Haiti known as voodoo (also spelled vodou, vodoun and several other variants), which combined African animist beliefs with borrowings from Catholicism such as the worship of various saints. The spectacular centrepieces of voodoo religious practice were ceremonies where priests (the men were known as *houngans*, the women *mambos*) would summon the gods, or *loa*, to possess the bodies of worshippers.

The American occupiers were terrified of voodoo and did their best to suppress it, breaking up ceremonies and confiscating drums and other ritual objects. Of course, this just drove it underground. The suppression of Haitian culture also had the unintended consequence of uniting Haitians. The mulattos, who copied the ways of Europeans, had always looked down on their darker-skinned fellow citizens with what amounted to unabashed racism; but the Americans were so openly contemptuous of the Haitians, considering them barely human, that mulattos and blacks were drawn together in hatred of *them*, and a new Haitian nationalism was born. Meanwhile, ethnologists in Haiti and elsewhere were beginning to study voodoo in earnest, giving the religion a

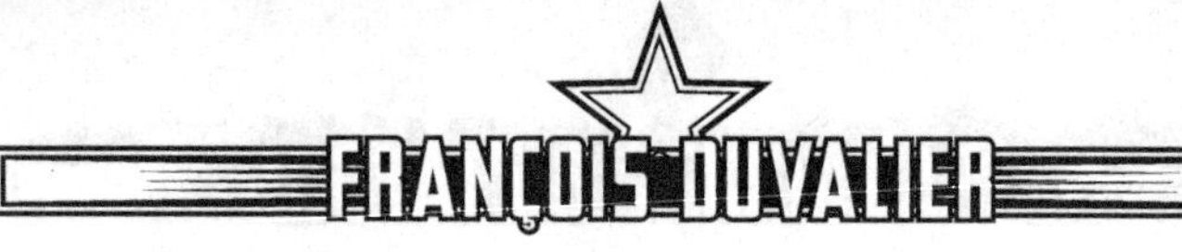

respectability it had previously lacked.

Duvalier worked as a doctor after graduating, but his practice suffered because he spent so much time writing academic articles about voodoo and promoting *negroisme*. Nevertheless, like many ambitious blacks, he chose to marry a light-skinned woman, Simone Ovide, in 1939. She was the illegitimate daughter of a mulatto merchant and a black domestic servant, and had been raised as a mulatto, but thanks to her mother's influence she was also a passionate believer in voodoo.

Duvalier's fortunes changed dramatically in 1943, when the U.S. government decided to fund a medical campaign to combat the awful tropical disease yaws, which causes the flesh to rot. Up to two-thirds of Haitians were afflicted by the disease, predominately blacks living in rural areas, but it could be cured with penicillin. Duvalier was installed in a clinic in the province of Gressier, where the disease was particularly prevalent, and had spectacular success. Over the next two years he cured hundreds of thousands of people, became famous throughout Haiti, and was given the affectionate nickname 'Papa Doc'. He later spent time in America, studying public health at the University of Michigan, but his imperfect command of English prevented him from gaining any qualifications.

A moderate black politician and former teacher of Duvalier's, Dumarsais Estimé, became president in 1946, and instituted some modest reforms which promoted the interests of the black middle class. Although Duvalier's friends had never detected any political ambitions in him, he served in two ministries in Estimé's government, eventually becoming Minister for Public Health and Labour, but achieved little in the role. Estimé's reforms proved too much for the elite, and although he was not personally corrupt, the same couldn't be said for his government. He was toppled in a coup in 1950 and replaced by a black colonel, Paul Magloire, who was backed by the mulattos and demonstrated a taste for pomp and fancy uniforms. During his rule things improved a bit, though. Relations with the U.S. — Haiti's chief source of foreign aid — were better, and there was some economic development, although this was almost entirely confined to the capital. Tourism also increased, and for a brief period Haiti became a fashionable destination, with the likes of Truman Capote and Noël Coward jetting in to sample the local colour. But after six years, rising black resentment and Magloire's increasingly dictatorial manner led to his overthrow.

Following Estimé's downfall, Duvalier had been forced to go into hiding. Having invested all his hopes for the advancement of black Haitians in Estimé, he was devastated by what had happened to him. He began to plot a political comeback, but this time he would be president, and he wasn't going to suffer the same ignominious fate as his friend. It is said he studied a copy of Machiavelli's *The Prince* until it fell apart.

Once Magloire was gone and an interim president had taken over, Duvalier began his campaign in earnest. He presented himself as a humble country doctor and friend to the peasants who would continue the reforms begun by Estimé, and the favoured candidate of both the U.S. and the military. Always immaculately dressed in a tailored suit and hat, no matter how hot the weather, the diminutive doctor was no orator, but he managed to project an air of calm and integrity, and his well-known interest in voodoo would have done him no harm among the black majority. After much political chaos and a series of bombings (in which some suspect Duvalier had a hand) the election was held on 22 September 1957. Duvalier won over twice as many votes as his opponent Louis Déjoie, a wealthy mulatto, and while there was considerable intimidation and vote rigging on both sides, most observers felt his victory reflected the will of the people. A month later, Duvalier was sworn in and took up residence in the National Palace.

In his first presidential address, Duvalier painted a rosy future for Haiti under his government. There would be political pluralism, redistribution of wealth, a free press and trade unions. Many expected that the softly spoken doctor, with his thick glasses and sober black suits, would simply be another puppet of the military, but 'Papa Doc' soon disabused them of this notion.

The chief objective of all dictators is to maintain power, and Duvalier was quicker off the mark than most. The first months of his rule were characterised by a harsh crackdown on his enemies and the closure of several newspapers. He also set about emasculating the army, which he hated and feared because it had toppled his beloved Estimé. He sacked its chief of staff, sent other officers he mistrusted to distant posts, had the armaments stored in the main army barracks moved to the palace, and generally kept it in disarray. Meanwhile, he recruited his own private secret police force who would eventually become the notorious Tontons Macoutes (the name is Creole for 'Uncle Knapsack' — in Haitian folklore a bogeyman who kidnaps children and stuffs them into his bag). They were mostly drawn from the rural poor, and many were also *houngans*. Only irregularly paid by the government, the Macoutes were given free rein to terrorise and kill people (including soldiers and wealthy mulattos), extort money and stamp out the slightest sign of dissent. They were easily recognised by their dark sunglasses (worn day and night), denim uniforms, red scarves and the holsters on their hips. Their female counterparts, the Filettes Laleau, were less numerous but equally feared.

While the Macoutes did most of their bloody work at night, they were not averse to going after supposed enemies of the state during the day, and were known to let rip with machine guns in crowded streets. Bullet-ridden bodies were left where they fell, and sometimes the heads of enemies were paraded through towns and villages on pikes.

By now, many had come to believe Duvalier's interest in voodoo was no longer purely academic, if it ever had been. In March 1958, according to a story often repeated by Haitians, Duvalier paid a visit to a large cave called Trou Foban, located in the mountains near Port-au-Prince. It was said to be the home of some particularly malevolent spirits which only the most powerful *houngan* would dare to go up against, and Duvalier had brought just such a *houngan* with him, accompanied by his assistants. The spirits were duly summoned, and agreed to move house. When Papa Doc and his men returned to the palace late that night, the spirits followed them, and took up residence in the room he had set up for voodoo rituals. And there they remained, protecting him from enemies until his death.

Whether there is any truth in this tale, it seems that the 'voodoo room' may have existed, for we have a description of it, or something like it, from an American ethnomusicologist named Harold Courlander. He had been visiting Haiti since the 1930s, travelling round the country making recordings of Haitian music and collecting musical instruments. He had donated some of them to the Bureau of Ethnology, where he had met Duvalier, and the two had often met for long talks. Returning to Haiti in 1958, Courlander sent a message to the palace and received an invitation to visit his old colleague, who was now president. After arriving at the palace, and being kept waiting for a while, he was led into a darkened room with black curtains on the windows and black candles providing the only light. He could just make out Duvalier, wearing a dark suit, sitting behind a long trestle table, flanked by impassive Tontons Macoutes wearing their inevitable dark glasses. Courlander spent about fifteen minutes discussing ethnological matters with an unsmiling Duvalier before

taking his leave, thoroughly bemused by the experience.

Voodoo was central to one of the most notorious events of Duvalier's early years, the fate of Clémente Jumelle. He had run as a presidential candidate against Duvalier, but had dropped out before the election. Upon coming to power, Duvalier issued a warrant for his arrest — as he did with all his other political opponents. After going on the run for a while, Jumelle became very ill and took refuge in the Cuban embassy, where he died from a lack of proper medical care. Two days later, as the hearse carrying his body made its way through the streets to the cathedral where the funeral was to be held, a police wagon appeared. Gun-toting policemen leapt out, commandeered the hearse and drove it away at speed, leaving mourners battered and astonished in the street. The body was taken to the palace, and at least three stories (and probably many more) were told in Haiti about what happened next. In one, Duvalier attempted to coax Jumelle's spirit out of his corpse, and was disappointed to find it had already departed. In another, he was keen to examine Jumelle's brain, so as to better understand the intentions of his enemies. And in yet another, perhaps the most popular, he had wanted Jumelle's heart to make an *ouanga* or voodoo charm. Whatever happened, a group of Tontons Macoutes later delivered a sealed coffin to Jumelle's family, and told them to bury it without opening it, but when they refused, the Macoutes took the coffin to the cemetery themselves. When Jumelle's family dug it up later, they found it contained someone else's corpse.

Although his impregnable image belied it, the diminutive Duvalier was already a very sick man when he became president. He suffered from diabetes, heart disease, circulatory problems and arthritis that made his hands swell up and caused so much pain he sometimes couldn't lift a telephone. On 24 May 1959, he suffered a massive heart attack that almost killed him. When he recovered, those who knew him agreed he had changed, and surmised that he had suffered brain damage while in a coma. He would go into terrible rages, spluttering and raving incoherently at his enemies in a way that terrified his aides. Even his close friend and leader of the Tontons Macoutes, Clément Barbot, was heard to say that the president had gone mad.

The persecution of his enemies became even more ferocious. Many were interrogated and tortured in rooms in the palace, and holes were reputedly drilled in the walls so Duvalier could secretly observe the proceedings. He knew his most potent enemy was the Catholic Church, and he declared war on it. Barbot and a band of Tontons Macoutes were despatched to Port-au-Prince Cathedral to beat up worshippers with nightsticks, and many priests were expelled from the country. When one monsignor was bundled onto a plane, wearing only his underpants, the Pope was so incensed he excommunicated Duvalier, but this is unlikely to have cost the dedicated voodooist much sleep.

It had by now become apparent, even to most of his staunchest early supporters, that all the idealism, humanitarianism and desire to improve the lot of poor black Haitians had drained out of François Duvalier, leaving a sort of husk. It was noted that even his physical appearance changed after he became president. Katherine Dunham, a famous American dancer and anthropologist who spent a lot of time in Haiti, met Papa Doc several times during the 1950s. Returning in 1962, she encountered him again at ceremony in the palace, and wrote that he looked like an entirely different person. (While he didn't recognise her, or pretended not to.)

Of course, in devoting most of his energies to maintaining power, Papa Doc was merely emulating every Haitian leader

since the country gained independence, and it wasn't hard for him to see threats everywhere. Beginning in 1958, the year after his election, there were regular incursions onto the country by Haitian rebels (in groups as small as eight and as large as two hundred) intent on triggering a revolt that would bring his regime down. All of these invasions, which ranged from the poorly planned to the downright farcical, were easily put down by Papa Doc's security forces, which increased both his reputation of impregnability, and his paranoia. For a week or so in 1964, foreigners arriving at François Duvalier International Airport emerged from the arrival hall to be confronted by the rotting corpse of the leader of the latest invasion, Yvan Laraque, seated in an armchair by the road, beneath a Coca-Cola sign reading "Welcome to Haiti".

In the greed that he began to display after coming to power, Papa Doc was also following time-honoured Haitian traditions, but once again, he raised things to a new level. Extortion was the basis of Papa Doc's regime, its only real

ideology. Everyone from American businessmen down to Haitian schoolchildren were squeezed for cash in the name of 'national reconstruction'. Much of this money was supposed to go to the building of Duvalierville, a model 'resort town' north of Port-au-Prince which was to symbolise all that Papa Doc had done for his country. It was the sort of grandiose scheme that dictators routinely come up with to justify their existence, but decades after construction began, Duvalierville remained little more than a collection of ramshackle concrete bungalows and a cockfighting ring. In fact the only major building project completed during Papa Doc's rule was the international airport in Port-au-Prince, and the Americans paid for that. Papa Doc was a master at obtaining U.S. aid, representing himself as a bulwark against communism in the region. Whenever the U.S. baulked at providing more aid money, or tried to exercise some control over the way it was spent, Papa Doc played the communist card, hinting that the country might need to turn to the Eastern Bloc for aid. In the end, the U.S. always coughed up. At one point it was estimated that 80 per cent of the many millions of dollars of aid it provided for Haiti either disappeared through mismanagement, or went straight into the pockets of Papa Doc and his cronies. Meanwhile the country lacked basic infrastructure. The electricity supply was intermittent. The telephone system rarely worked.

Papa Doc was nevertheless unanimously re-elected president in October 1961 (that he was the only presidential candidate on the ballot paper no doubt contributed to this result). But forces were gathering to bring him down.

On the morning of 26 April 1963, Papa Doc's children, sixteen-year-old Simone and twelve-year-old Jean-Claude, were being driven to school when another car approached and shots rang out. Their chauffeur and two bodyguards were killed, but the children scrambled out of their car and made it to the schoolyard and safety.

Papa Doc was insensate with rage. He believed a military man must have been responsible for such an attack, and the Tontons Macoutes went on a bloody rampage, murdering hundreds, perhaps thousands, of soldiers and their families. Papa Doc suspected that a former lieutenant, François Benoit, might have been the assassin because he was a champion sharpshooter. He wasn't at home when the Macoutes arrived, so they shot his parents, young son, servants, a few other people who happened to be there, and the dog. (As they left they encountered a passing stranger whose first name happened to be Benoit, and shot him too for good measure.) When Benoit took refuge in the embassy of the neighbouring Dominican Republic, this too was attacked. In retaliation, the new, democratically elected Dominican president, Juan Bosch, threatened to go to war, and Dominican troops started to amass on the border.

Papa Doc's aides had been telling him from the beginning that the likely assassin was Clément Barbot. The former Macoute leader, who had run the country when Papa Doc was recovering from his stroke, had fallen out with him when he extorted money from businessmen and failed to pass on some of it to the president. He had been arrested and tortured, then thrown into the hellhole of Fort Dimanche prison for eighteen months. On his release, he vowed revenge. Following their attack on the Duvalier children, Barbot, his brother and a few others continued to defy the regime with a campaign of bombings and assassinations. They were hiding out in

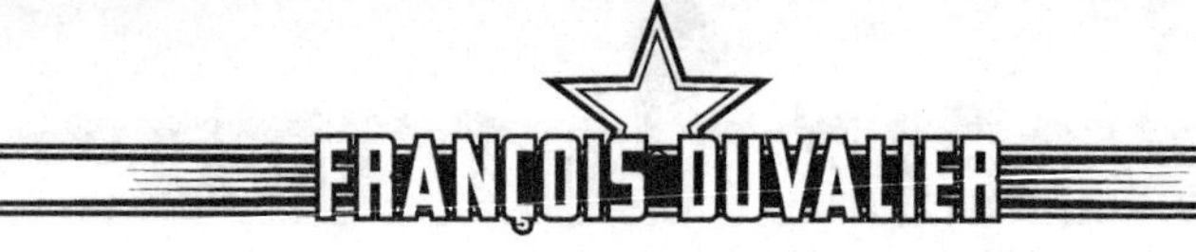

a canefield when a peasant informed on them. Macoutes surrounded the canefield and set it ablaze, and Barbot and his comrades were shot as they staggered out.

The U.S. looked on this explosion of violence with dismay. President Kennedy, who had a particular loathing for Papa Doc, despatched warships to Haiti, cut off almost all aid to the country, and, it seems, gave the Dominicans permission to invade. Papa Doc declared martial law. In the midst of this turmoil, he appeared on the balcony of the palace to give a remarkable speech. Standing preternaturally still, he declared, "I am the personification of the Haitian fatherland." He said he had no fear of bullets and machine guns, and uttered for the first time what would become a favourite line: "I am already an immaterial human being." Yet Papa Doc's fall seemed imminent, apparently to himself as well. He booked a flight to Paris on an American airline for himself and his family.

And then…nothing happened. The Dominican army proved less eager to invade Haiti than their president, and they overthrew him in a coup. Kennedy was assassinated. (Papa Doc privately took credit for this — having, he said, called on voodoo spirits to attack him.) A few more poorly planned rebel invasions were easily put down.

Papa Doc had seen off his opposition, both internal and external, and now decided to do away with the tiresome need to hold elections. The government whipped up a campaign designed to persuade the supposedly reluctant and humble 'country doctor' to become 'president-for-life'. Delegation after delegation arrived at the palace to plead with him to assume the title, and newspaper editorials heaped grandiose praise on his head. Papa Doc was ready to take up the challenge. "I will be lord and master," he said in one speech. "I have always talked with wild energy which characterises me; with all the savagery that characterises me." A new constitution was drawn up, enshrining the 'president-for-life', and the result was confirmed by a referendum. This was another Duvalier special, with all the ballot papers having 'oui' printed next to the proposal.

The cult of personality surrounding Papa Doc was in full swing. Perhaps the most striking manifestation of it was a booklet issued by the government entitled 'Le Catéchisme de la Révolution'. Written in question and answer format in the style of the Catholic catechism, it included hymns, litanies and even a bizarre re-working of the Lord's Prayer penned by Papa Doc himself.

> *Our Doc who art in the National Palace for life, hallowed be thy name by present and future generations. Thy will be done at Port-au-Prince and in the provinces. Give us this day our new Haiti and never forgive the trespasses of the antipatriots who spit every day on our country; let them succumb to temptation, and under the weight of their venom, deliver them not from any evil...*

If Papa Doc here takes on the trappings of Catholicism, it is with voodoo that he will always be associated. His habitual black clothing and strangely impassive, inscrutable manner led to him being identified with the *guédé* or spirits of death, and in particular with the top-hatted, black-coated Baron Samedi, haunter of graveyards. Others elevated him to the status of a god, and his photograph became a fixture in voodoo *houmforts* or temples. Certainly, the longer that he stayed in power and the more enemies he saw off, the more it seemed he had divine help on his side. Before we get too carried away with all this admittedly exciting stuff, however, it should be noted that the extent of his involvement in voodoo as an actual practitioner remains unclear. The identification of Papa Doc with Baron Samedi, which became commonplace in accounts of Haiti published in the West, can largely be traced to writers like Bernard Diederich, a *Time* journalist and co-author of an early Duvalier biography, and his friend Graham Greene, whose 1966 novel *The Comedians*, set in Haiti, infuriated its president. Such tales fitted right in with Haiti's centuries-old image as a country gripped by a unique brand of irrational and deadly superstition, and I would say there's certainly an element of Western condescension here.

What is not in doubt is that Papa Doc understood the efficacy of cloaking himself in voodoo as a control mechanism, and did nothing to scotch rumours that he was a powerful *bocor* or sorcerer. It's hardly surprising then that some of his opponents decided the only way to attack him was with voodoo. One night a gang of them broke into the tomb of his father and stole the heart from the corpse to make an *ouanga* (as Papa Doc was rumoured to have done with Jumelle's heart). They left after smearing both corpse and tomb with excrement.

In addition to his ambiguous relationship with voodoo, Papa Doc often stated that he was the living embodiment of some of Haiti's previous black rulers, and in particular its first, the revolutionary hero Jean-Jacques Dessalines. This led to the rumour that he spent one night a year sleeping on Dessalines's tomb.

967 was Year 10 of the 'Duvalierist Revolution', and celebrations were held across the country to mark the momentous occasion. Papa Doc issued a pocket-sized book of his wisest and pithiest pronouncements, *Brevier of a Revolution*, in emulation of Mao's Little Red Book.

The British TV presenter Alan Whicker arrived in Haiti the following year to conduct a rare series of interviews with the ageing dictator. He found Papa Doc frail and so scared of assassination attempts that he rarely left the palace, yet he still inspired absolute terror in everyone around him. One morning, Whicker and his crew arrived at the palace to find that Papa Doc's secretary was away, and none of the other staff had the authority to knock on his office door and tell him they were there. After waiting several hours in frustration, Whicker left the palace, walked to the local telegraph office, and sent Papa Doc a telex message that read "Mr President, I am waiting outside your door." The highlight of the visit came when Papa Doc suggested that Whicker accompany him on his 'Christmas shopping'. This consisted of Papa Doc, his wife Simone (a.k.a. Mama Doc) and one of their three daughters doing the rounds of Port-au-Prince's jewellery shops and picking out their finest items, none of which, needless to say, they paid for.

Even a dictator with an iron grip on his country may have trouble controlling his family, as Papa Doc found out. His oldest and most headstrong daughter, Marie-Denise, had decided she wanted to marry a tall, imposing thirty-four-year-old army officer, Max Dominique, who was a member of the Palace Guard. With his usual distrust of army men, Papa Doc was bitterly opposed to the marriage with Dominique (who was already married with children), but Marie-Denise had made up her mind. After they were married, he promoted Dominique to military commander of Port-au-Prince, but remained suspicious of him, and came to believe that he was planning a coup.

While tempted to eliminate Dominique, Papa Doc instead decided to cut him down to size, and had nineteen Palace Guard officers — all of them friends of Dominique — arrested and imprisoned in Fort Dimanche. One morning a few weeks later, he ordered Marie-Denise, Dominique and his other staff officers to gather at the palace. They then drove in a cavalcade to the prison. While Marie-Denise waited in her car, the men trooped inside, and Papa Doc, wearing an army helmet, led them to the rifle range where the nineteen officers were tied to stakes. Dominique and eighteen other officers were told to each stand in front of one of the prisoners, then handed rifles. When Papa Doc yelled "Fire!" they shot their comrades.

Marie-Denise was greatly relieved when Dominique emerged from the prison alive. It has been claimed that she had a machine gun hidden under her car seat, and if he had not reappeared, she planned to use it on her father.

The next day, Papa Doc changed his mind, and announced that that he was going to have Dominique killed after all. When his wife and Marie-Denise got down on their knees and begged him to reconsider, he relented and ordered him to be sent into exile. When he went, Marie-Denise and her sister Simone went with him. Devastated by the loss of his daughters, Papa Doc was seen weeping at his desk.

Two years later the exiles were in Spain when Papa Doc relented and offered to pardon Dominique. Marie-Denise was wary, but agreed to return by herself so she could assess the situation. Appalled by the dysfunction in the palace, she set about clearing up the mess, firing Papa Doc's secretary (and mistress) Francesca Saint-Victor, and taking over the role herself. She eventually gave the all-clear for her husband to return with their young son.

Every year Papa Doc was in power, Haiti's GDP fell. The life expectancy of the average Haitian dropped to around forty-two years, and the country had record levels of infant mortality and illiteracy. As his people suffered and starved, he used government funds to buy up properties across the country and fatten his overseas bank accounts, while his wife and children splurged on luxury goods. Perhaps his most reprehensible single act was to make a deal with the

Dominican Republic to send Haitian workers there to cut sugar cane. It was a very lucrative deal for him, but the workers were lucky if they were ever paid the wages they had been promised. Papa Doc, who had come to power with the promise of improving the lot of black Haitians, had effectively reintroduced slavery.

Papa Doc seemed well aware that his former friends and supporters were aghast at how the 'Duvalier Revolution' had unfolded. As the years went by, he banished competent advisers from the palace, replacing them with illiterate Tontons Macoutes who offered him nothing but blind loyalty. In his last few years, he rarely left his office.

His physical condition had deteriorated so much by 1970 he was no longer able to chew food (his wife had to spoon it into his mouth then move his jaw up and down). Even he could see he needed to decide on a successor. He knew that the best hope for the survival of 'Duvalierism' (whatever that was supposed to mean) lay with one of his children, with the obvious choices being his son, Jean-Claude, or his daughter Marie-Denise. She was initially the frontrunner, having proved herself capable and tough-minded in running his office. The spoilt, overweight Jean-Claude, on the other hand, loved sports cars and girls but had absolutely no interest in politics. Papa Doc, who had a habit of promoting women to powerful positions, clearly favoured his daughter, but was persuaded that Haitians would never accept a female president. And so, when he was too ill to attend the celebrations for his 64th birthday, Jean-Claude appeared on the balcony of the palace in his father's place, looking bewildered.

A few days later, as he lay on his death bed, Papa Doc admitted to some of his military leaders that "My government has not been what I wanted it to be. I've had to do things, things that weren't what I set out to do."

He died on 21 April 1971, and his funeral took place three

days later, on the feast day of Baron Samedi. It was attended by a crowd of people making ostentatious displays of grief, real or feigned. When a strong wind suddenly blew up and filled the air with dust, the mourners scattered in panic, believing it was Papa Doc's soul leaving the earth.

It's estimated that forty to sixty thousand Haitians were murdered during the rule of François Duvalier. That he personally took part in the torture and murder of some of them was widely attested. Many thousands more fled the country, including most of its professionals. Doctors, teachers, scientists and engineers left *en masse*. When the country's terminal corruption eventually became apparent and foreign aid dried up, Haiti became the poorest country in the Western Hemisphere, and remains so today. Perhaps the best epitaph for Papa Doc came from a resident of Port-au-Prince who told a visiting American journalist, "He has taught us to live without money and eat without food. No, that's not all. Duvalier has taught us to live without life."

The question remains, how could an idealistic doctor who had travelled around the country saving the lives of many thousands of Haitians end up murdering them in comparable numbers? There doesn't seem to be a satisfactory answer to this (unless you subscribe to the Baron Samedi theory). Papa Doc has retained his impenetrability — and that's just how he would have liked it.

Jean-Claude was appointed president the day after Papa Doc's death. Dubbed 'Baby Doc', he was certainly a milder fellow than his father, and may even have wanted to improve things for his people. Sadly, Baby Doc was completely under the thumb of his mother and, later, his wife Simone, who rivalled Papa Doc himself in avarice, and the country remained as corrupt as ever. The regime staggered on until 1986, when Baby Doc and his family were forced to flee to France (taking with them upwards of $300 million from the Haitian treasury). Their plane was scarcely in the air before a mob descended on Port-au-Prince's main cemetery, extinguished the eternal flame on top of Papa Doc's tomb, then began to take it apart using stones and their bare hands. But mindful of what had happened to the corpse of Papa Doc's father, someone had ensured that they would find the tomb empty.

CHAPTER 5

NICOLAE CEAUŞESCU

NICOLAE CEAUȘESCU

Attained power in 1965
Hastily tried and efficiently shot in 1989

One day, a brash young Nicolae Ceaușescu said to his brother-in-law, who was trying to teach him shoemaking. "I won't need a trade. I'm going to be Romania's Stalin."

And so it came to pass. In achieving his goal, Ceaușescu was just the latest in a long line of tyrants who have blighted Romania. The country, originally three principalities — Moldavia, Wallachia and Transylvania — had been sliced and diced by invaders for two millennia. In 107 AD, the Roman emperor Trajan and his legions overran Transylvania, relieving the local Dacians of so much gold and other treasure that he was able to give the rest of the Roman Empire a year off paying tax. The Romans were followed by a host of others, including the Goths, the Huns, the Bulgars, the Magyars, the Mongols and the Turks (who stayed the longest). Among the Romanian strongmen who did their best to fend off these invaders was the fifteenth-century prince of Wallachia, Vlad Tepes, or Vlad the Impaler, known for his art installation of a forest of Turks impaled on stakes. He was feted as one of Romania's greatest heroes during the Ceaușescu era, and after Ceaușescu's death it was reported that he had planned to demolish Vlad's former castle and build a palace of his own on the ruins.

Vlad is, of course, often said — rather dubiously in my opinion — to have been the inspiration for Bram Stoker's Count Dracula, and it's perhaps no coincidence that Ceaușescu was widely rumoured to be a vampire in his lifetime. One popular story was that blood was extracted from newborn babies and sent to nourish him. It was only if they survived this ordeal that their births would be registered three days later.

icolae Ceaușescu was born in the village of Scornicești on 26 January 1918. His father, Andruță Ceaușescu, owned a small farm, made a little extra money as a tailor, and was so habitually drunk when he registered his children's births that he ended up naming two of his sons Nicolae. His mother, Alexandrina, was a pious woman who maintained her faith long after her son had declared her country atheist. Nicolae, the third of their ten children, is said to have been conceived when Andruță was AWOL from the army.

Romania had entered the First World War late, in 1916, on the side of the Allies, a decision that backfired spectacularly when the Germans made mincemeat of the ill-prepared Romanian army and comprehensively plundered the country. After the war it regained its former provinces of Transylvania and Bessarabia, doubling its size and making it the fifth largest country in Europe, but its economy was in ruins. Its oil reserves were largely in foreign hands, and the peasantry lived in the same dire poverty that had been their lot for centuries. (The last of its so-called 'peasant revolts' had taken place as late as 1907, and was crushed with the usual ferocity.)

At the age of eleven, like many peasant children, Nicolae was despatched to Bucharest to look for work. While most Romanians were dirt poor, Bucharest in the 1930s was a cosmopolitan city known as 'the Paris of the Balkans'. It was ruled over by King Carol II, a feckless and erratic monarch who loved fancy uniforms and the high life, and was obsessed with grandiose building plans (as Ceaușescu would be years later). His major project, never completed although a great

many buildings were knocked down to make way for it, was a palace that would be larger than Buckingham Palace. Ordinary Romanians were both fascinated and appalled by their king and his mistress, Elena Lupescu, who lived in a large and luxurious country house.

In Bucharest, Nicolae lived with his sister Niculina, who was married to a shoemaker. Nicolae was supposed to become his apprentice, but it's doubtful he did much cobbling. He spent most of his time on the streets, and his first arrest was for brawling. He was short, ungainly, barely literate, devoid of humour and prone to violent rages, and he stammered so badly that people avoided him. One of his contemporaries, Mihai Popescu, recalled that "His stammering spasms were sometimes so violent that his leg would twitch uncontrollably to the rhythm of the stammer and this got on people's nerves." Ceaușescu spent years trying to overcome his stammer, but never quite managed it. In later years, his peculiar brand of oratory, complete with mispronounced words, odd facial expressions and inappropriate gestures, would often be mimicked by Romanians (so long as they were behind closed doors and among well-trusted friends).

As a teenager, Ceaușescu flirted with a number of political organisations before joining the Communist Youth League in 1933. The Romanian Communists were a motley band who never numbered more than seven hundred during the '30s and enjoyed virtually no popular support. Their leadership included many Germans, Hungarians and Jews (the latter fact being enough to damn them in the eyes of anti-Semitic Romanians), and they were mostly known for their subservience to Russia. They didn't quite know what to make of the hyperactive young Ceaușescu, although they were impressed by his energy and obvious dedication to the cause.

In February 1934, a Communist railway worker, Gheorghe

Gheorghiu-Dej, was arrested after organising a strike. The following day, workers occupied the railway workshops at Gristana, a suburb of Bucharest, the army was sent in and several workers were killed. The bluff and bearlike Gheorghiu-Dej became one of Ceaușescu's two heroes (the other being Stalin), and he was arrested at the trial of the strike leaders for distributing pamphlets supporting them. After a brief spell in jail, he was told to get back to Scornicești and stay there, but he returned to Bucharest and was arrested again in 1936. While in jail in Brasov he did everything he could to ingratiate himself with the senior Communists who were his fellow prisoners.

He was released in 1938, the same year that Carol II scrapped the Romanian constitution, banned political parties and declared himself 'Royal Dictator'. When war broke out the following year, the King's instinct, like that of most Romanians, was to side with Britain and France, but the fall of France made this position untenable. After Hitler and Stalin signed their 'Pact of Steel', Hitler demanded that Romania return Bessarabia to Russia and Transylvania to Hungary, and Carol acquiesced. This caused so much anger in the country that he was forced to abdicate in favour of his 18-year-old son Michael, while General Ion Antonescu became de facto ruler of Romania. He steered the country into an alliance with Hitler, and Romanian soldiers were soon fighting alongside the Germans to claw back Transylvania.

Ceaușescu spent most of the war years in prison. He acted as servant and bodyguard to Gheorghiu-Dej and boned up on Marxist-Leninist jargon. Gheorghiu-Dej reportedly treated him like a son, but the other Communists were far less enamoured of him. His cellmate for a couple of months was Pavel Campeanu, who would rise high in the ranks of the Communist Party after the war. Decades later, he recalled the horror of sharing a shower with Ceaușescu. "He was very ugly," he said, struggling to find the right words. "Not deformed, just unpleasant to look at." According to Campeanu, "His most striking feature, though, was the deep hatred he showed his fellow inmates, even though they were fighting for the same cause at the risk of death... It took the form of a free-floating anger and contempt for other people, particularly people his own age or in positions he considered inferior to his own. In his relations with the rest of us he seemed strangely empty of any normal human feelings." He was also notorious for cheating at chess.

The imprisoned Communists were treated fairly leniently — and even more so when Russian military victories indicated the Allies were going to win the war. In August 1944, with the Red Army advancing into Romania, King Michael demonstrated an unexpected steeliness by ordering Antonescu's arrest, forming a new government and declaring war on Germany. The following day, German bombers flew over Bucharest, inflicting much damage and destroying the palace.

The Russians soon occupied the country, to the delight of the Romanian Communists who now began to infiltrate the government. At a meeting in Moscow in August 1944, Churchill and Stalin had divided up post-war Europe between them, with Russia having 90 per cent influence over Romania in return for Britain having 90 per cent influence over Greece. Stalin imposed crippling war reparations on Romania, plunging much of the peasantry back into a state of starvation.

eaușescu had been released from an internment camp in the town of Tirga Jiu (though former inmates described conditions there as more like a sanatorium) two months before King Michael's coup. His whereabouts during this crucial period are unknown, although he may have been with his girlfriend for, improbably, he had acquired one. This was Elena Petrescu, the daughter of a ploughman who had been born in a village not far from Ceaușescu's birthplace of Scornicești. They had met, probably at a Communist Youth League gathering, in the late '30s. Contemporaries described her as a good-looking girl, but impossibly stupid.

Gheorghiu-Dej was anointed as leader of the Communist Party, which was of course good news for his protégé, Ceaușescu. In 1945, the Soviets installed a Communist-dominated government with just enough members from other factions to give it a veneer of legitimacy. A new secret police force, the Securitate, was created, and liquidation of the party's enemies began in earnest, with tens of thousands murdered over the next few years. In November 1946, the Communists gained power outright in an election characterised by intimidation and vote rigging on a monumental scale.

Ceaușescu, now married to Elena, was appointed a regional party secretary. A few days before the election he was in the town of Slatina, looking after electoral matters there, when he paid a visit to a local bank manager and demanded a large donation to the party. The bank manager demurred, a fight broke out, and Ceaușescu (or possibly his bodyguard) stabbed him to death. He was also involved in the huge project to collectivise farming throughout the country. Most of the peasants were dubious about the idea, to say the least, and Ceaușescu had those who objected the most vehemently shot. He was given the rank of major-general in 1948 and put in charge of indoctrinating the army. He loved the uniform and took to his new military status in an almost comical way. Never a drinker before, he began spending the evenings with his fellow officers, knocking back the booze and telling bawdy stories.

Ceauşescu continued to rise through the party ranks during '50s. He was appointed to the Central Committee, joined the delegation that attended Stalin's funeral in 1953, and in 1955 was put in charge of hiring and firing within the party bureaucracy, giving him considerable influence. Meanwhile, Elena had begun her absurd masquerading as a chemist. While her closest brush with chemistry had been a stint in a dodgy patent medicine factory in the '30s, party ties got her a speedy doctorate (without her having to go through the tiresome process of obtaining a degree first), and a job as a researcher at the Institute of Chemistry in Bucharest. In 1960, she became its director, despite the fact that she was still virtually illiterate. She spent her time there being mean to the staff, cutting their pay, purging those who had questioned her scientific credentials, and generally making their lives a misery.

After Khrushchev denounced the excesses of Stalin in his 1956 'secret speech', Gheorgiu-Dej, like other Eastern Bloc leaders, began to distance himself from the Kremlin. This first became apparent when cultural life was liberalised, with Romanian artists freed from the straightjacket of socialist realism, and foreign books and movies allowed into the country for the first time since the war. Gheorgiu-Dej also refused to bow to Khrushchev's demand that Romania concentrate on oil and gas production to the virtual exclusion of heavy industry (which Stalin had based his own economic plans on). The process culminated in a 1964 speech in which he basically declared Romania's independence from the Soviet Union. This was music to the ears of nationalists who had never been able to stomach the Russians, and the Romanian Communist Party experienced something new — a glimmer of popular support.

A year later, Gheorgiu-Dej was dying of throat cancer (he was convinced the Russians had caused it by exposing him to radiation). Although Ceaușescu had been his protégé for many years, he made it clear that his chosen successor was the easy-going Gheorghe Apostol, one of his old cronies from the railway trade union. It was not to be. The Central Committee was full of ambitious men who despised each other, and the exact nature of machinations that went on are unclear, but with the endorsement of foreign affairs minister Ion Maurer, they elected Ceaușescu as first secretary. Some believe they thought that, as the youngest of them, he would be the easiest to manipulate. Others argue that Ceaușescu, who for all his youthful worship of Stalin hated Russians in general, was seen as a man who would continue to stand up to them.

Ceaușescu initially made a pretence of ruling in a collegiate manner, but over the next few years he sidelined or discredited his rivals. He continued — and even extended — Gheorgiu-Dej's liberal cultural policies (by the late '60s, the most popular shows on Romanian TV were British programs like *The Avengers* and *The Saint*). Above all, he continued to distance Romania from the Soviet Union, which gained him kudos in the West. He was often bracketed with Alexander Dubček, the Czech Communist leader who was attempting to introduce 'socialism with a human face'. And on 21 August 1968, when Soviet tanks rolled into Czechoslovakia to crush the so-called 'Prague Spring', Ceaușescu rose to the occasion. Addressing a huge rally in front of the palace in Bucharest, he declared the Russian invasion "a great mistake and a grave danger to peace in Europe…a shameful moment in the history of the revolutionary movement." This was undeniably a brave move, for the Soviets could have easily invaded Romania, too. (That they didn't was no doubt because they realised that, despite his sheen of liberalism, Ceaușescu

remained a hardline Marxist-Leninist.) Ceaușescu's defiance saw his stocks in the West rise even higher, and the likes of Charles de Gaulle and Richard Nixon were soon beating a path to his door. All this fawning inevitably went to his head. “A man like me,” he remarked to one of his ministers in the early ’70s, “only comes along once in every five hundred years.”

With the constant coaching and prodding of the fiercely ambitious Elena, Ceauşescu had transformed himself into a reasonable facsimile of a national leader. He had managed to almost completely banish his stammer and facial tics while speaking in public (although the content of his speeches never rose above the level of banal) and became addicted to the adulation of crowds. Elaborately stage-managed tours of Romania’s towns became a regular part of his schedule, with regional party chiefs competing to put on the best show. In one celebrated incident, when a row of specially planted trees died before an impending visit, a team of workers was despatched to paint their leaves green.

A pivotal event was the Ceauşescus’ 1971 visit to China and North Korea. Mao’s Cultural Revolution, then in full swing, opened his eyes to the possibilities of social engineering, but it was his experience of North Korea that would prove the most fateful for his country. Ceauşescu observed the extraordinary regimentation of North Korean society, the endless rows of identical buildings in Pyongyang, and the grandiose personality cult of Kim Il-sung, and liked what he saw. All observers agree he arrived home a changed man, and the effects for ordinary Romanians were almost immediate. Western pop music and TV programs were suppressed, books were banned and press controls tightened. It would eventually become illegal to own a typewriter which had not been registered with the police. Ceauşescu also became far more autocratic. To ensure loyalty he appointed members of his extended family to important government posts, and in 1974 made himself the first president of Romania. At the inauguration ceremony he wore a rather fetching sash and was presented with a kingly sceptre, a detail which tickled

that ardent monarchist Salvador Dalí so much that he sent the dictator a congratulatory telegram.

Elena had also been changed by the trip to China and North Korea. She was impressed by the political power wielded by Mao's wife, Jiang Qing (who took a shine to her when they met), and on her return began a rise through the party ranks which culminated with her being made deputy premier in 1980.

Ceauşescu could be charming to people if he felt it was necessary. This was not the case with Elena, who treated everyone around her like dirt. Nothing their underlings did was ever good enough, and they lived in fear of her. Those closest to them were convinced that Nicolae did, too. If it looked like he was going to be late for an appointment with her, he became visibly flustered.

In dealing with his enemies, Ceauşescu displayed a greater subtlety than many of his fellow Communist leaders, preferring demotion and internal exile to imprisonment and torture (while a favourite ploy was to have dissidents declared insane and placed in psychiatric hospitals). Meanwhile his secret police, the Securitate, maintained their hold on the country by creating an all-encompassing climate of paranoia. It was commonly believed that most — if not all — the country's phones were bugged, and that as many as one in four people was a Securitate informer. Whether such tales were really true hardly mattered. People were so cowed they avoiding uttering the names of Nicolae and Elena in public — they were 'Him' and 'Her' or 'Them'. And although it seems some of them never realised it, the most closely watched Romanians of all were the highest-ranking members of the party — the so-called *Nomenklatura* — whose homes were invariably bugged. Elena eventually took charge of their surveillance. She had an office near Ceauşescu and spent most of her working day locked away in it, listening to tape recordings of government officials and their wives, enjoying in particular the ones of them having sex.

Advancement in all areas of society came to depend on paying lip service to the Ceauşescus. With all printing presses controlled by the state, it became virtually impossible to have a book published without a reference to — and preferably a quote from — the turgid speeches of the self-styled 'Genius of the Carpathians', while the country's bookshelves strained beneath the weight of the great man's collected works — a compulsory purchase for all party members. Elena's career as a chemist followed a similar pattern, with countless research papers issued under her name. When visiting scientific institutions in other countries, she was always accompanied by a translator who was also a trained chemist and could turn the gobbledegook she spouted into something coherent. Just as Ceaușescu believed himself a great statesman, Elena got it into her head that her scientific achievements were real. "I feel that the scientific mind I was blessed with shouldn't be used just for the well being of my own country but for all mankind," she once said. "I should invent something that will last forever, like fire or nuclear energy."

Dictators are known for their love of kitsch, especially when it comes to interior decoration, and Ceaușescu was no exception. He and Elena had over forty palaces and villas scattered around the country, characterised by cavernous rooms, huge chandeliers, gilt furniture, marble floors, gold-plated bathroom fittings and wardrobes bursting with clothes (Elena's dress collection rivalled Imelda's Marcos's, while Ceaușescu, fearful of germs and poison, is said to have never worn clothing or shoes more than once). Each residence had a screening room where they could watch foreign TV shows and movies (which were, of course, denied to ordinary Romanians). Among their favourites were the America cop show *Kojack* and the 1974 film version of *The Great Gatsby* starring Robert Redford, while they were also said to be partial to soft-core porn. Their principal home in Bucharest, Primavera Palace, had an indoor swimming pool, as did Neptun, their holiday house on the Black Sea. All this opulence stunned Romanians when it was revealed after Ceaușescu's downfall. But look closer, and everything was gimcrack, done on the cheap. The fabrics were synthetic, the Persian carpets factory-made, the electronic equipment outdated, the rooms full of the sort of tawdry china figurines and bric-a-brac you wouldn't look at twice in a junk shop. None of the Ceaușescus' homes looked like anyone actually lived in them (and indeed they never set foot in some of them).

Ceaușescu also had numerous hunting lodges, with large expanses of countryside set aside for his greatest passion — blasting away at animals large and small. Thousands of wild goats and bears, some imported for the purpose, were fed until they were docile, sometimes drugged, then herded together so they could be despatched by Ceaușescu *en masse*. Foreign politicians invited on hunting trips with him were invariably amused by the blatant way his ever-present Securitate men ensured that he always bagged the most game.

Ceaușescu travelled around the world endlessly and was welcomed by leaders of every political stripe, from France's Giscard d'Estaing to Cambodia's Pol Pot. Undoubtedly his greatest propaganda coup was his state visit to Britain in 1978. Arriving at London's Victoria Station, Nicolae, Elena and their entourage were greeted by the Queen, the Duke of Edinburgh and a host of lesser royals. Ceaușescu, with the Queen beside him and crowds cheering him on, was taken by landau to Buckingham Palace, where he was given a fancy hunting rifle with a telescopic sight, while Elena was presented with a gold and diamond brooch. (She was notorious for demanding expensive gifts when on state visits.)

The extreme paranoia of the Ceaușescus was much in evidence during this visit. They were terrified of germs, so whenever they had to shake hands with anyone, a Securitate man was ready to pour alcohol on their hands and wipe them with sterilised cloths. As they always did on foreign visits, they brought their own bedding with them, and the Queen was mightily offended when Ceaușescu deployed his food taster during dinner at the palace. Assuming the building was bugged as any public building in Romania would be, he also held early morning meetings with his security team in the garden. Giscard d'Estaing (who called a visit by Ceaușescu

an "unavoidable calamity") had warned the Queen that his entourage would steal anything that wasn't nailed down, so she ordered her staff to be particularly vigilant.

As well as demanding expensive gifts when visiting other countries, Elena liked to receive scientific honours. After much wheedling by the Romanians, the Royal Institute of Chemistry gave her a fellowship, and the Central London Polytechnic an honorary degree. She also had a two-hour meeting with the opposition leader, Margaret Thatcher, during which they supposedly discussed Romania's chemical industry. As Thatcher was a trained chemist rather than a pretend one, Elena's interpreter would have had his work cut out for him.

While the British government was as keen as any to cosy up to Ceaușescu, his invitation to Buckingham Palace had an ulterior motive: British Aerospace thought they were close to selling £300 million worth of aircraft to Romania. But when Ceaușescu left England the contract was still not signed. Back home, reluctant as ever to pay for anything in hard cash, he instructed his negotiators to offer payment in substandard Romanian steel and textiles. When the British understandably baulked at this, they were offered part-payment in ice cream and strawberries — seriously! The contract, needless to say, was never signed.

Ceaușescu's British visit received blanket media coverage in Romania, and caused genuine despair among its people. Romanians admired Britain, and to see its monarch fawning over their dictator and presenting him with an honorary knighthood (Knight Grand Cross of the Order of Bath, the highest honour that could be given to a foreigner) was a bitter pill to swallow. How would they ever be rid of this man?

On July 1978, Ceaușescu suffered his biggest setback so far. This was the defection to the United States of Ion Mihai Pacepa, the deputy head of Romania's foreign intelligence agency, the DIE. Pacepa had spent much of his time in close proximity to Ceaușescu and his family, and knew all the secrets.

Pacepa was debriefed by the CIA for months. In 1987, he published a book, *Red Horizons*, in which he revealed in copious detail the activities of the DIE, which were largely centred on the wholesale theft of technology from the West by infiltrating Romanian agents in foreign companies (Ceaușescu thought it a moral imperative to steal from the capitalists). He also described Ceaușescu's dealings with the likes of Yasser Arafat and Gaddafi. For years, he desperately tried to become the mediator in the Middle East conflict (and pocket a Nobel Peace Prize in the process). But it was the book's vivid descriptions of the private lives of the Ceaușescus and their children that garnered the most comment.

Valentin, their eldest child, maintained the most distance from his parents. After studying in London, he worked quietly as a physicist at the Central Institute of Physics in Bucharest, and was regarded as a decent fellow by ordinary Romanians. Zoia, their daughter, was a mathematician. The Securitate kept a close eye on her, and Elena took an unhealthy interest in her boyfriends (she invariably disapproved of them, and ordered at least one to be exiled). In defiance, Zoia took other boyfriends and gained a reputation, probably undeserved, for promiscuity. But it was the Ceaușescus' youngest son, Nicu, for whom the Romanian people reserved their greatest contempt. A heavy drinker from the age of fourteen, Nicu was a notorious playboy known for crashing cars, fighting in bars and raping women. While some of the stories about him were no doubt exaggerated, Pacepa's book has more than enough vignettes to back up the image: Nicu with a machine gun in one hand and a bottle of whisky in the other; Nicu leaping onto a table at a banquet and urinating on a plate of oysters to 'season' them; Nicu groping the wives of government ministers — in front of them.

Despite this behaviour, Nicu was Ceaușescu's heir apparent. He was the head of the Communist Youth League (as his father had been) and later a district secretary in the city of Sibiu. To give credit where it's due, Nicu was genuinely appalled by how badly ordinary people in Romania were suffering, and perhaps the only man in the country willing to say this to Ceaușescu's face. He was once heard shouting at him, "The country will be destroyed. It's freezing cold and no-one has anything to eat. You'd better fucking resign!"

Pacepa's defection unhinged Ceaușescu. He overreacted by ordering a wholesale purge of his staff, and completely dismantled the DIE, an organisation that had been fiendishly well organised and successful in what it did. The result was the departure from his inner circle of the last individuals with any integrity and independence in their thinking. They were replaced by sycophants who only told the dictator what he wanted to hear, and kept him insulated from the realities of life in Romania. The only person with any influence over him now was Elena.

eaușescu's adherence to Stalinist central planning and insistence on industrial growth at the expense of agriculture had driven Romania's economy into the ground, especially when the oil crisis hit in the early '70s, but things became much worse after 1980 when he made a snap decision to pay off all Romania's foreign debt. This was largely achieved by increasing exports, particularly of food, leading to such serious shortages that rationing had to be

introduced. Petrol and electricity were also in short supply. Ceaușescu's solution to the energy crisis was to decree that people could only use 40-watt light-bulbs.

Another government policy that caused agony for ordinary people dated back to 1966, when Ceaușescu was still being hailed around the world as comparatively liberal. Keen to increase Romania's population, he had declared that all couples should have four children. Rigid restrictions on contraception and abortion were announced, and divorce became almost impossible. The birth rate soared, but as Romania lacked the doctors, nurses and medical infrastructure to handle this, so did the infant mortality rate. Thousands of unwanted babies — many of them handicapped or suffering from infectious diseases including AIDS (which officially didn't exist in Romania) — were banished to understaffed clinics in out-of-the-way places where they died a slow death from neglect and malnutrition.

With Romania's economic and social problems deepening, the Ceausescus became increasingly preoccupied with grandiose building plans inspired by their visits to North Korea. As part of a strange, neo-Marxist desire to efface the differences between town and country, villages were levelled and hundreds of churches and historic buildings torn down to make way for hideous, poorly-built apartment blocks that lacked electricity and running water. The culmination of their building program, and perhaps the greatest architectural folly of all time, was the gargantuan People's Palace, designed to hold, for no good reason, all the arms of government under one roof. A fifth of old Bucharest was levelled to make way for the palace and the Boulevard of Socialist Victory leading to it — longer and wider than the Champs-Élysées. Some seven thousand buildings, including houses, monasteries and the magnificent Brâncovenesc Hospital, all disappeared at a wave of the dictator's hand. To add insult to injury, many people were forced to sign documents in which they requested their homes be demolished, and sometimes they were given only a few hours' notice that it was about to happen. Some, losing the houses they had been born in, committed suicide.

Nicolae and Elena oversaw every detail of this monstrous building with its lumpen clash of architectural styles. They constantly changed their minds about its design, driving the team of architects working on it to distraction. Ceaușescu was incapable of envisaging a design feature until a large-scale model of it was built, and even then he could never make up his mind. One feature he never bothered to add were toilets for the fifteen thousand workers who toiled on the building every day. It was literally full of shit, and before a visit by the Ceaușescus, a team would go along the route they would likely take, scooping it up so they wouldn't have to step in it.

Towards the end, Ceaușescu was at the building site up to twice a day. It was as if he realised, in the foggy recesses of his brain, that the ground in Romania was shifting, and it was only here that he remained in absolute control.

The vast People's Palace was unfinished when he died. Today it serves as the Palace of Parliament, and is still mostly empty.

s the 1980s rolled on, the queues outside shops grew ever longer and increasing numbers of people perished in winter from a lack of heating, but Ceaușescu's grip on power seemed as firm as ever. It is true there were occasional ruptures in the system, such as the time in 1987 when striking workers at a truck factory in Brasov ransacked the local party headquarters. Nevertheless, the mass rallies continued, with tens of thousands of workers regularly bussed in to Bucharest, handed placards with Ceaușescu's face on them, and made to watch and cheer the distant figure of the

Conductator ('leader' — the title he had adopted) giving speeches lasting three hours. In truth, it was only the Securitate men up the front, dressed as workmen, who were really cheering. No matter, they were backed up by tape recordings of cheers.

Ceaușescu's photos in the state newspaper *Scientia* were always retouched so he appeared twenty years younger than he actually was, and Romanians were acutely aware that his father had lived to the ripe old age of eighty-three. (On one occasion, the elderly Andruță, as drunk as ever, had been heard to criticise his son's policies in a bar in Bucharest. The next day, the bar had disappeared, building and all.) In reality, the 'Genius of the Carpathians' was now a decrepit old man, suffering from diabetes for which he refused to take proper medication, his mind visibly slipping. With the homely Elena by his side, this once imperious pair had become a couple of frumps who had, as Peter York memorably put it, "an air of suppositories and liver tonics".

While a few of the people around him saw the end was near, it took the collapse of the Soviet Union and the revolutions of 1989 to create the necessary conditions for Ceaușescu's removal. The trigger came on 17 November with demonstrations in support of a Hungarian-speaking dissident priest, Laszlo Tokes, who was holed up in his house in the Transylvanian city of Timisoara. A rumour had gone around that the government was trying to expel him. (In fact, it was his bishop trying to do that — Romania's various churches had always been in bed with Ceaușescu.) But once there, the demonstrators refused to leave. While all of this was going on, the 14th Congress of the Romanian Communist Party was held in Bucharest. In his usual rambling speeches, Ceaușescu recited the latest fabulous economic figures, but

made no mention of the unpleasantness in Timisoara, or the fact that the Berlin Wall had fallen days earlier (beyond noting that there were anti-Communist forces about). At the end of it, the 3,308 members of the congress unanimously re-elected him.

The number of demonstrators surrounding Tokes's house grew to 5,000. On the evening of Saturday, 15 December, shouting anti-Ceaușescu slogans, they began moving towards the city centre. They broke into a bookshop and set fire to the dictator's books, then ransacked the local party headquarters.

Ceaușescu called an emergency meeting the following morning. He berated the defence minister, General Vasile Milea, for failing to order his men to fire at the demonstrators. "What kind of defence minister are you?" he asked. Elena pitched in: "You should shoot them so they fall and put them in basements. Not even one of them should see the light of day again." The deputy defence minister, General Stănculescu, was despatched to Timisoara, and that evening, the army and security forces started shooting. In the information vacuum that was Ceaușescu's Romania, rumour soon inflated the less than one hundred killed into tens of thousands, inflaming the rest of the country. Ceaușescu was dimly aware that something was happening, but insisted on leaving for a scheduled two-day trip to Iran.

On his return on 20 December, he gave an address broadcast on television and radio. He looked haggard and sounded incoherent. The following morning, he appeared on the balcony of the Central Committee building to address a hastily-convened rally. As he started to speak there could be heard an unaccustomed murmuring among the huge crowd that became a low rumble, then the chanting of slogans and the word 'Timisoara'. Ceaușescu, who had long believed he had a mystical connection with the Romanian people when he spoke to them, stopped speaking. It was all being broadcast live on television, and the expression on his face as he saw his power draining away was something to see. Elena, standing beside him as always, urged him to "Promise them something." He started muttering about wage increases but was drowned out by people shouting "Down with the murderer!" and singing pre-war patriotic songs. The broadcast was terminated as security men ushered Nicolae and Elena back into the building.

It was the signal for Romanians to take to the streets. There was rioting in Bucharest through the night, and dozens of people were shot by the Securitate and units of the army. Once again, rumour greatly inflated the death toll.

The Ceaușescus spent a restless night in the Central Committee building. In the morning, they peered through the windows and saw that the building was surrounded by tanks, but the massive influx of troops Ceaușescu had ordered to secure the city were nowhere to be seen. He blamed General Milea, and later that morning, Radio Bucharest announced that the general had committed suicide. Whether he did, or whether he had been shot on Ceaușescu's orders (as was immediately assumed by everybody), the announcement was the catalyst for the army, seemingly instantaneously and to a man, to switch sides. The tanks turned around to face the Central Committee building, then began rumbling towards it, accompanied by cheering crowds who could not believe the speed at which events were unfolding. Romanian television was back on air and covering everything.

Inside the Central Committee building, there was pandemonium. Beneath it, and honeycombing the surrounding area, lay a network of tunnels guarded by the Securitate through which Ceaușescu and his cronies could have easily escaped. It was apparently General Stănculescu who suggested they go by helicopter instead. Four were summoned but in the end only one, under the command

of Ceaușescu's personal pilot, landed on the roof just before midday. With the first demonstrators inside the building, the Ceaușescus, Prime Minister Bobu, Deputy Minister Manescu and two bodyguards squeezed into a lift. It stalled on the top floor and the bodyguards had to force the doors open, but eventually they made it to the roof and piled into the helicopter. It was dangerously overloaded but the pilot managed to get it airborne.

They could have gone to the international airport at Otopeni where they may have been able to board a plane and flee the country, but Ceaușescu still couldn't grasp that it was all over. He thought if he could regroup with loyalists outside the capital, perhaps in Sibiu where Nicu was in charge, the situation could be turned around. So he ordered the pilot to take them to his villa in Snagov, where he had often hosted hunting parties for foreign dignitaries. Ceaușescu rang one district secretary after another and asked about the situation in their regions, but received mostly frosty replies. Meanwhile, Elena was rushing around, stuffing valuables into bags. A little over an hour later, the Ceaușescus and bodyguards were in the helicopter and on their way again, leaving Bobu and Manescu behind.

When the pilot, who had learned from his radio operator that the army had joined the rebellion, told Ceaușescu he was worried they would be shot down, he was ordered to land immediately. The helicopter came to rest next to a main road, and the bodyguards flagged down a couple of cars. With Nicolae, Elena and one bodyguard in the first car, and the other bodyguard in the second, they set off, with Ceaușescu still unsure where to go. They soon came to a village where the driver of the first car, a doctor named Deca who just wanted to be anywhere else in the world at this point, pretended they were running out of petrol. They stopped next to a house where a factory worker named Nicolae Petrisor was washing

his car. On realising who the new arrivals were, he shouted excitedly to his wife, "They're here! It's them!"

Petrisor was ordered into his car, and the Ceauşescus and one of the bodyguards got in after him (the other bodyguard had taken the opportunity to scarper). As they drove off, Ceauşescu told Petrisor to turn the radio on, and they heard a dissident Romanian poet named Mirceas Dinescu breathlessly proclaiming the fall of the dictator. Ceauşescu told Petrisor to turn it off. Petrisor later claimed that Elena was pointing a gun at his head while this was going on, but this seems unlikely to me — the bodyguard was there for such menial work. Ceauşescu then told him to drive to a factory he had often shown off to foreign visitors as a paragon of Romanian industry, but when they arrived there the workers were on strike and threw stones at the car.

The most farcical flight of a despot since Louis XVI and Marie Antoinette fled from Paris dressed as servants continued. The streets were now so crowded with demonstrators it was difficult to get anywhere, but Petrisor eventually dropped the Ceauşescus off at an agricultural institute in Târgovişte and made his escape. The director there rang the local militia, and two militiamen arrived that afternoon to pick them up. Forced to take side streets to avoid the crowds of demonstrators, it took them four hours to drive the 492 yards (450 metres) to the militia headquarters, where a contingent of soldiers were waiting to take them to the local army barracks. Ceauşescu arrived there barking orders and it took him some time to realise he was now a prisoner.

During the three days they were at the barracks, the Ceauşescus were true to type. Nicolae railed at the foreign powers he blamed for his downfall, and demanded to speak to the demonstrators who could be heard outside, confident he could still weave his magic. Elena, meanwhile, behaved as if she was back in one of her palaces, surrounded by incompetent servants. They both railed at the army rations they were given to eat, calling them inedible. When an officer told him it was what they always ate, Ceaușescu refused to believe him.

A makeshift bedroom was set up for them, and a guard assigned to watch them during the night. He was embarrassed to see the elderly couple clinging to each other, while bickering about which one of them was most to blame for their predicament.

The army may have sided with the people, but the Securitate weren't about to give up. They could be heard firing at the demonstrators outside. (It later transpired that, in a sort of final homage to the blatant fakery that had characterised the Ceaușescu regime, many of the gun shots were tape recordings.) On the night of 24 December, when it seemed the Securitate might overrun the barracks, the Ceaușescus, wearing army greatcoats, were bundled into an armoured car and spent the night in it, lying face down on the floor.

In the years leading up to 1989, a number of plots to overthrow Ceaușescu had been hatched by senior military and government figures. Among them was Ion Iliescu, who had been a government minster during the '70s before being sidelined by Ceaușescu. None of the plots had come to anything, but as soon as the dictator fled the plotters realised their time had come, and Iliescu and some of the others gathered in the Central Committee building.

Meanwhile, General Stănculescu, who just days before had been overseeing the murder of people in Timisoara, was holed up in the Ministry of Defence building. He had always been a Ceaușescu loyalist, but was keeping his options open. (He had even turned up for work that morning with a plaster cast on his leg — a ruse to justify inaction that even

Ceaușescu saw through.) It was only when he received the news of the dictator's arrest that he phoned Iliescu and told him to form a new government.

On the morning of 25th December, Stănculescu and a team of lawyers flew to Târgoviște in a helicopter. They were accompanied by a four-man firing squad, which gives some indication of how they expected the trial about to unfold would end.

A small room, originally a school room, was set up as a makeshift court, and the Ceaușescus were brought in. The lawyers assigned to their defence advised Nicolae to plead insanity, a suggestion he vehemently rejected. He repeatedly said that he did not recognise the court, and denied all the charges laid against him. He rejected the claim that he had starved his people, and spouted fictitious government statistics to refute it. Ironically, two of the charges — that he had committed genocide in Timisoara and hired foreign mercenaries to fire on demonstrators (it had been rumoured he had brought in Arabs for the purpose) were actually false. "This is outrageous!" Elena shouted, and for once she had a point. The prosecutor also spent some time taunting Elena about her scientific pretensions. This wasn't, strictly speaking, relevant to the proceedings, but you can hardly blame him. When someone asked Ceaușescu why they had fled from Bucharest by helicopter, he said that he had been advised to by people plotting against him, and stared coldly at Stănculescu.

After a five-minute recess, the judge and the lawyers (who were also the jury) returned, and the Ceaușescus were sentenced to death. Soldiers stepped forward and began to tie their hands behind their backs. "Don't tie us up!" Elena screamed. "It's a shame, a disgrace. I brought you up as a mother. Why are you doing this?" The trial had lasted just under an hour.

The Ceauşescus were led out into the yard, and it was probably only then that they realised what was about to happen. They were taken to a spot Stănculescu had picked before the trial began and made to stand facing a wall, but turned around just as the soldiers began to fire. Elena fainted and her body was riddled with bullets where it lay. Ceauşescu was held upright by the stiff overcoat he was wearing as the bullets tore into him. The firing squad had been ordered not to aim above his chest so his corpse would be easily recognisable.

In the Securitate, Nicolae Ceauşescu had the most efficient security force in the Eastern Bloc, more pervasive and feared than the KGB. Phones and buildings in Romania were bugged in vast numbers, an army of censors went through every letter dropped into a post box. Ion Pacepa records a meeting of Ceauşescu's inner circle in 1979 where he declared, "In a very short time we will be the only country on earth able to know what every single one of its citizens is thinking." The supreme irony of Ceauşescu's regime is that, by the end, he didn't know what anyone was thinking, for no-one, not even the Securitate, had the nerve to tell him.

Oh, he knew there were a few pesky dissidents around, and that some Romanians insisted on listening to Radio Free Europe (at one point he demanded the names of all those he did). But the idea that most of the population did not share his vision — and never had — was inconceivable to him. Ceauşescu had lived in a Communist bubble since his teens. He had never held a job outside the party, or mixed with people who weren't Communists. When shown entirely spurious statistics on economic progress by his fawning officials, year after year after year, he believed them, for he had ordered them. They were the inevitable result of the political system he had devised, so how could such statistics be doubted? He was well aware that there were a few problems with food shortages and blackouts and such, but these minor setbacks could only be expected as the perfect socialist society was built.

"They were surprised by events, astonished," said Valentin Ceauşescu after his parents' downfall. "They couldn't believe what was happening. I think they never realised it. They never realised that they were not loved."

CHAPTER 6

JEAN-BÉDEL BOKASSA

JEAN-BÉDEL BOKASSA

Attained power in 1965
Crowned himself emperor in 1977
Died in obscurity in 1996

On 4 December 1977, the world gained a rare thing: a new emperor. His coronation took place on a sweltering morning in a sports stadium given an imperial makeover, in Bangui, the capital of the landlocked, impoverished nation known until the year before as the Central African Republic.

The country's former president, Jean-Bédel Bokassa, now Emperor Bokassa I, stood erect in front of his golden throne, an extraordinary affair in the shape of an eagle with outstretched wings. He wore a fetching, full-length gown embroidered with thousands of pearls, and matching pearl-encrusted slippers. Draped over his shoulders and trailing across the floor was a crimson velvet mantle 30 feet (9 metres) long and trimmed with a generous expanse of ermine. In his right hand he grasped a sceptre of ebony encrusted with jewels, while a ceremonial sword hung from his waist. And on his head sat the imperial crown, another splendid creation of gold and diamonds, topped by an eagle perched on a blue globe representing the earth. A few minutes earlier, Bokassa had placed the crown on his own head, just as his hero, Napoleon, had done at *his* coronation ceremony a hundred and seventy years earlier.

Bokassa, previously known to the outside world for his penchant for cutting off people's ears, had invited two hundred foreign journalists along to his big day, hoping for maximum coverage. He received it, but the tone wasn't quite as positive as he was hoping for.

Jean-Bédel Bokassa was born on 22 February 1921, in the village of Boubangui, in what was then known as Oubangui-Chari. It had been a French colony since the 1880s, one of a cluster of territories known collectively as French Equatorial Africa. Like most African colonies, its people were ruthlessly exploited as free labour for the production of rubber, hardwood, coffee, cotton and other commodities.

Bokassa's father, Mindogan Mgboundoulou, was a village headman who had the unenviable task of forcing his fellow villagers to work. But there was rebellion in the air by the 1920s. A prophet named Karnu had emerged who claimed to have a magic plant that would turn the French into gorillas, and distributed hoe handles to his followers which would protect them from bullets. Caught up in the excitement, Mindogan released some villagers held captive so their relatives would agree to work. He was arrested and beaten to death in a square outside the Prefect's office. Bokassa's mother Marie was so traumatised that she committed suicide a week later.

Bokassa, aged six, was placed in a mission school where he excelled as a student, then moved to a secondary school whose principal suggested he become a priest. Bokassa had always been fascinated by soldiers and uniforms, though, and upon graduating in 1939 he joined the French army.

After France fell to Germany, French Equatorial Africa allied itself to Charles de Gaulle's 'Free French' government in exile. Bokassa, now a sergeant, saw action in France and Germany in 1944. Although only five feet (152 cm) tall, he was physically tough and courageous in battle, and was awarded the *Légion d'honneur* and the *Croix de guerre*. He stayed in the army when the war ended, and served in France's ill-fated war in Indochina. He fell in love with the Vietnamese people, and married seventeen-year-old N'guyen-Thi-Hué;

with whom he had a daughter. He went back to France on leave in 1953, expecting to return to Indochina shortly, but he never did, and it was years before he saw his daughter again. He left just in time, for the following year many of the soldiers he had fought beside were killed in the Battle of Den Bien Phu.

1959 found him back in his homeland for the first time in twenty years. While he was away, France, in a desperate attempt to preserve its empire in the face of rising African nationalism, had granted its colonies semi-autonomy. Oubangui-Chari had been rechristened the Central African Republic (or Centrafique), and a charismatic former priest, Barthélemy Boganda, had become its first premier. A few months before Bokassa's return, Boganda died in a plane crash believed to have been an assassination. The French authorities installed a replacement more to their liking, the former interior minister, David Dacko. He was far less popular than Boganda, and wasted no time banning opposition parties and imprisoning his enemies.

Bokassa, who considered himself a man of destiny, had come back at just the right time. Dacko's government was corrupt from the start, with an endless number of cronies given lucrative government jobs. Meanwhile, the process of putting together an army for the new nation had begun, and Bokassa, who had attained the rank of captain in the French army — and was also a cousin of Dacko — was the obvious man to head it. In 1963, he was named commander-in-chief. His army may have consisted of a mere five hundred poorly trained and equipped men, but they gave him a power base.

Dacko sensed his ambitions, but he also found the notoriously vain Bokassa a rather absurd figure. He made little secret of this, and once declared, at an official dinner where foreign diplomats and Bokassa were present, "Colonel Bokassa only wants to collect medals, and he is too stupid to mount a coup d'etat." Dacko nevertheless created a five hundred-strong police force to provide a counterbalance to his potential rival's army, as well as appointing a hundred and twenty security guards. In 1965, while Bokassa was in France as part of a delegation, Dacko banned him from re-entering the country. Bokassa spent months mustering support from the French, and eventually Dacko relented and allowed him back.

Bokassa was also dithering. He wasn't sure whether his soldiers were up to mounting a coup, and feared that if he toppled Dacko, the French would step in and restore him to power. But he knew Dacko's position was weakening. The country was almost bankrupt, and the French had been forced to bail it out. They were also unimpressed when Dacko, looking for other sources of income, invited Chinese investment in the country.

Bokassa made his move on the evening of 31 December 1965, ordering his troops to seize the presidential palace and the radio station. Dacko wasn't in the capital, Bangui, but he was quickly located and arrested. When he was brought to the Palais de la Renaissance, Bokassa embraced him and said cheerily, "I tried to warn you — but now it's too late." It was all over in hours and relatively bloodless, with the casualties limited to eight policemen who died in shootouts with soldiers, and a hapless security guard at the radio station who had been armed with a bow and arrow. Shortly after 2 a.m., Bokassa issued his first order: that all the prisoners in Bangui's dreaded Ngaragba prison were to be set free, and a couple of hours after that he was on the radio. "This is Colonel Bokassa speaking to you," he said. "The Dacko government has resigned. The hour of justice is at hand. The bourgeoisie is abolished. A new era of equality for all has begun."

aving seized control with remarkable ease, Bokassa sang from the song sheet usually deployed after a successful coup d'etat — he promised the people there would be elections soon. In the meantime, he abolished the National Assembly, tore up the constitution and ruled by decree.

Bokassa characterised his regime as a revolutionary movement, but one also committed to fighting corruption and promoting austerity. He lambasted greedy civil servants, saying they spent most of their time in their offices having sex, and cut their pay. He banned his ministers from going to bars. He also lost no time in expelling the Chinese, whom he accused of plotting to take over the country. All of this was calculated to reassure the French. His political survival ultimately rested on their recognising his regime, but he was also proud of his service in the French army and idolised President de Gaulle. The French government watched and waited for a while, but ten months after the coup, Bokassa was invited to Paris where he was received at the Elysée Palace.

Bokassa's austerity program got off to a promising start when he appointed his right-hand man during the coup, Captain Alexandre Banza, as minister of finance. Banza instituted some important reforms, including cutting ruinous taxes for farmers, but the anti-corruption crusade was never going to last long. Bokassa knew that he couldn't survive without keeping civil servants and the army happy, while a man with the extravagant tastes he was now beginning to demonstrate was hardly the person to spearhead an austerity program. He was also terminally unwilling to delegate. He reserved no less than twelve cabinet posts for himself, while constantly shuffling his other ministers, dispensing favours, then firing them on a whim. Knowing that their time in cabinet would likely be short, ministers busied themselves

funnelling as much state money into their bank accounts as possible.

As the first anniversary of his coup approached, there was no more talk of an election. And why should there be? Bokassa knew he was the only person qualified to lead his country, a man of almost supernatural abilities. "I am everywhere and nowhere," he said gnomically. "I see nothing yet I see all. I listen to nothing and hear everything."

When Banza clashed publicly with the President over the budget, he was demoted to health minister. He began to make preparations for a coup, but Bokassa got wind of it, and in April 1969, Banza was arrested and tried by a military tribunal. There are many versions of how he died, from the mundane — being shot by a firing squad, to the baroque — Bokassa slashing him to death with a razor during a cabinet meeting. Such a hands-on approach to meting out punishment wouldn't have been at all out of character. Bokassa was rarely without his favourite ebony cane with ivory knob, the so-called 'cane of justice', which he used to beat subordinates who displeased him — sometimes fatally. In 1974 he would use the cane on a British journalist, Michael Goldsmith, who had been accused of spying, badly injuring him and causing an international outcry.

Bokassa may have ordered Ngaragba prison, known locally as 'the Devil's Hole', emptied on the night of his coup, but it soon began to fill up again with his enemies. They were kept in chains, four men in cells designed for one, given meagre meals and regularly beaten. Almost every evening saw summary executions in the prison's courtyard, and no-one knew who might be next. Some were kept in there for years, yet there was always the possibility that Bokassa might suddenly order their release. In June 1972, feeling very pleased with himself after his latest trip to France, he once again ordered that everyone in the prison be freed.

This sort of capriciousness was a hallmark of Bokassa's regime. In 1972, after a brazen robbery at the palace, he decided that thieves should be punished by having their ears cut off. A couple of days after signing the decree, he arrived at Ngaragba with his retinue, and the forty-six thieves it housed — all now minus ears — were brought into the courtyard. Bokassa gave them a good telling off, then ordered the prison guards to beat them all to death with their nightsticks. He told them to stop five minutes later, but by then three prisoners were dead.

Bokassa liked to be known as a ladies man. When he came to power, he had six wives who all had their own houses (never mind the fact that one of his first decrees had been to ban polygamy). The total number of wives would eventually rise to seventeen, while the children he fathered ran into the hundreds, although only forty or so were officially recognised.

His principle wife was Catherine Denguiade, who was a beautiful thirteen-year-old schoolgirl when he first noticed her walking through the streets of Bangui. They married three years later. Like many dictator's wives, Catherine, known to the Central Africans as 'Maman Cathy', loved shopping for luxury goods. The other wives were generally referred to by their nationalities. While on state visits to other countries, Bokassa had a habit of acquiring wives as others would souvenir tea towels, and their number included the Romanian, the Gambonese, the Swede, the German, the Libyan and the Chinese. After Catherine, his most visible wife was Gabriela Drimba — the Romanian. Bokassa was visiting his good friend Nicolae Ceaușescu in Bucharest in 1972 when he noticed the blonde-haired Gabriela performing with a folkdance troupe. She was married and rejected his advances, but she turned up unexpectedly at Bangui airport a few weeks later (no doubt after a little pressure from the Ceauşescu regime). She was given a particularly fine villa to live in, was regularly seen in public with Bokassa, and by all accounts came to enjoy her strange new life.

Bokassa liked to present himself as a good father (albeit one not above having his sons thrown into Ngaragba prison for a while if they misbehaved). Shortly after coming to power, he had asked the French authorities in Vietnam to look for the daughter, Martine, he had fathered in the 1950s. In 1970, they told him they had found her — a dark-skinned girl living in the slums of Saigon. Bokassa organised a plane for her, and she was greeted at Bangui airport by a guard of honour. Days of celebration followed, with Martine paraded around the country amid much music and dancing. Alas, a few weeks later a Vietnamese newspaper revealed that this Martine was an impostor. After a host of other girls came forward claiming to be Martine, Bokassa's former wife emerged — with photos of herself with Bokassa and a birth certificate for her daughter to prove it. The real Martine was duly flown to the Central African Republic, where she was greeted with rather less fanfare than the first one.

Bokassa had been furious when he learned of the imposture, believing that the French had orchestrated it to make him look foolish. At first he wanted to hand the fake Martine over to the French ambassador, but then relented and agreed to adopt her. She eventually married an army officer named Obriou who secretly hated Bokassa and, in 1976, mounted an abortive coup against him. A few hours after his execution, the fake Martine gave birth to a baby boy who was killed by lethal injection on Bokassa's orders. His mother survived for another year before disappearing.

To be fair, Bokassa's high regard for women did result in some material gains for female Central Africans. As well as polygamy, he banned dowries and female circumcision, and made it an offence for parents to limit their daughters' educational opportunities. And on Mother's Day, 1971, he managed to combine two of his greatest loves — women and homicide — by ordering the immediate execution of all male prisoners in the country found guilty of raping or murdering women.

okassa could never have survived without the support of the French, who for years propped up his country's shambolic economy with massive injections of aid. But the relationship was often fractious. President de Gaulle was happy enough to welcome Bokassa to the Elysée Palace, but made fun of him in private. He is supposed to have coined the nickname 'Papa Bok', which was both a play on Haiti's 'Papa Doc', and a snide reference to Bokassa's size (in French, 'un bok' is a small glass of beer).

Despite his professed love for De Gaulle (at the French leader's memorial service in 1970, he had embarrassed himself in front of other dignitaries by repeatedly bursting into tears and declaring he had lost his true father), Bokassa wasn't always happy with the French either. He complained they weren't providing enough aid, and wanted to keep his country a backwater they could continue to exploit. Searching for other sources of funds, he put feelers out to various communist countries, including the Soviet Union and China, an interesting move given that one of the main reasons he had given for mounting his coup was to kick the Chinese out. At one point, apparently to burnish his new Marxist credentials, he expelled a host of French agricultural advisers, and began to collectivise farming. As inevitably happens with collectivisation, this resulted in a sharp drop in agricultural production, but it did serve to divert more money from the sector into the pockets of Bokassa and his cronies.

Bokassa was a canny businessman, and owned a host of enterprises including a textile factory, a saw-mill, an abattoir, a restaurant and retail stores. He expected to be made a director of any large company in the country, and received a hefty cut from its export industries, including the lucrative diamond trade. When on overseas visits, he liked to have a pocketful of diamonds he could hand out to people he wanted to cultivate. (He once tried to slip some into the hand of Madame de Gaulle, who was shocked.) Much of his wealth went in the direction of Swiss banks, while he also spent a fortune on lavish properties in France. The largest of these was the chateau of Saint-Louis Chavanon, which had sixty rooms and was set in 124 acres (50 hectares) of lush grounds. His wife Catherine preferred to stay at the chateau of Hardricourt, conveniently close to Paris and its shops.

Bokassa gained a valuable ally when Giscard d'Estaing became the French president in 1974. He was a patrician fellow whose family flaunted its aristocratic roots, and had a love of extravagance and high-living to rival Bokassa's. His family also had investments in the Central African Republic, giving him a vested interest in keeping its economy afloat. Giscard became a regular guest of Bokassa, and was allowed to indulge his passion for hunting. His particular pleasure was shooting elephants — Bokassa said that he had probably accounted for fifty of them. He was allowed to ship the accumulated ivory to France, tax free.

The Central African Republic's economy was on its knees by 1975. Giscard sent a team of experts to evaluate the situation, and their report detailed such woeful financial mismanagement that even he baulked at providing more aid. In desperation, Bokassa turned to another possible economic saviour, Libya's oil-rich Colonel Gaddafi. Always keen to spread his revolutionary message, he was amenable, and to press his case, Bokassa converted to Islam, despite the fact that the country was largely Catholic, and in the public mind Islam was largely associated with Arab slave traders. The result of this was the ludicrous spectacle of Bokassa (now rebadged as Salim Addin Ahmed Bokassa) and some of his more pliable ministers kneeling on goatskins provided by the Colonel, praying to Mecca.

Bokassa had always been known for his vanity. As an officer in the French army, he loved to swan about in a flash uniform decorated with medals. Once he became president, the medals grew exponentially. To those he had won during World War II and in Indochina were added various decorations bestowed on him by other countries, plus a host of medals he had essentially awarded himself — and on state occasions he like to wear *all* of them. Such an assemblage of metal required a reinforced shirt.

For a man of such overweening ambition as Bokassa, it was galling to have the mere title of president. Surely there was another title more appropriate. Emperor, perhaps?

The idea was not quite as outlandish as it might seem, for Bokassa had a model in the form of Haile Selassie. Perhaps best known today as an unlikely figure of veneration for Rastafarians the world over (who believe him to have been the Messiah), Selassie had ruled Ethiopia since 1916, and assumed the title of emperor in 1930. Bokassa had met Selassie, and would have been impressed by his regal bearing — and fabulous uniforms. In 1974, after a famine in Ethiopia claimed some two hundred thousand lives, Selassie was deposed in a coup, placed under house arrest for a while, then unceremoniously strangled. This turn of events only made Bokassa even keener on his plan. Africa, he must have

reasoned, had a vacancy for an emperor.

Giscard d'Estaing was decidedly lukewarm when Bokassa broached the idea. The French press had been highly critical of the Central African leader's extravagance, and this

development was wasn't going to help. Bokassa had some leverage, though, because the French government hated his deal with Libya. It was finally agreed that, if he cut his ties with Gaddafi, the French would recognise his new 'empire' and even bankroll his coronation. That suited him just fine. Gaddafi hadn't honoured most of his promises anyway, and Bokassa was tiring of Islam — its ban on alcohol in particular. A new constitution was drawn up, and it was announced on 4 December 1976 that the country would henceforth be known as the Central African Empire. (How a nation can be considered an empire without having any colonies is a question I can't answer and nobody seems to have asked at the time.) Its first ruler would be Emperor Bokassa I, and his coronation would take place exactly a year later.

A host of French designers and craftsman were set to work creating all the trappings for the ceremony. Guiselin, the company that had designed Napoleon's uniforms, were responsible for Bokassa's coronation gown and mantle. Arthus Bertrand, an equally venerable firm which specialised in making medals and decorations for the French government, fashioned his crown, which was valued at $2.5 million. And the all-important eagle throne was the work of the sculptor Olivier Brice. Fashioned from sheets of bronze attached to a sturdy metal framework then plated with gold, it was 11 feet (3.5 metres) tall and weighed two tonnes. An arch-shaped hollow at the front contained a red velvet-lined seat on which the imperial posterior could rest. The total bill for all of this, plus a few other bits and pieces including an imperial coach, came to about $22 million.

Meanwhile, Bokassa had to decide which one of his wives would be his empress. The contenders were his principle wife, Catherine, and his more recent favourite, Gabriela. Catherine argued that the empress should be a Central African, while she had also given him sons who could be his heirs. Bokassa agreed and Gabriela retired to her villa, where she consoled herself with the attentions of her guards. Bokassa, apprised of the situation, arrived one evening with a party of soldiers. After threatening to feed the guards to crocodiles, he ordered they be taken to Ngaragba prison where most were eventually shot. However, in another demonstration of his indulgent attitude to women, he merely sent Gabriela back to Romania.

n the morning of the coronation, Bangui was looking its best. The streets had been cleaned, the buildings painted, the beggars ejected.

Bokassa originally wanted his coronation to take place in Bangui's cathedral, with Pope Paul VI presiding (just as Pope Pius VII had done at Napoleon's coronation). Sadly, the Pope was indisposed, and the venue was changed to the city's sports stadium. It had been jazzed up with tapestries, banners and swathes of red drapery. The eagle throne stood at one end on a raised dais.

The guests had taken their seats by 8.30 a.m. Two-and-a-half-thousand invitations had been sent to foreign dignitaries but only six-hundred had accepted, and the most senior politician Bokassa managed to snare was the prime minister of Mauritius. Even his buddy Giscard d'Estaing wasn't there.

Bokassa was due to arrive at 9 a.m., but he was late as always. The air conditioning in the stadium had broken down and the guests dressed in all their finery were sweating. An hour later, the imperial carriage, a French antique decorated in gold and drawn by eight white horses, drew up outside. The guests stood as two guards wearing Napoleonic uniforms and bearing the national flag and imperial standard entered and took their places on each side of the throne. They were followed by four-year-old Prince Jean-Bédel, wearing a white admiral's uniform, and his mother Catherine, looking elegant in a gold lamé Lanvin gown, its train carried by ladies-in-waiting. Then, as the band played the 'Imperial March', Bokassa appeared, a golden laurel wreath on his head, and moved at a stately pace to his throne.

A deafening twenty-one gun salute rang out as Bokassa

donned his crown. He then took the oath of office, and everyone sang the national anthem. Afterwards, there was a mass in the cathedral, and all the guests reconvened that evening for a banquet at the palace.

The international press covered this spectacle with undisguised mockery. The French in particular were indignant about Bokassa's wholesale appropriation of their national symbols and his absurd channelling of Napoleon. African newspapers were, if anything, even more scathing, with many writers accusing him of making Africans look like fools.

The reign of Emperor Bokassa I lasted barely two years, his downfall triggered by, of all things, school uniforms.

Bokassa was ambivalent about education. Having come to power with a promise to develop his country, he had no choice but to improve its education system, and established new secondary schools and Bokassa University in Bangui. But he knew that education posed a risk because educated citizens might come to question his one-man rule. The problem was made more acute because many teachers had to be brought in from France, and it was inevitable that they would transmit ideas about political freedom to their students. Several university professors were sacked for doing this in 1974. When students boycotted classes in protest, their leaders were carted off to Ngaragba where they were held for several days and beaten. Two years later, after further protests when a college teacher was arrested, Bokassa signed a degree making it illegal for teachers to discuss politics or criticise the government.

While Bokassa was wary of education, he wasn't pleased when Central African students did poorly in their final exams in 1977. Some blamed the French teachers, but

Bokassa thought the students lacked discipline, and one way to rectify that would be to make them wear uniforms. It was therefore announced that the wearing of school uniforms — designed by Bokassa — would be compulsory from 1 October 1978. There was an added bonus for Bokassa in that the uniforms would be manufactured in his textile factory, and sold in his stores. The main problem with the plan was that, as the deadline approached, the country was facing an economic crisis so severe that the government hadn't paid soldiers, teachers and civil servants for two months. People simply couldn't afford to buy the uniforms, so few students were wearing them 1 October. There were no immediate consequences, but in January two of the largest secondary schools announced they would no longer admit students without uniforms.

School students across the country went on strike, and university students joined their protests. On 19 January, three thousand of them gathered at the university, then marched to the palace where they were met by soldiers. They retreated to the suburbs, smashing shops along the way (including a boutique owned by Empress Catherine). With workers joining in and helping to set up barricades, and the army unable to restore order, Bokassa sent in his highly-trained imperial guard who, with the aid of a couple of Soviet-built tanks and armoured cars with mounted machine guns, were able to restore order.

The situation was outwardly calmer for the next few months. An injection of French cash allowed the emperor to pay civil servants, and schools reopened, but many students and teachers refused to return to them and several were arrested. Meanwhile, the organisation representing university students was planning further protests. On 12 April, Bokassa ordered the closure of all schools, while soldiers took over the university. Five days later, dozens of students were arrested at a rally, and a curfew was imposed. Security forces fanned through Bangui in the early hours of the morning, moving from house to house and arresting any students they found. Many of them, some as young as fourteen, were sent to Ngaragba prison where they were stripped, beaten and thrown into cells. In one instance, thirty were crammed into a cell designed for one, and by the following morning, many were dead. With parents clamouring for answers, Bokassa tried to downplay what had happened. He said that around fifty people had been arrested for looting, but claimed that the missing students had fled across the border into Zaire.

News of the crackdown slowly spread to the outside world, and Amnesty International released a report on it in April 1979 which was particularly embarrassing for the French government. At a Franco-African summit in Rwanda the following month, Bokassa found his old friend Giscard was suddenly not so friendly, and even worse, leading the calls for an international commission of inquiry into the events in Bangui. While he initially resisted the idea, Bokassa ultimately had no choice but to agree to it.

The commission, composed of magistrates from several African countries, arrived in Bangui on 12 June. Bokassa welcomed them with open arms, assuring them that they would have the full co-operation of government officials. These, they soon learned, were empty words. All the officials they spoke to stuck to the emperor's version of events: nothing to see here, only a few dead, everything back to normal now. The commissioners, to their credit, therefore concentrated on talking to ordinary people, including students who claimed to have been present at Ngaragba on the night of the beatings.

Bokassa received a phone call from President Bongo of Gabon in late July. Bongo told him that a French official would be coming to Gabon with a message from Giscard d'Estaing, and he needed to be there to hear it. Bokassa was suspicious, but agreed to make the trip. The official's message was blunt: the commission's soon-to-be-released report would hold Bokassa responsible for mass murder, and Giscard wanted him to abdicate immediately. Bokassa flatly refused, and when Giscard rang him the next day, he hung up on him.

The Commission found that at least a hundred and fifty people had been killed during the January protests, while the victims in April numbered up to two hundred, including a hundred children. And it accepted the testimonies of three students that Bokassa was present at Ngaragba on the night of 18 April, and had taken an enthusiastic part in the beatings, although other witnesses disputed this.

wo days after the report was released, France cancelled all but humanitarian aid to the Central African Empire. Bokassa — or to use the new title the French press had bestowed on him, 'the Butcher of Bangui' — turned back to Gaddafi in desperation. The Colonel was willing to forgive his short-lived embrace of Islam, for he still had his eye on the empire's hitherto under-exploited uranium deposits and a strategically useful military base in Bouar, so on 12 September, Bokassa and an entourage flew to Libya. Gaddafi kept him waiting for a day and a half — to make it clear who was boss — then received him in his tent in Benghazi. After listening patiently as Bokassa poured out his tale of woe, Gaddafi gave the diminutive emperor a hug and offered him a deal. He would bankroll Bokassa's army and civil service for two years, in return for control of the military base. A mightily relieved Bokassa returned to his hotel, confident that his empire was safe. In fact, it was already history.

What he didn't know was that the French had spent months putting together a detailed plan — Operation Barracuda — for his overthrow. They had been wary of activating it, fearing that Bokassa might order reprisals against the thousands of French citizens working in his country, but as soon has his plane had touched down in Libya, this fear evaporated. Hundreds of French troops stationed in Zaire and Chad crossed into the Central African Empire, where they encountered no resistance whatsoever and quickly secured Bangui. All that remained was to install a new leader, and the French had one up their sleeve — although he was actually more of an old leader. Having evaluated the various Central African self-styled opposition leaders, they had decided that the best of a bad lot was the ineffectual David Dacko, the man Bokassa had deposed in 1964. After years in prison, he had been rehabilitated and served in Bokassa's government, before going into exile in France. Just before midnight on 20 September, Dacko went on the radio and told Central Africans, "The regime of Bokassa I has disintegrated."

Bokassa was woken in his hotel room in Benghazi at 2.30 a.m. and told of these events. He faced an immediate dilemma: where to go? He could remain in Libya in the uncertain embrace of Gaddafi, return home and rouse his loyal forces for a comeback (even he realised that was a long shot), or go to France where he could at least retire in comfort to one of his chateaux. He chose the latter course, and next morning boarded his plane and headed for France.

For all their meticulous planning for his overthrow, the French don't seem to have foreseen this eventuality, and there was something like panic in the government. As Bokassa's plane approached Orly airport it was refused permission to land, and the same thing happened when it flew on to Roissy. It was only when Bokassa threatened to land on a highway that the French relented, and the plane was ordered to land at a military airport near Paris, where it was immediately surrounded by soldiers. Bokassa and his entourage spent a cold and hungry night in the plane, glued to the radio —

their only source of information about what was going on.

Bokassa wasn't a French citizen so the French had no obligation to take him, but they didn't know where to send him either. Argentina, Brazil and a host of African countries they approached didn't want him. When told that he had been refused permission to go home, he expressed the desire to go to Zaire or Libya, but they too said no (Gaddafi pointed out that he was already looking after one deposed African dictator, Idi Amin, and that was quite enough). Finally, President Houphouët-Boigny of the Ivory Coast agreed to take him on humanitarian grounds.

While all this diplomatic toing-and-froing was going on, the French forces in the Central African Republic (as it was again) were trying to claw back some of the billions of francs gifted to Bokassa over the years. Soldiers raided his imperial compound in Berengo, 50 miles (80 kilometres) from Bangui, and carried off cash and diamonds, the contents of Bokassa's personal museum, and all the paraphernalia from his coronation. They also took reams of government documents, including many incriminating letters from Giscard d'Estaing to his former favourite dictator. Meanwhile, ordinary Central Africans were doing their bit, tearing down Bokassa's statues and pictures. Finding his golden eagle throne still in the stadium, they tore it apart, and individual feathers from it could later be found on sale in markets for four francs each. The ornate carriage that had taken Bokassa to his coronation was driven through the streets and trashed.

he fallen emperor was installed in a villa in Ivory Coast's capital, Abidjan. Guarded by soldiers, he was initially forbidden to leave the villa, and his letters and phone calls were monitored. He was bewildered and lonely — all his wives had suddenly made themselves scarce, the foreign ones returning to their respective countries while Catherine remained in France. She drew money from Bokassa's Swiss bank account and sold some of his expensive cars — there was still shopping to do. A few weeks after he was deposed, she did visit him in Abidjan, but came bearing a doctor's note stating that, due to some unspecified medical condition, she wasn't allowed to have sex with him.

The French press continued to have great sport with Bokassa as further reports (not all of them reliable) filtered in of his various outrages. According to one tale, when the crocodile-filled pond in one of his villas in Berengo was drained, the well-chewed remains of some thirty people had been found at the bottom of it. Longstanding rumours that he was a cannibal were also aired again — rumours which Bokassa had never taken much trouble to deny during his rule. This may seem odd, but there is a widespread belief in Africa that someone who eats the flesh of another human assumes their spirit and becomes more powerful, so Bokassa thought it would do his fearsome image no harm. (In the same way, all those wives were a visible demonstration of his virility). Bokassa was even known to have joked about cannibalism to foreign visitors — during the banquet that followed his coronation, he had turned to a French government minister, Robert Galley, and whispered, "You never noticed but you ate human flesh." Now, the reinstalled President Dacko cheerily confirmed to journalists that this was a specialty Bokassa had often served his guests. Wanting to distance himself from the former regime, Dacko also announced that Bokassa would be tried in absentia for his crimes. Held over just four days in early 1981, the trial was a farcical affair in which anyone was welcome to stand up and say whatever they wanted to about Bokassa without fear of cross examination. One of his cooks recalled how he had often served up the testicles of the emperor's enemies — "cooked to a turn", but the highlight was the testimony of a doddering old soldier named Phillipe Linguissa. He told the court he had been working in a military canteen in 1977 when he was ordered to fetch a casserole dish, salt, spices, onions and some wine, then driven to Berengo. A soldier took him into Bokassa's kitchen and opened the refrigerator to reveal a male corpse missing its head, hands and feet. When Linguissa baulked at cooking a man, the soldier pointed a revolver at him. Linguissa continued:

> *I put myself to work as I would prepare a chicken, stuffing it with rice and onions and sewing the skin with a needle and thread which Bokassa had given me. I sprinkled it with gin and Pernod and placed the entire body in a large vat which I slid into an immense oven. When I pulled it out later to see how it was cooking, the body started to move, sat up, and pointed at me with one of its arms. It struggled so much that it messed up the entire kitchen. I begged its forgiveness and pushed it back in the oven.*

Linguissa's marvellous Grand Guignol tale was reported in newspapers around the world.

The French press were also scathing about the role Giscard had played in propping up Bokassa. The satirical newspaper *Canard enchaîné* mocked the President's aristocratic pretensions, his acceptance of diamonds and his marathon safaris. Over in Abidjan, Bokassa was greatly enjoying his former friend's discomfiture. He had regained his fighting spirit and was planning a comeback. He had an ally in a former French soldier turned journalist Roger Delpey, who had written a book in which he claimed that Hitler and Eva Braun had survived the war. After interviewing Bokassa prior to his downfall, and deciding that he was innocent of the crimes of which he had been accused, Delpey visited Bokassa in Abidjan and the pair cooked up 'Operation Revenge'. Delpey smuggled out letters from Bokassa to African leaders, asking for their help (a request that fell on very deaf ears), and kept the press supplied with documents (some probably forged) which further discredited Giscard. When the government realised what Delpey was up to, he was arrested and charged with acting in a way that would damage "France's military or diplomatic position". He spent months in prison with no sign of a trial, and many viewed this as Giscard trying to silence an enemy. Facing a presidential election in May 1981, Giscard bowed to pressure to have Delpey released. He went on to lose the election to François Mitterand, a result that delighted Bokassa. "Now he is unemployed like me," he said. There was even more good news for him two months later when Dacko, who had been no better as president the second time round, was deposed in a coup led by the army commander, General Kolingba.

Bokassa's life in Abidjan had also improved. Some of his children had come to live with him and he was free to roam the city, frequenting nightclubs where he drank whisky and picked up girls. He also found a new wife, a local woman named Augustine Assamat.

Roger Delpey's spell in prison didn't dampen his enthusiasm for Bokassa. He helped raise millions of francs from Bokassa's supporters (mainly army veterans), and came up with a new comeback plan. This would involve a private plane flying from Paris to Abidjan, carrying armed Bokassa supporters and twenty French journalists to record the momentous events. After Bokassa and Delpey joined the plane in Abidjan, it would fly to Bangui, where its pilot would feign engine trouble and request permission to land. As all this was going on, helicopters would be flying over Bangui dropping a million leaflets with the message "Bokassa is at the airport. He awaits you, come and find him!" People who picked up these leaflets, overjoyed at the return of their beloved emperor, would flock to the airport and take him to the palace in triumph, while President Kolingba and his government would flee the country.

The plan was activated on 25 November 1983, but fell down at the first hurdle. Some of the journalists, briefed by Delpey, couldn't keep their lips sealed, and when the French security services heard about the plan they contacted President Houphouët-Boigny. When the plane landed at Abidjan it was surrounded by soldiers and ordered back to Paris.

Bokassa was dejected, but this fiasco did have one positive outcome for him in that Houphouët-Boigny, fed up with his unwanted guest's antics, urged France to take him. They eventually agreed, and Bokassa and his wife Augustine were installed in one of his former properties, Chateau Hardricourt, where he was kept under house arrest. He was allowed a few visitors who found him in straitened circumstances. The chateau was rundown, and as winter approached, Bokassa couldn't afford to heat it. He busied himself writing a book, to be called *Ma Vérité* (My Truth), in which he would vindicate himself, while also sticking it to Giscard. Bokassa claimed in the book that Giscard had ordered his overthrow because he wanted to make Empress Catherine his mistress, and that she later became pregnant with his baby, which had been aborted. When Giscard heard that the book contained this sort of thing, he applied successfully for an injunction against its publication, and all but a handful of copies were pulped.

Bokassa never gave up hope of returning home, and events during 1986 made it seem possible. There was unrest in the Central African Republic, where President Kolingba's administration had turned out to be as inept and corrupt as Bokassa's, while Paris was wracked by a series of terrorist attacks. Busy dealing with these, the police stopped guarding Bokassa's chateau, and he decided to make a break for it.

If his previous comeback plan had been a victory for

optimism over reality, there wasn't even a plan here. Having crossed the border into Belgium in two cars, Bokassa, Augustine, five of his children and a few advisers boarded a plane to Rome, then took another flight to Bangui. Bokassa was travelling on a false passport and no-one recognised him until they had all passed through security. It wasn't until they were collecting their luggage that someone cried out, "It's Bokassa! The boss is back!" He chatted happily to people as airport security, confused about what was going on, fled in terror. The fun was not to last. Informed of the unexpected arrival, the government despatched soldiers who carted Bokassa off to the army headquarters, Camp de Roux.

While Bokassa had already been sentenced to death in absentia, the law required another trial now that he had returned. This would last five months and involve dozens of people testifying. It began on 7 November 1986 and was much more rigorous than the first trial, with Bokassa's defence lawyers subjecting witnesses to cross examination. This meant that it didn't go as straightforwardly as President Kolingba had hoped. As witnesses stood up to give evidence about Bokassa's atrocities, two things became apparent. Firstly, some of them were clearly complicit in the crimes themselves (indeed, a few were subsequently arrested, which naturally made other witnesses reluctant to come forward). Secondly, nobody could provide proof that Bokassa had ordered, say, the murder of children. Bokassa, when questioned by the prosecution, blamed everything on his subordinates being over-zealous. The accusations of cannibalism got a good airing, of course. This was the charge that riled Bokassa the most, for he knew how damaging it had been to his reputation internationally. Phillipe Linguissa made a much-anticipated reappearance, this time describing how he had flambéd a body with gin and whisky.

Bokassa was found guilty of embezzling the equivalent of

$10 million from the state, and complicity in at least twenty murders, the arrest and detention of children, and torture leading to death, but not guilty of cannibalism. He was again sentenced to death. He had attended every day of the trial, and was visibly exhausted by the end of it, but confident the sentence would never be carried out. He was right. After an appeal process lasting several months, during which other African leaders had quietly lobbied Kolingba, the sentence was commuted to life imprisonment. He remained in his small bare cell in Camp de Roux, where he received few visitors. None of his wives ever showed up, even his most recent one, Augustine, which was particularly galling for him.

There were many ironies in Bokassa's life, the last one being that he was saved from this plight by the coming of democracy to the Central African Republic. After much stalling, and France threatening to cut off funds, the deeply unpopular Kolingba agreed to hold a free and fair election. Embittered after losing the first round and wanting to make mischief, he announced that all prisoners in the country would be freed — including Bokassa.

He was assigned a luxury suite in the palace, where he received a flood of curious visitors. He told them that if his country called again, he was ready, and walked around Bangui wearing his marshal's uniform. The eventual winner of the election, Ange Patassé (who had served as Bokassa's prime minister after he had made himself emperor), became so annoyed by these airs that he had Bokassa moved to a dilapidated villa. He spent much of his time there reading the Bible, and wore a long white robe like a priest's, with a crucifix around his neck. He told the Italian journalist Riccardo Orizio, who visited him at the villa, that he had experienced visions of Christ when he was twelve years old, and while on a visit to the Vatican in 1970, Pope Paul VI had secretly nominated him the "thirteenth apostle of Holy

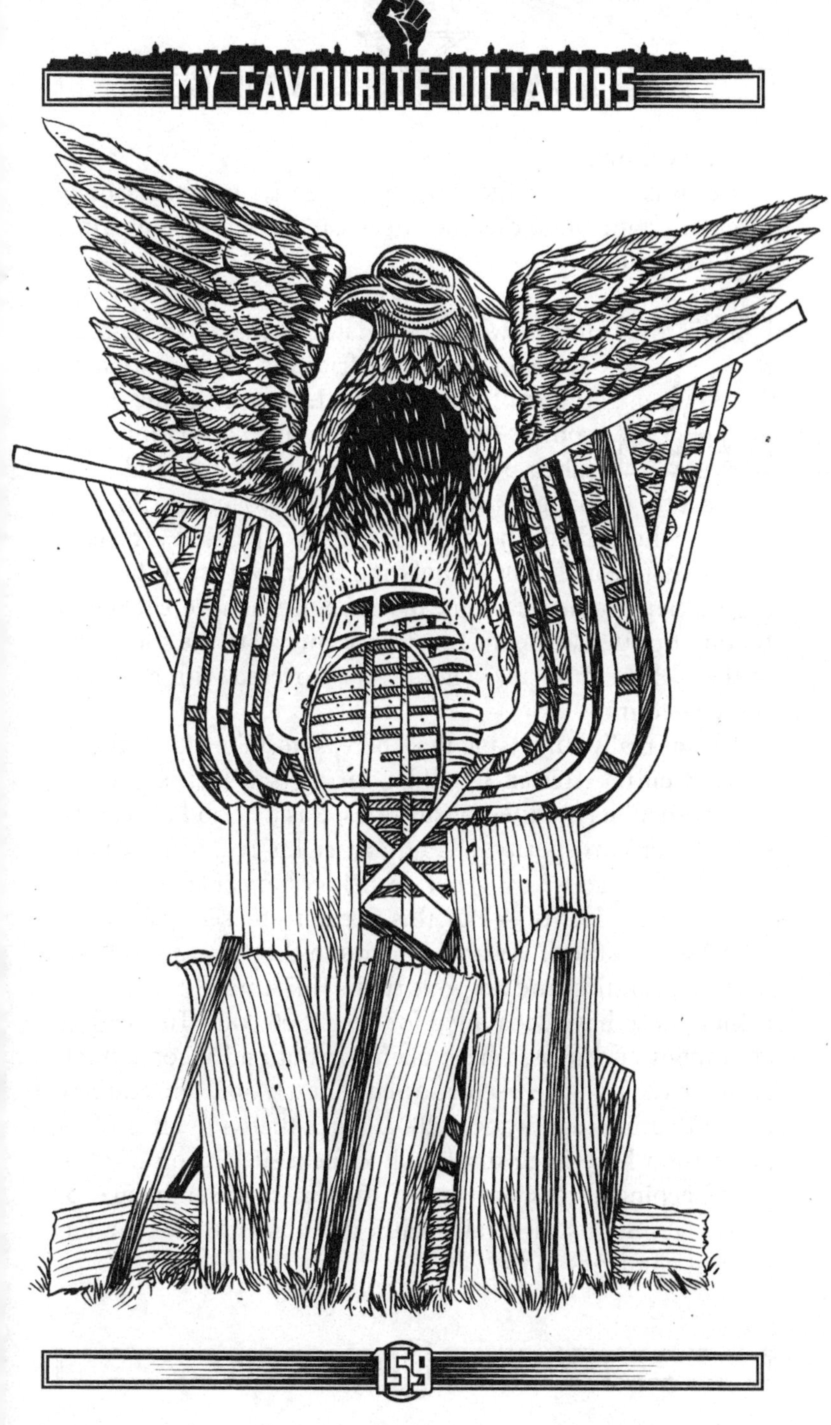

Mother Church".

He was in the villa for three years, an increasingly forgotten figure, and died of a heart attack in a Bangui clinic on 3 November 1996.

lmost twenty years later, in July 2016, a group of young Central Africans found the rusting frame of Bokassa's golden eagle throne in the sports stadium where his coronation had taken place. They painted it yellow and set it up on one of Bangui's main streets. A spokesman for the group, who called themselves patriots, praised Bokassa, noting that he had built schools and the university. When the government found out, some of the young men were taken in for questioning, while the throne was moved to the courtyard of the Culture ministry, where it was covered with sheets of corrugated iron.

It's not really surprising that there is nostalgia for Bokassa in the Central African Republic, for the sad fact is that his rule, with all its manifest absurdities, was a period of relative stability and prosperity. His human rights record may have been deplorable — he is generally held responsible for around five hundred deaths — but this needs to be set against the casualties in other African countries in the same period due to ethnic conflicts and despotic rulers (Idi Amin, for example, is thought to have accounted for up to 500,000). The leaders who followed Bokassa have been corrupt and incompetent, ethnic rivalries have been allowed to fester, and the country descended into civil war in 2004. Since then a quarter of its population have been displaced, while a succession of U.N. peacekeeping forces have tried to impose a semblance of order. Despite its mineral wealth, it remains one of the ten poorest countries in the world.

CHAPTER 7

FERDINAND MARCOS

FERDINAND MARCOS

Attained power in 1965
Died in exile in 1989

Ferdinand Marcos thought he would be remembered as one of the great statesmen of the twentieth century. In his mind's eye he was a man touched by God, a war hero and the saviour of democracy in the Philippines (even if saving it had meant suspending it for a while). Instead, he is remembered for his wife's collection of shoes.

That's not surprising, for it was no ordinary collection of shoes, and she was no ordinary wife. Standing next to Imelda in her colourful, butterfly-sleeved dresses, Ferdinand in his white barong shirt cut a comparatively dull figure, but in reality they were perfectly matched. She was the glamorous frontwoman of their 'conjugal dictatorship', on a self-proclaimed mission to erase all the ugliness in her country and make it as beautiful as herself. He was a ruthless political operator from way back, a master manipulator of others, a behind-the-scenes man. What he was doing behind the scenes, for over two ruinous decades, was parting an already poor nation from much of the wealth it had.

And when it all came tumbling down in 1986, with the kleptocratic couple and their retinue fleeing hastily in American helicopters, the shoes were left behind. At least twelve hundred pairs of them (some say three thousand), neatly arranged on shelves of polished wood in Manila's Malacanang Palace.

The dictatorship of Ferdinand Marcos can only be understood in the context of the long, curious and ambivalent relationship between the Philippines and the United States.

In 1896, Filipinos rebelled against their colonial masters in Spain, a year after a similar revolt had broken out in Cuba. With anti-Spanish fever being whipped up in America by the newspapers of William Randolph Hearst, President McKinley sent the battleship *Maine* to protect U.S. citizens in Cuba in 1898. When it blew up (somewhat mysteriously) in Havana Harbour, America declared war on Spain. Thousands of U.S. soldiers and the Pacific Fleet were despatched to Manila where they made short work of the Spanish. The Filipino rebel leader Aguinaldo formed a new government and declared independence, but there was a slight hitch: Manila Bay was still full of Yankee battleships, and they weren't going anywhere soon. Under the terms of the Treaty of Paris that formally ended the Spanish-American War, the U.S. gained possession of the Philippines, and Aguinaldo declared war on the U.S.

The Philippine-American War was a far more protracted and bloody affair than the war with Spain. American troops mounted a ferocious campaign against the Filipino insurgents, who were often armed with little more than bows and arrows. They destroyed whole villages, threw civilians into concentration camps, and committed numerous atrocities. Estimates of the number of Filipino casualties range from 200,000 to over a million, with most being victims of disease or starvation. Eventually, the country's landowners grew tired of the slaughter and went over to the American side, while the middle class were attracted to jobs in the civil service the Americans had created. After three years, the rebellion petered out.

The U.S. gave Filipinos a semblance of autonomy. They

could elect their own congress and president, but all laws had to be ratified by the U.S. Congress. In return, the Philippines received economic benefits, with the U.S. agreeing to import its sugar duty-free. The arrangement benefitted the elites enormously, while the peasants were more exploited than ever. As a result, most Filipino politicians paid lip service to the idea of independence for their country over the next few decades, but few wanted it in a hurry.

Ferdinand Marcos was born on 11 September 1917 in Sarrat, a town in the province of Ilocos Norte. His mother was Josefa Edralin and, according to the official record, his father was Mariano Marcos. His real father was Ferdinand Chua, a law student and member of one of the wealthiest Chinese clans in the country. He had been having an affair with Josefa (possibly while she was working as a servant in his family home), and when she became pregnant wanted to marry her, but his family wouldn't allow it. A marriage was instead hastily arranged between Josefa and Mariano, a swaggering young hooligan from a poor family who was a fellow student at her high school.

Agreeing to marry Josefa was a lucrative move for Mariano. Ferdinand Chua — who was officially Ferdinand Marcos's godfather — went on to become a judge with immense wealth and influence. With his help, Mariano was elected to the Philippine Congress. He threw himself into his political career and was away from his family for months on end. When he returned, he inflicted harsh discipline on Ferdinand and his brother, whipping them and locking them in a cupboard if they misbehaved, but praised them when they did well. Above all, he was determined that they would grow up to be as tough as him, and taught them boxing, shooting and fencing.

After two terms in Congress, Mariano was defeated in the 1931 election. He ran again in 1935, and was beaten again, this time by a man named Julio Nalundasan. To add insult to injury, Nalundasan's supporters left a celebration party and drove to the Marcos home with an open coffin in which one of them was lying, labelled Mariano Marcos. The next day, a furious Mariano, his brother, brother-in-law and Ferdinand (who was now eighteen and studying law), held a meeting. According to the court testimony of another man present, they discussed killing Nalundasan, and young Ferdinand, a crack shot with a pistol, volunteered to do it. Mariano immediately left for Manila to create an alibi for himself. That evening, as Nalundasan stood on the porch of his house, brushing his teeth, he was shot in the back and died a few minutes later.

There were no immediate repercussions for the Marcoses, and Ferdinand continued with his studies, but three years later he was arrested and charged with murder. In December 1938, he was convicted and sentenced to between ten and seventeen years in prison, but just days later, the judge told him that President Quezon had decided to pardon him (Judge Chua had clearly been pulling strings again). He refused the pardon, though, and said he would appeal his conviction.

Ferdinand Marcos was blessed with a phenomenal memory, the sort of photographic recall associated with *idiots savant*. He could read a lengthy text, then recite it word for word, then recite it backwards. This gave him a huge advantage when studying law. During the year it took for his appeal to be heard, he sat for the bar exam and scored so highly he was suspected of cheating. He demanded to be re-examined, and was given an oral exam by the justices of the Supreme Court, again achieving a very impressive score. At the end of it, the justices asked him to do one of his party tricks — reciting the Constitution backwards.

Marcos was called up for army service in November 1942. The attack on Pearl Harbour came a month later, and the first Japanese troops were on Philippine soil a few days after that.

There are two versions of his war years. In the officially sanctioned (by Marcos) version, the young lieutenant quickly proved himself a resourceful officer and tactician, leading small bands of men on intelligence-gathering missions and guerrilla-style attacks on the Japanese. In one engagement, Marcos and three privates overwhelmed an artillery battery and killed more than fifty Japanese. On another occasion, he was shot in the hip by a sniper, dug the bullet out with a knife, then dragged himself miles back to his comrades. He was captured by the Japanese several times, tortured horribly, and survived the Bataan Death March. His exploits earned high praise from General Douglas MacArthur, and there were calls

for him to be awarded the Congressional Medal of Honour. Towards the end of the occupation, Marcos was leading a secret guerrilla organisation, the Ang Mga Maharlika (the 'Noble Studs') that wrought havoc on the Japanese.

Tales of Marcos the highly-decorated war hero would prove invaluable as he embarked on a political career, and were recycled endlessly by the likes of *Time* magazine when he became America's favourite dictator and best friend in the Pacific. As his military records mysteriously disappeared from the U.S. archives in the 1950s, it was difficult for anyone to refute them. But they turned up again decades later, and along with the accounts of those who knew Marcos during the war, they paint a different picture. Instead of being involved in espionage during the early days of the occupation, Marcos and his men spent most of their time looting, and far from being the scourge of the Japanese, there is evidence that he collaborated with them. (Mariano Marcos certainly did — he was hired by them as a full-time propagandist.) As for his much-vaunted Maharlika force, it was little more than a band of black marketeers.

After the U.S. landed in the Philippines in 1944, Mariano was arrested and charged with war crimes. As some of the Filipino soldiers who had captured him were friends of the murdered Nalundasan, they gave him a special send-off — his hands and feet were tied to four carabao water buffalos which were steadily lead in opposite directions, tearing him limb from limb. Ferdinand was also arrested and came close to being executed too, until some influential friends intervened.

The U.S. finally granted the Philippines independence in 1946, but continued to keep a tight grip on the country. General MacArthur refused to let in American aid until his preferred presidential candidate, Manuel Roxas, was safely installed in Malacanang Palace. When Roxas died suddenly in 1948, his deputy, Elpidio Quirino, assumed the presidency. He had been one of the country's most ruthless and successful politicians before the war, as well as the head of an extensive criminal organisation to which the Marcoses were linked. In the 1949 election, Quirino's army of thugs tortured and murdered hundreds of his political opponents. This intimidation, combined with extensive vote rigging, saw him elected. Also elected to Congress that year was his ally, that great hero of the Philippine resistance, Ferdinand Marcos.

Marcos immediately threw himself into the task that would occupy him for most of the next three decades — amassing obscene wealth. He was hardly alone here, for most of the American aid now flowing into the country went straight to politicians and the landowning elite. Appointed to head the Committee of Commerce and Industry, Marcos extorted large sums of money from Chinese businesses, while also involving himself in tobacco smuggling and many other lucrative ventures.

arcos was in the Congress building one day in 1954 when he saw a pretty young girl named Imelda Romualdez in the visitors' gallery. He recognised her from the Central Bank, where she worked as a clerk, and asked someone to introduce him. Wasting no time on small talk, he told her he was in love with her, he was going to marry her, and one day he would be president of the Philippines.

Imelda, born in Tacloban in 1929, was one of eleven children of Vicente Romualdez. The Romualdez family were well known and politically connected (Imelda's uncle was a congressman) but Vicente was a feckless and workshy member of it, and Imelda grew up in poverty — for some years living in a garage. A noted beauty, she had been a runner-up in the Miss Manila beauty contest (although she always claimed to have won).

Marcos pursued her relentlessly. At one point, he took her to his bank and showed her a safe deposit box containing around a million dollars in cash. Just eleven days after being introduced to Marcos, Imelda gave in and signed a marriage certificate, and they were married two days later. Yet she was still ignorant about many aspects of his life — not least the fact that he had a mistress who had borne him three children (and would become pregnant with a fourth shortly after Ferdinand and Imelda's wedding). When Imelda discovered this, she was devastated. With divorce impossible in the heavily Catholic Philippines, she had a nervous breakdown and was packed off to the U.S. where she underwent psychiatric treatment for three months. Back in Manila, she pulled herself together and resolved to make the best of it.

Over the next few years, Marcos continued to enrich himself with countless shady deals while consolidating his political career. He was elected to the Senate in 1959, and became Senate president two years later. Along with this office came control of the military budget, and he attended to some unfinished business by having twenty-one medals awarded to himself for bravery during the war.

Despite her marital woes, Imelda threw herself into the campaign to make her husband the Nacionalista Party's nominee for the 1965 presidential election. She travelled tirelessly around the Philippine archipelago, throwing tea parties and handing out gifts. Wearing brightly coloured dresses and always ready to burst into a syrupy love song, Imelda charmed peasant and politician alike. Marcos won the nomination.

His reputation was further burnished during the presidential campaign by a movie about the exploits of his brave Maharlika. The U.S. threw its support behind Marcos, with glowing articles appearing in the American press and the CIA helping out behind the scenes. Calling in all the favours he was owed and outspending all other candidates, Marcos won the election.

He paid his first official visit to America in 1966, when President Johnson stood next to him and gushed about his wartime record. LBJ knew it was all bullshit, but he was mired in the Vietnam War and needed the support of every Asian leader he could get. Marcos agreed to send non-combat Filipino troops to Vietnam, and host a 'peace summit' in Manila. In return, Johnson authorised a host of deals which would see hundreds of millions of dollars flow to the Philippines over the next couple of years. The U.S. also bent over backwards helping Marcos achieve one of his primary goals — turning the Philippines into a police state. The municipal police force and rural constabulary were centralised under his command, with the CIA and other U.S. agencies providing extensive training in surveillance, computerised record-keeping and interrogation techniques.

Among the first foreigners to experience the new reality of the Philippines under Marcos were, of all people, the Beatles. They arrived in Manila in July 1966 to play two concerts, and were met at the airport by grim-faced, gun-toting policemen. They were driven to their hotel in a limousine accompanied by a motorcade, but hardly had time to put their bags down before they were invited to a reception for Imelda. Jetlagged, they politely declined the invitation. The concerts, where they played to 80,000 people, went off without a hitch, but they woke the next morning to footage of crying children on television and newspapers reporting their insult to the President and his wife. There was no motorcade, just a solitary car to take them back to the airport, where they were greeted by an angry mob of people who punched and kicked the band and their entourage as they struggled to

board their plane, with security staff looking on dispassionately. They weren't allowed to take off until they paid a 'leaving tax', which just happened to be the same amount as the proceeds of the concerts. Ringo later called it the worst experience of his life.

Marcos had promised to crack down on corruption when he ran for president, but by 1969 the CIA was aware that he and his cronies had siphoned off almost all the millions in U.S. aid and war reparations that had poured into the Philippines since his election. Imelda was equally adept at extracting money from people, both to fund her increasingly ambitious shopping trips (in one two-month spree in America, she and her daughter Imee managed to spend $3.3 million), and as donations for the many building projects she masterminded, including a grandiose Cultural Center. Imelda seemed to be on a one-woman mission to beautify the Philippines with these projects, but nothing was done to reduce the endemic poverty of the country. Indeed, between 1965 and 1975, when both Ferdinand and Imelda were busily salting away millions in foreign bank accounts, the wages of ordinary Filipinos halved in value.

The 1969 presidential election was a very bloody affair, with hundreds murdered and whole villages razed. Marcos spent $168 million on his re-election campaign, which he raised by simply printing money. This caused inflation to rise so steeply that the country was literally bankrupted, and Marcos was forced to seek an emergency loan from the IMF. On election day, when another forty-seven people were killed, rampant vote rigging ensured that Marcos won 74 per cent of the vote. He had so obviously stolen the election that he faced his first concerted opposition, with huge demonstrations in Manila that lasted for days. In January 1970, students seized a fire truck, drove it through the gates of Malacanang Palace, and stormed into the building. Six were killed in the ensuing riots. Marcos stayed holed up in the hastily fortified palace for the next few weeks, and retaliated with a brutal crackdown on students and other 'subversives'. The demonstrations subsided eventually.

In the run-up to the election, Marcos had decided that another film glorifying the Maharlika was needed. This was to be a full-blown, Hollywood-style production, and two American actresses were flown to the Philippines to audition for the part of Evelyn, Marcos's wartime love interest who had supposedly saved his life by taking a Japanese bullet for him. They were taken to a party where Marcos was introduced to them as 'Fred'. One of the actresses, the engagingly named Dovie Beams, hailed from Nashville and had acted in a few soap operas. She was thirty-six but said she was twenty-three, and she and 'Fred' talked for hours. At the end of the night he cut to the chase, as he had done with Imelda years before, told her that she had the best legs he had ever seen, and he was in love with her. Dovie was soon installed in her own house, with a full retinue of servants, bodyguards and even a social secretary. Elaborate precautions were taken to keep Marcos's affair with her a secret from Imelda.

The film role required Dovie to speak Spanish and Tagalog, so Marcos gave her lessons, and she bought a cassette recorder to record them. Sometimes when the lessons broke off so they could have sex, the tapes kept rolling. Dovie, who was no fool, put the tapes carefully aside, while also helping herself to documents from Marcos's desk. One night, Marcos took nude photographs of her with a Polaroid camera, then asked for some of her pubic hair. She said yes, but only if he gave her some of his. She sent some of the tapes and papers, along with the presidential pubes, to America for safekeeping.

After almost two years, with Marcos's domestic problems increasing, their relationship began to sour. Dovie was angered by his decision not to release the Maharlika film, for which she had not been paid, and began demanding large sums of money. It culminated in a shouting match between the two of them in the palace, witnessed by others, in which she accused him of being a liar. Afterwards, she was taken by some of Marcos's men to a hotel room where, she alleged, she was tortured. She later checked herself into a hospital under an assumed name.

Dovie's disappearance was reported in the papers, and there were rumours she had been killed. Imelda was now fully aware of her husband's affair, and of course she was enraged. Through the American Embassy, she offered Dovie $100,000 to go quietly. Instead, Dovie held a press conference where she played one of the tapes, on which the unmistakable voice of Marcos could be heard singing (Filipinos love singing), then begging for a blow job. A couple of journalists managed to make copies of the tape, which was soon circulating throughout the country. Students at the University of the Philippines played it on a loop on campus radio, and it blared out over the university's loudspeakers. Troops sent to get the situation under control couldn't stop laughing.

Marcos lost some serious face in this debacle, but it strengthened Imelda's hand immeasurably. Ferdinand had had his fun, and now she was going to have hers. She became a fixture of the 'jet set', travelling around the world, hobnobbing with socialite friends like Christina Ford, the wife of Henry Ford II, with whom she was rumoured to be having a lesbian affair. Another favourite was the perma-tanned American actor George Hamilton, to whom she reportedly gave $1.2 million which he used to buy Charlie Chaplin's former house in Beverly Hills. Whenever she got the urge to travel, Imelda simply commandeered a jumbo jet from Philippine Airlines (sometimes taking an extra one for her luggage). A chastened Marcos had signed over to Imelda and her family the Philippines' largest gold mine, and wherever she went she spent up big on property, artworks, jewellery, lingerie and, of course, shoes. Imelda also acquired real political power for the first time — she became the Mayor of Metro Manila — and a new nickname, the 'Iron Butterfly'.

When she wasn't partying, Imelda was acting as a roving ambassador for the Philippines. She paid visits to Chairman Mao, Premier Kosygin in the USSR and Gaddafi in Libya. Given Gaddafi's penchant for seducing the wives of other political leaders, there is no way he wouldn't have made a move on her, but she always denied having sex with him. (She told people privately he was gay, demonstrating some psychological insight.) The wife of the staunchly anti-communist Marcos mixing with people like Mao raised a few eyebrows in Washington. Some thought Imelda was merely being capricious, but it was really a ruse thought up by Marcos. If the Americans saw the Philippines moving into communism's orbit, they might come through with some more money.

nder the Philippine Constitution, Marcos was prevented from running for a third term in the election due in 1973. There was much speculation that Imelda would run in his place (although it is doubtful whether Marcos ever really wanted that). Others believed he would rig a scheduled constitutional convention so that the rules were changed. He tried his best to do this, with many envelopes of cash thrust into the hands of delegates, but anti-Marcos feeling was now running so high that the customary bribery didn't seem to be working.

Dictators rarely keep diaries, having far too many secrets to hide, but Marcos began keeping one after he won his second presidential election. He handwrote it on Malacanang Palace stationery, and it was found a year after he had fled the country. Even allowing for the fact that he was writing for posterity, so was at pains to present himself in the best possible light, the diary makes it clear that he had succumbed to his own mythology (including the fiction that he was a war hero), and it gives a fascinating insight into his mind during this crucial period. He was paranoid, superstitious, a hypochondriac (the merest ache or pain was a medical emergency), and thought he had telepathic powers (or a "strange capacity to receive messages"). He prayed daily, and believed that God spoke to him.

Marcos could not accept his own actions had caused his popularity to plummet, and blamed it on the communists. In reality, the main communist group in the country, the New People's Army, was tiny and ineffectual, but in his mind, they were part of a vast conspiracy against him which included his political opponents and the media. He decided that the only way to save democracy in the Philippines was to suspend it — by declaring martial law.

Such a drastic step could only be credible if there was a credible threat to national security. So he manufactured one. On 21 August 1971, two hand grenades were tossed onto the stage at a Liberal Party rally at Plaza Miranda in Manila. All eight Liberal candidates for the upcoming senatorial election were badly wounded, and nine others were killed. Numerous opposition figures were arrested over this but never charged. Over the next year, there was a spurious report of a communist arms cache being found, and a spate of bombings and kidnappings. On 23 September 1972, a convoy of cars carrying the defence secretary, Juan Ponce Enrile, was attacked by gunmen (an attack Enrile had organised himself). This was the final provocation Marcos needed, and he declared martial law two days later. Government troops seized newspapers and TV and radio stations, closed schools and arrested opposition politicians including Marcos's fiercest and most fearless critic, Senator Benigno Aquino. Richard Nixon and Henry Kissinger, forewarned of his intention to declare martial law, had thrown their support behind him. American businesses operating in the Philippines agreed that the country could do with a little discipline.

Martial law continued for months, then years. Opponents of the regime were systematically arrested, tortured and murdered. Filipino exiles in the U.S. did their best to bring these atrocities to the attention of politicians and the American public, but the Nixon administration remained steadfastly behind Marcos. Even the explosive testimony given by journalist Primativo Mijares to a Congressional subcommittee in 1975 had little effect. Mijares, formerly a trusted Marcos insider, gave a comprehensive account of Marcos's career, from the murder of Nalundasan, to his fraudulent war record, to the nightmare of martial law. He went on to write a book which mysteriously vanished from U.S. bookshops and the Library of Congress. A few months later, after inexplicably returning to the Philippines, Mijares also vanished (it was rumoured that he had been thrown from a helicopter into the sea by Marcos's security forces). The Justice Department conducted a desultory investigation into his claims but decided he was an untrustworthy witness, and that was that.

On declaring martial law, Marcos had vowed to stamp out crime, and crime did indeed virtually disappear from Philippine newspapers during these years (because they were now forbidden to report on it). In reality, Marcos divided up and sold off the rights to various criminal enterprises — gambling, drug running, prostitution

— to international criminal organisations, in particular the Japanese Yakuza. The Philippines became one of the world's most popular destinations for sex tourism, with paedophiles being particularly well catered for. (At one point, it was estimated that there were forty thousand child prostitutes in Manila alone.) While ordinary Filipinos were subject to a midnight curfew, the police turned a blind eye to the sight of children as young as six offering oral sex to tourists in the street. Whenever anyone had the temerity to raise the subject with Ferdinand or Imelda, they pointed out that prostitution was illegal in the Philippines, so the problem didn't exist.

Marcos was being called the richest man in Asia even before his first presidential term had ended, and while much of his wealth could be attributed to graft and corruption on an epic scale, some commentators believed even this could not fully explain it. That led to a persistent rumour that he had discovered 'Yamashita's Gold'. Named after the Japanese general who was stationed in the Philippines towards the end of the war, this was the collective term for a vast quantity of gold and jewels plundered by the Japanese from their conquests in Asia. It had supposedly been stockpiled in the Philippines with the intention that it be shipped on to Japan, but the presence of American submarines in the Pacific made this untenable. As U.S. forces closed in on the Philippines, the Japanese hid their treasure by dumping it in the sea or stashing it in tunnels dug by Allied POWs (who were then killed to prevent them revealing the locations).

In 1970, a treasure hunter named Rogelio Roxas, armed with an old Japanese map and a metal detector, unearthed a gold Buddha statue weighing some 2,000 pounds (907 kilos), with a head that opened and hollow torso filled with jewels. He made the mistake of announcing his discovery, and the Buddha was seized by soldiers and taken to Marcos. Roxas spent two years in jail. Later, after Marcos's fall, he

filed a suit against him in an American court, alleging theft and claiming damages. This was eventually upheld, although Roxas had died by then.

The discovery of the statue apparently rekindled Marcos's interest in Yamashita's Gold (which some said he had been seeking since the 1950s). In 1977, an American mining engineer named Robert Curtis went public with an interesting story. He said he had travelled to the Philippines two years earlier, after being engaged by Marcos to help locate hidden gold and process it for sale on the international market. Curtis had contacts with Republican politicians and the far-right John Birch Society, and together they had cooked up a scheme to extract and sell up to $2 billion worth of gold, taking a hefty cut for themselves. In the Philippines, Curtis was taken to two locations where gold was supposed to be hidden, one a sunken ship, the other on land. They had been pinpointed by Olof Jonsson, a Swedish psychic imported for the purpose (Ferdinand and Imelda were both big on psychics). However, the searches were aborted for reasons which are unclear, and the whole scheme eventually fell apart.

Over the next few years there were many more stories linking Marcos to Yamashita's Gold. There were people who claimed to have seen tunnels containing huge stacks of bullion, and evidence of unorthodox gold trading around the world, with Marcos's fingerprints on it, on a scale so vast it could not be explained by the dictator selling off his own country's gold reserves. Yet none of this has been proved conclusively, and there are many who believe that Yamashita's Gold was a myth all along.

he Marcos regime was a hollow structure erected for the enrichment of a few, and in the early 1980s, as it drew to an end, there were two events that perfectly encapsulated that hollowness.

The first was the completion of a concrete bust of Marcos, 98 feet (30 metres) high, which was erected on the side of a mountain in Bengue province. It had cost an estimated $1.5 million, and in order to build it the government had confiscated a vast swathe of farmland from the local Ibaloy people, paying them a pittance in return.

The second was the International Film Festival that Imelda held in Manila in 1982. To house the festival, she ordered a grand new Film Center to be built at a cost of $100 million. As much of the money allocated to building it disappeared into various pockets, the work was shoddy. Two months before the festival was due to begin, two floors collapsed and up to thirty labourers were killed. A rumour spread that the bodies were simply cemented over to prevent delays in the construction schedule, and Imelda was forced to exorcise the building to mollify the superstitious.

Imelda had confidently predicted that 4,500 celebrities would attend the festival. The actual number was considerably lower, although Brooke Shields and George Hamilton turned up.

n 1981, a Chinese-Filipino businessman named Dewey Dee left for Costa Rica, leaving debts of $90 million dollars behind. In a country the size of the Philippines, that should have caused barely a ripple, but so much of its capital had been moved offshore by Marcos and his cronies that the coffers were almost empty. When the institutions Dee owed money to called in other debts to

cover themselves, and their debtors also defaulted, the entire financial system began to wobble. It was a situation that called for decisive action, but Marcos was now gravely ill with lupus. He had been diagnosed with the disease in 1971, and it had reached such an advanced stage that he was often incapacitated and in desperate need of a kidney transplant.

After his arrest following the declaration of martial law, Marcos's great political rival, the charismatic Benigno Aquino, spent seven years in prison. At one point he went on a protracted hunger strike which ended with him having a profound religious experience. He had eventually been allowed to leave the country, and went to the United States. With Marcos seemingly close to death, he decided that it was time to return, despite warnings from Imelda and others within the regime that this would be a dangerous thing to do.

On 21 August 1983, a plane carrying Aquino and a party of journalists touched down at Manila International Airport. Aware of the dangers he faced, the former senator was wearing a bulletproof vest. When the door of the plane opened, three military men escorted a smiling Aquino off it and down a flight of steps. Before he reached the end of it, one of them shot him in the back of the head. Other soldiers appeared with a corpse they had prepared earlier — belonging to one Rolando Galman — dumped it on the tarmac next to Aquino's body, and fired a few more shots into it.

The feared head of the secret police and army chief of staff, General Fabian Ver, and several others went to the hospital where Marcos was recuperating from a failed kidney transplant to tell him what had happened. He was furious. "You fools," he shouted at them. "They will all blame me!"

Marcos appeared on television the next day, his face puffy and yellow, and declared that Galman had been a communist and the lone assassin.

Over in Washington, the reaction to these events was

mixed. There had been a brief hiatus in America's slavish support for the Marcos regime when Jimmy Carter was elected president in 1977. Carter had even asked Marcos to improve human rights in his country, a plea that had been ignored. But Ronald Reagan was in the White House now, and he and his wife Nancy had been close friends of Ferdinand and Imelda ever since they attended the opening of Imelda's Cultural Center in 1969. However, while Reagan seemed oblivious to the idea that Marcos had any faults at all, others in his administration could see that his time was up. Indeed, the very messiness of Aquino's murder showed that he was losing control.

Marcos set up a commission to investigate the murder, and a year later, surprisingly, it fingered General Ver and other officers as being behind a conspiracy to kill Aquino. Their subsequent trial was rigged, though, and quickly resulted in their acquittal. American officials put pressure on Marcos to cut Ver loose, but he refused. They also began to have quiet discussions with General Fidel Ramos, the head of a group of dissident soldiers called the Reform the Army Movement (RAM), and Juan Ponce Enrile, who was seen as a possible successor to Marcos. RAM began to plan a coup, with tacit support from elements in the CIA.

Reagan and some of his advisers persuaded Marcos to hold a snap election in 1986. They expected him to win it easily. What they hadn't counted on was Benigno Aquino's widow Cory declaring herself a candidate. All the country's opposition parties promptly fell in line behind her, and a million people turned up for one of her rallies in Manila. Marcos followed his usual election script, distributing millions of dollars in bribes and preparing thousands of bogus ballot papers, but on election day, 7 February, there was far more scrutiny of the voting than in previous elections, with nuns bravely guarding ballot boxes from the soldiers who tried to snatch them. Reagan was stunned when told that on any fair assessment Aquino had won.

Marcos refused to concede, though, and the National Assembly declared he had won by 1.5 million votes. Aquino, at another rally which attracted a million people, declared she had won. She urged her followers to begin a non-violent protest campaign which gained the support of the head of the Catholic Church in the Philippines, Cardinal Sin. The Reagan administration, still hoping to save Marcos, urged him to make concessions, but he refused. They also urged Aquino to concede, a suggestion she treated with the contempt it deserved. Meanwhile, RAM's coup plan, put on hold until the election had been held, was reactivated.

On Saturday, 22 February, Ramos was at the constabulary headquarters at Camp Crame in Manila, while Enrile was across the road at the defence ministry. Both men worked the phones all day, urging their troops to get to Manila as soon as possible (Enrile had his own private army, not actually that uncommon in the Philippines). They held a joint press conference at 6.30 p.m. where they explained how the election had been rigged, apologised for their roles in the Marcos regime, and threw their support behind Aquino. As they were speaking, Cardinal Sin was on the radio, urging people to get out onto the streets and support the rebels.

That evening, three hundred heavy crates, perhaps containing — who knows? — some of Yamashita's Gold, were taken to the jetty beside Malacanang Palace and loaded onto a barge. They were later transferred to the presidential yacht, and apparently taken to Hong Kong.

In Washington on Sunday morning, Reagan was finally persuaded that Marcos was finished, and the White House issued a statement saying that all American aid to the Philippines would end if the situation turned violent. That afternoon, Ver despatched a contingent of marines in

armoured personnel carriers to Camp Crame to capture Enrile and Ramos. They were met by a solid wall of over 120,000 people who were crying, singing and trying to give them flowers. Ordinary Filipinos were experiencing something they never had before — a chance to have a say in their own destiny. It was soon dubbed 'People Power'.

A defiant if barely coherent Marcos held a press conference on Monday, declaring a state of emergency and his intention to have himself inaugurated as president the following day. At one point, Ver took him aside and begged for permission to bomb Camp Crame, but Marcos said no. He was hatching a plan to escape in American helicopters to his stronghold of Ilocos Norte, were he could plot his return to power. That evening, however, he was crushed to learn that Reagan had vetoed the idea. In desperation, Imelda rang Nancy Reagan and begged her to help, but all she could offer was asylum in America.

The inauguration took place on Tuesday as planned. Ferdinand and Imelda stood together and sang 'Because of You'.

Because of you,
There's a song in my heart.
Because of you,
My romance had its start.

It was all broadcast live on a TV channel controlled by Imee Marcos (until rebels stormed the station and cut off the broadcast half-way through).

On Wednesday, shots were fired at Malacanang Palace, and Marcos finally gave in to reality. At 9 p.m. that evening, Marcos, Imelda, their four children and some of their friends boarded four U.S. helicopters. He still wanted to go to Ilocos Norte, but was told that was not possible. Instead they were taken in two jumbo jets, their holds laden with more crates of cash, gold and jewels, to Hawaii, and exile. A few hours later, people stormed Malacanang Palace. Some of them made their way to Imelda's private quarters, where they found her shoes and five hundred bras, including a bulletproof one.

The Marcoses settled in Honolulu, were Ferdinand tried, and failed, to orchestrate a political comeback. Suffering from heart, lung and kidney ailments, he died in 1989.

After Marcos's fall, the Presidential Commission on Good Government was established and given the task of recovering the money stolen by the Marcoses. It has so far recovered around two billion dollars, so has a lot more work to do. In an exquisite irony, it has itself been accused of corruption.

The Philippines must surely be one of the world's most

forgiving nations. In 1991, Marcos's only son, Ferdinand Jr, known as 'Bongbong', decided to risk going back, and was welcomed at the airport. He rang Imelda and said, "Mom, it's time to come home." Bongbong became a senator, and ran unsuccessfully for president in 2015; his sister Imee is governor of Ilocos Norte province; and Imelda, who had a seat in the House of Representatives for years, also ran for president. Ferdinand Marcos came home too — for many years his embalmed corpse could be seen in a refrigerated glass case in a museum in Ilocos Norte. In 2016, however, following a ruling from the Supreme Court, it was transferred to the cemetery for war heroes in Manilla. (Some believe, though, that it was actually a wax replica, the dictator's body having disintegrated years before.)

The concrete bust of Marcos fared less well — in 2002 it was blown up by persons unknown. Some thought they had hoped to find treasure inside it.

CHAPTER 8

MUAMMAR GADDAFI

MUAMMAR GADDAFI

Seized power in a coup in 1969
Pulled from a drain, poked with a stick and shot in 2011

here have been few dictators more precocious than Muammar Gaddafi. He was dreaming of taking over his country while still a schoolboy, and at the age of twenty-seven, with the help of some friends, he did it.

And there have been few dictators who came to power with such natural advantages. With Libya's huge oil reserves and relatively small population, its people should be among the richest on earth.

But Gaddafi had other ideas — big, flaming, epochal, revolutionary ideas that would turn his country — and he hoped the world — upside down. And so, for over four decades, the people of Libya became reluctant participants in one of the strangest political experiments in history.

ew people could have deserved someone like Gaddafi less than the Libyans, whose country has been subject to waves of colonisers for millennia. First came the Greeks, then the Romans, the Vandals, the Arabs (who had by far the greatest influence on it), the Ottomans and finally the Italians, who arrived in 1911. But none of them ever had complete control over it. Libya is mostly desert and the bulk of its population clings to the coast. Its vast interior is the home to nomadic Bedouin tribes for whom a central government has always been a distant and largely meaningless concept.

Muammar Gaddafi was born into one of these tribes, the

Qadhafiyya (which literally translates, strangely enough, as those who spit or vomit). He came into this world in a tent on the outskirts of the coastal town of Sirte, probably in the early 1940s (he never knew his birth date). He was the only son of an illiterate goatherd, Mohammad Abdul Salam bin Hamad bin Mohammad. Gaddafi would later make much of his austere Bedouin beginnings, and on official visits to other countries often insisted on taking his tent and few camels and horses.

Of all the invaders who had attempted to subjugate the tribes of Libya, the Italians were the worst. They dealt ferociously with resistance, especially after Mussolini came to power in 1922, and during their years of occupation some 750,000 Libyans were killed, equivalent to half the country's population. Those who weren't killed were denied an education and any role administering their country. By the time British and French forces defeated the Italians in 1943, much of Libya's infrastructure was in ruins and 90 per cent of Libyans were illiterate. After the war, there was talk of carving up the country between the British and French, but following fierce opposition from the Libyans themselves, the U.N. declared it an independent state in 1951. The leader of the Senussi, a fundamentalist Islamic movement which had led resistance to the Italians, was somewhat reluctantly installed as its first monarch, King Idris I.

Unlike most of his generation, Gaddafi received an education, having commenced school at the age of fourteen. He was known as a serious young man, a good student and a pious Muslim, and his political ambitions were clear. His hero was Egypt's President Nasser, whose nationalist, anti-colonial stance was causing huge excitement through the Arab world. The young Gaddafi hung on Nasser's every word as it was broadcast over his radio station, Voice of the Arabs, and his schoolmates carried a stool around so he could make impromptu speeches in the manner of his hero. He decided the fastest path to power was the one taken by Nasser — a military coup — so he enrolled in a military academy in 1963, and persuaded some of his friends to join him there. Like Nasser and his associates, they called themselves the 'Free Officers'. They would form Gaddafi's inner circle when he came to power, and some of them were with him until the end. As part of his military training, which was supervised by British officers who he was rude to, Gaddafi spent several months in England in 1966. He despised the country and said he suffered racial abuse there. In an assertion of Bedouin pride (and an early instance of his love of costume) he was photographed striding down Piccadilly wearing flowing white robes.

Gaddafi now began to plot his revolution in earnest. He sent his men across the country to hold secret meetings and form anti-government cells. They had little trouble doing this, for Idris's Western-backed regime was corrupt and unpopular. Oil had been discovered in Libya in the late 1950s, but when commercial production began in 1963, little of the proceeds trickled down to the general population. In 1969, when an ill and ageing Idris left to spend the summer in Greece and Turkey, Gaddafi and his men seized their chance. They occupied the royal palace, government offices, police stations and airports, and Gaddafi appeared on the radio to announce that Libya was now a republic.

It was a textbook 'bloodless coup' and accepted by most of the population. Gaddafi, who quickly promoted himself to the rank of colonel and commander of the armed forces, was handsome, charismatic and an apparently plausible facsimile of Nasser. Completely inexperienced in government, he and the other eleven officers who formed the Revolutionary Command Council (RCC) moved slowly at first. Living up to his anti-Western rhetoric, Gaddafi closed British and

American oil bases, banned alcohol and Western books, closed nightclubs, introduced sharia law and deported twelve-thousand Italians (forcing them to dig up and take their dead with them as well). He held talks with Nasser about unifying Libya and Egypt, part of his dream of forming a united Arab nation which could take on the West (under his leadership, of course). Nasser was keen (especially to get his hands on Libyan oil revenues) but he died in 1970. His successor, Anwar Sadat, was much less impressed by Gaddafi, and they eventually became bitter enemies, with the Egyptian leader declaring him to be "100 per cent sick". (Libya and Egypt would briefly go to war in 1977.) Gaddafi's attempts to form a union with Syria were equally fruitless.

Meanwhile, the Libyan economy was stagnating. Gaddafi grew increasingly angry that change wasn't happening fast enough, and publicly criticised the other members of the RCC. When anyone disagreed with him, he would have a tantrum, then head off to the desert to sulk for a while. He was angry with the Libyan people, too, for not embracing his revolution. The trouble was, most people didn't understand it.

He decided to make himself perfectly clear, or as clear as he could make himself about anything. In a speech in the town of Zuwara in 1973, Gaddafi for the first time outlined the extent of his aims, which were nothing less than a total transformation of Libyan society. It would all be based on what he called the Third Universal Theory (the first two being capitalism and communism) and elaborated in his political manifesto, *The Green Book*, the first part of which appeared in 1975.

Allow me a brief digression. When I was a child, I thought I had figured out everything about "life, the universe and everything", as Douglas Adams put it, and in bed at night would patiently explain it all to my toy lamb. I can't remember what I said to him, but I imagine the tone in which I said it must have been something like that of *The Green Book*. It's the work of a man whose stupendous ego eclipses any shortcomings in education or worldly experience.

The Green Book is a slim volume in three parts. In the first, Gaddafi outlines (none too coherently) the new political system he had devised, in the second he expounds on socialism, and in the third he weighs in on social issues. This last is by far the most entertaining volume. Here, for example, is the Colonel on the subject of women.

> *It is an undisputed fact that both man and woman are human beings. It follows as a self-evident fact that woman and man are equal as human beings. Discrimination between man and woman is a flagrant act of oppression without any justification. For woman eats and drinks as man eats and drinks ... Woman loves and hates as man loves and hates ... Woman thinks, learns and understands as man thinks, learns and understands ...*

So, equality for women, then. But not so fast, for it seems there are differences between men and women.

> *Woman is a female and man is a male. According to a gynaecologist, woman menstruates or suffers feebleness every month, while man, being a male, does not menstruate and he is not subject to the monthly period which is a bleeding. A woman, being a female, is naturally subject to monthly bleeding. When a woman does not menstruate, she is pregnant. If she is pregnant she becomes, due to pregnancy, feeble for about a year, which means that all her natural activities are seriously reduced until she delivers her baby... The man, on the other hand, neither conceives nor breast-feeds. All these innate characteristics form differences because of which*

man and woman cannot be equal.

With that sorted, Gaddafi turns his attention to the issue of 'the black race'. At the moment, the blacks are enslaved by the whites, he writes, but the natural cycles of history mean that the table will be turned. Blacks also have another advantage.

The black race is now in a very backward social situation. But such backwardness helps to bring about numerical superiority of the blacks because their low standard of living has protected them from getting to know the means and ways of birth control and family planning. Also their backward social traditions are a reason why there is no limit to marriage, leading to their unlimited growth, while the population of other races has decreased because of birth control, restrictions on marriage and continuous occupation in work, unlike the blacks who are sluggish in a climate which is always hot.

On the subject of education, Gaddafi is unequivocal.

Compulsory education, of which countries of the world boast whenever they are able to force it on their youth, is one of the methods which suppresses freedom. It is a compulsory obliteration of a human being's talents as well as a forcible direction of a human being's choices. It is an act of dictatorship damaging to freedom because it deprives man of free choice, creativity and brilliance.

The book ends with a chapter on melodies and art which mentions neither melodies nor art, and a denunciation of spectator sports, which Gaddafi finds incomprehensible.

Few authors have been as in love with their work as Gaddafi was with his *Green Book*. After its publication, he declared that other writings on democracy "are all in the rubbish bin".

He was proudest of his new system of government, which he called the Jamahiriya. All authoritarian, hierarchical systems are bad, he argued, and democracy is a sham. Politicians and political parties exist only to exploit people, and the solution is to get rid of them. Instead, a system of local working parties would be formed, whose members would meet at larger district congresses. Representatives of these district congresses would form the General People's Congress, which would be Libya's legislature, while a second body, the General People's Committee, would be its executive branch.

Gaddafi abolished the Libyan republic in March 1977 and instituted his vision, calling it the Great Socialist People's Libyan Arab Jamahiriya. It was to be a democracy from the ground up. But the reality, as Libyans soon discovered, was rather different. The General People's Committee, which theoretically governed the country, had no powers over the military, the police, the oil industry, the budget or foreign policy. And the various people's congresses were soon overtaken by fanatical Gaddafi supporters and became instruments of government surveillance. As all people's needs were taken care of by the new system, there was no need for other organisations, so professional associations, trade unions and political parties were banned. A year on in, Gaddafi abolished sharia law, declaring its endorsement of private property incompatible with socialism. Meanwhile, he adopted nebulous titles like 'Guide of the Revolution' and 'Brother Leader', and kept up the charade that he was not really in charge.

The only upside for the Libyan people in all of this was that Gaddafi was serious about equality. Having nationalised the oil industry, he had vast wealth at his disposal, and used it to make improvements to infrastructure and provide free education, housing and healthcare, which for a time made him very popular.

MUAMMAR GADDAFI

But Gaddafi was not content to reshape Libya — he wanted to take his revolution to the world. One of his earliest supporters, Omar al-Meheishi, who became his minister for planning, said that Gaddafi was never the same after receiving a rapturous welcome at the Islamic Summit Conference held in Pakistan in 1974. When he returned from it he told al-Meheishi he was now the "leader of the world". He set about transforming his vast but sparsely populated country into a major player, making military service compulsory for all men up to the age of forty-five and purchasing huge amounts of armaments, chiefly from France and Russia. (There were few Libyans with the technical skills to service these weapons, however, so warplanes were sometimes left in their crates.) But Gaddafi would make his biggest mark on world affairs through his enthusiastic and utterly indiscriminate funding of terrorist organisations.

The plight of the Palestinians was the cause dearest to his heart. Early on he had a falling out with Yasser Arafat and his Fatah organisation, believing them insufficiently extremist, but he bankrolled innumerable other Palestinian groups over the years, including Black September (responsible for the 1972 Munich Olympics massacre) and the organisation of Abu Nidal, a notoriously brutal terrorist responsible for many hundreds of civilian deaths. Gaddafi grew particularly close to Abu Nidal, who lived in a luxurious residence in Tripoli during the 1980s.

Gaddafi had a long relationship with the IRA, which he supported with huge amounts of money and arms. One arms shipment in 1986 included Sam ground-to-air missiles and six tons of the explosive Semtex, which afterwards found its way into numerous IRA bombs. Other groups showered with Gaddafi's largesse included the Black Panthers, the Red Brigades, the Sandinistas, the Nation of Islam, the Basque

separatist movement ETA and the Japanese Red Army. It seems that no vaguely anti-imperialist group who beat a path to Gaddafi's tent, no matter how crazed or unfocused their aims, came away empty-handed. Gaddafi also provided training, so that Tripoli became, as Daniel Kawczynski put it, "a sort of international university of terror".

When Gaddafi's dreams of a pan-Arab state came to nothing, he turned his attention to Africa. This saw him injecting funds into the coffers of numerous corrupt African governments, and cosying up to other dictators like Bokassa and Idi Amin. He managed to persuade some thirty countries to sever relations with Israel, but saw little else in return for his huge investment. (To give Gaddafi his due, some of the money he pumped into impoverished countries certainly saved many lives.) Most damaging was his support of Islamic rebels in a messy civil war in Libya's southern neighbour Chad. Gaddafi lost around 9,000 troops and most of his military hardware in this ill-advised venture. His mighty war machine had been trounced by one of the world's poorest countries.

Perhaps the strangest international relationship Gaddafi developed was with the Christian cult the Children of God, notorious during the 1970s for its female members' practice of 'flirty fishing' (or luring people into the movement by offering sex). Gaddafi corresponded with the group's leader, David Berg, known as Moses David or 'Mo', and Berg spent a month in Tripoli in 1975. He wrote of Gaddafi, "There has not been another such worldly political leader in modern times as this young prophet of the seemingly impossible. There has hardly been such a Godly world political leader since the days of his own prophet, Mohammed...and the prophets of ancient times, including Jesus." A number of Children of God members travelled to Libya where their singing, accompanied by guitar and flute, was said to have been much appreciated by the locals, and Gaddafi is even supposed to have written a song for them. Berg also devoted one of his 'MO letters' (the cartoon-illustrated leaflets in which he shared his thoughts with his followers) to the Libyan leader. In 'Gaddafi's Magic Lamp' he praised the Arabs and said that the story of Aladdin and his lamp was a prophecy of Gaddafi and his oil.

In the late 1970s, eager to keep the momentum of his revolution going, Gaddafi announced the formation of 'revolutionary committees'. Initially composed of students who had embraced his political theories, the committees rapidly expanded and infiltrated every organisation and institution in Libya, including the army, police and media. Newspapers ceased to report foreign news and printed little more than government propaganda and extravagant praise of the Brother Leader. ("His teeth are naturally immune to stain, so that when he releases a full-blown smile, the naturally white teeth discharge a radiation pregnant with sweet joy and real happiness for those lucky ones who are fortunate to be around him.") TV was no better, with programming consisting largely of readings from *The Green Book*, endless footage of Bedouin women going about their daily chores, and more propaganda. After the evening news bulletin the announcer would say, "And now we will see the confessions of the stray dogs." Cut to footage of some poor, battered 'reactionary' being interrogated by a revolutionary committee. Live broadcasts of executions were another regular feature of the schedule. To ensure the continued loyalty of the revolutionary committees, Gaddafi appointed members of his family to lead them.

Similar havoc was wrought on Libya's economy. All land and housing was summarily confiscated by the state, with people only allowed to lease back enough land for their own needs. Most people lost their savings when they were forced to exchange their old currency for a new devalued one, but were only allowed a small amount of the latter. All private enterprise and commerce were banned in 1984, and people were forced to fight over the meagre goods to be found in state-owned supermarkets, their walls plastered with slogans from *The Green Book*. With private enterprise a thing of the past, most Libyans were forced to take jobs in the public service, and Gaddafi with his oil money was happy to expand it to soak them up. Never mind that most of the jobs they did were redundant or non-existent, or that the result was a grotesquely bloated bureaucracy which only served to further cripple the economy. Gaddafi had written of abolishing the state; the reality was that under his regime, the state had consumed the Libyan people body and soul.

Gaddafi was paranoid about Libyan dissidents in other countries plotting to bring him down. He despatched his revolutionary agents to deal with them, leading to a string of assassinations. As naïve as ever about the outside world, he could not understand why foreign governments would be upset by these killings — the victims were Libyan citizens, after all. Revolutionaries also took over Libyan embassies around the world. The London embassy, an elegant building in St James's Square, became a 'people's bureau' staffed by surly, long-haired young men wearing open-necked shirts and jeans. This had disastrous consequences in 1984 when a British policewoman, Yvonne Fletcher, was killed outside the embassy when its staff fired shots at demonstrating dissidents. PC Fletcher's police helmet sat abandoned on the ground during the ensuing ten-day siege, a poignant symbol of extremism. Shortly afterwards,

Britain broke off diplomatic relations with Libya.

The U.S. had already done that three years earlier. After Ronald Reagan was elected president in 1981, he made clear his personal loathing of the Libyan leader. He called him "the mad dog of the Middle East" and believed (erroneously) that he was a Soviet puppet. His administration piled pressure on Libya, introducing economic sanctions and shooting down two Libyan airplanes in disputed airspace over the Gulf of Sirte in 1981. In 1986, the bombing of a disco in West Berlin in which two American servicemen were killed (and to which Libya was tenuously connected) provided the pretext for a military strike. On 15 April, eighteen U.S. bombers took off from bases in the U.K. and hit Libyan targets, including Gaddafi's compound in Bab Al-Aziziya. Gaddafi survived the raid, but claimed that his six-month-old adopted daughter Hanna did not. In retaliation, Libya fired a couple of Soviet-built missiles at a U.S. coast guard station on the Italian island of Lampedusa, but these fell limply into the sea.

Gaddafi had so antagonised everyone in his region that even his fellow Arab leaders could muster only a muted response to the attack. Indeed, the Libyan people themselves seemed stubbornly less than outraged at the bombing of their Brother Leader's tent. Gaddafi ordered the bomb site left as it was, and erected next to it a kitsch sculpture of a huge gold fist crushing an American plane (made from pieces of the only plane which had crashed during the raids). But for all his show of defiance he was clearly rattled, and pulled his head in for a while.

He was facing other pressures as well. The price of oil had fallen and U.S. sanctions were finally biting — the state-owned supermarkets were even freer of goods than usual. With discontent rising, Gaddafi was forced to make a few concessions, and allowed a limited amount of free enterprise — Libyans were for the first time in many years able to gaze on a corner shop. He also publicly criticised the hated revolutionary councils, saying they had deviated from his ideology. To demonstrate he was serious about reform, the ever-theatrical Colonel climbed into a bulldozer and tore a hole in the wall of Furnash prison in Tripoli, through which four-hundred prisoners were allowed to escape. It was all a sham though. Libya remained as repressive a society as ever.

On 21 December 1988, a bomb on a Pan Am plane bound for New York detonated as it flew over the town of Lockerbie in Scotland. All 259 passengers and crew on board, and eleven townspeople, were killed. Iran initially was suspected of being behind the attack, but in 1990, evidence linking Libya to it emerged. In November 1991, the U.S. and U.K. charged two Libyans, Abdelbasset Al-Megrahi, who had been head of security for Libyan Arab Airlines in Malta, and Al-Amin Khalifa Fhimah, a security agent, with planting the bomb. Gaddafi dismissed the evidence against the two men as tenuous — and it's true that Libya's involvement in the bombing has never been proved. When he refused to hand them over for trial, the U.N. Security Council imposed further sanctions. An embargo was placed on exporting arms, airplane parts and other equipment to Libya, all air links to it were cut, and Libyan assets in other countries were frozen. To Gaddafi's fury, other Arab countries supported the sanctions. As Libya was still able to export its oil, these sanctions did not hit too hard at first. But Gaddafi was about to face a threat more serious than the combined forces of Western imperialism, and an ideology much more powerful than his Green revolution.

Gaddafi had a curious relationship with Islam. He presented himself as a devout Muslim, and Islam was supposed to be one of the pillars of his revolution. But from the beginning he regarded the Muslim clergy as another potential threat. He positioned himself as a sort of Islamic protestant who believed that people could have a direct communion with Allah without the need of clerics, and clerics who dared to criticise his regime were dealt with severely and sometimes murdered. As radical Islam was embraced by young people across the Arab world, it was inevitable that the tide would reach Libya. Many young Libyans went to fight in the jihad in Afghanistan, and by the mid-'90s the regime knew that Islamist groups had formed in the country — and were arming themselves. Gaddafi sensed the gravity of the threat and acted accordingly. The revolutionary committees killed suspected Islamists and dragged their bodies through the streets, hundreds more were arrested, and military attacks were launched against Islamist holdouts, which were thickest in the east of the country. In 1996, prisoners in the Abu Salim prison, many of them Islamists, took a guard hostage and demanded improvements in conditions. They released him when their demands were met. The next day, some twelve hundred of them were ordered into the prison's central courtyard, and security forces on the rooftops spent the next four hours shooting every last one of them dead. It was the worst single atrocity to take place during Gaddafi's rule.

He had crushed the Islamists, for the time being at least, but Gaddafi's regime had been severely destabilised, and Libya's economy remained a basket case. Corruption was endemic, inflation rampant and public services virtually non-existent. Realising a crunch was coming, Gaddafi buckled. He agreed to hand over the two Lockerbie suspects, on the condition that they be tried at a special court at The Hague. At the trial in 2000, Fhima was acquitted but Al-Megrahi was sentenced to twenty years jail. The U.S., still intent on turning the screws on Libya, demanded the Lockerbie victims be compensated. Gaddafi was incensed but, pressured by some of his more pragmatic advisers, agreed to pay each of the victims' families up to ten million dollars. The U.S. also demanded that Libya give up all its weapons of mass destruction, and cease its somewhat amateurish attempts to develop nuclear weapons. Gaddafi baulked at that for the moment.

Then came 9/11, and the wily Colonel was handed an unexpected opportunity. He came out strongly against the attacks, going so far as to order a 'blood drive' amongst the Libyan people to help the victims in New York. It was a brilliant PR move. Gaddafi pointed out that he been fighting the Islamists for years, and had condemned Osama Bin Laden as far back as 1995. He freely handed over all the intelligence Libya had gathered about Islamist groups, and backed the invasion of Afghanistan. Tony Blair's government had been keen to normalise relations with Libya for some time, and negotiations with the U.K. and U.S. continued behind the scenes. The U.S. invasion of Iraq was obviously playing on Gaddafi's mind as well, and in 2003 he finally agreed to dismantle his WMD programs.

The effect of this was immediate. In 2004, Blair visited Libya, and was photographed with a cheesy grin on his face as he shook hands with Gaddafi outside his tent (to his aides' immense relief, he was spared the traditional Bedouin greeting of kisses on both cheeks). The U.S. re-established diplomatic relations and removed Libya from its list of state sponsors of terrorism. International companies rushed to invest in Libya. Gaddafi was in from the cold.

The idea had taken hold among the Libyan people that these developments would be accompanied, finally, by some genuine political and economic reforms. Hopes were particularly high that an announcement would be made during celebrations for the 30th anniversary of the revolution in 1999. But instead of unveiling reforms, Gaddafi announced — you guessed it — his invention of a rocket-shaped car, the safest in the world. He had, it seems, been working on the design of the five-seater 'Jamahiriya Rocket' — described by the BBC as "sleek and surprisingly stylish" — for some years. The bureaucrat in charge of manufacturing it declared, "The invention of the safest car in the world is proof that the Libyan revolution is built on the happiness of man."

Gaddafi relished his re-emergence on the world stage. Always flamboyant, his clothes grew ever more bizarre, eliciting much mirth from commentators. "Drawing upon the influences of Lacroix, Liberace, Phil Spector (for hair), Snoopy, and Idi Amin, Libya's leader—now in his 60s—is simply the most unabashed dresser on the world stage," wrote Henry Porter and Annabel Davidson in a delirious Gaddafi fashion spread which appeared in *Vanity Fair* in 2009. Sometimes he went with a military look, with peaked cap, gold epaulettes and chest dripping with ribbons and medals. (For a visit to Italy, he added to these a large photograph of his greatest hero, the Libyan resistance leader Omar al-Mukhtar, who had been executed by the Italians in 1931.) At other times he headed in the opposite direction, donning the sort of garish costumes you might expect to see on an ageing drag queen. At the G8 summit in July 2009, he mingled with other world leaders, wearing a red-and gold embroidered kufi hat with matching silk robes. But this was nothing compared to the elaborate costume of shiny, peach coloured material he donned to meet the Portuguese prime minister in 2000, which made him look a bit like an animated shower curtain.

The rehabilitated Gaddafi also turned his attentions back

to Africa, pushing for a 'United States of Africa' (which would have its capital in his home city of Sirte). While he didn't get too far with that, African nations were still more than happy to take his money. In 2008, surrounded by an assortment of African rulers and tribal leaders, and wearing a flowing, gold embroidered gown, he was proclaimed the 'King of Kings of Africa'.

Adding to all this pizzazz were the glamorous members of his celebrated, heavily made-up, Kalashnikov-toting female guard. Known officially as the 'Revolutionary Nuns' but usually referred to in the Western media as his 'Amazons', they made their first appearance in 1982. They were supposedly all virgins, handpicked by the Colonel himself. They were said to be totally loyal to him, and at least one of them was, for she was killed when she threw herself over Gaddafi during an attack by Islamists in 1988. For a visit to Paris in 2007, he brought along thirty of them wearing blue camouflage uniforms (along with his tent, which was pitched next to the Louvre) and a camel.

Gaddafi was always happy to cultivate his reputation as a ladies man, and was notorious for hitting on female journalists (indeed, foreign news agencies used to send female journalists to him, knowing they were more likely to gain an interview). He had always presented himself as a great liberator of women in his country, denouncing polygamy, increasing the rights of divorced women, and encouraging women to join the military (which enraged the clerics). But after his downfall, a very different picture began to emerge, with reports that the female guards had been routinely sexually abused by the Colonel and his officers. But this was just the tip of the iceberg.

Whenever Gaddafi was out in public, visiting a school or university perhaps, his aides knew to watch him closely. If he touched a girl on the head, that was the signal. The next day, she would receive a visit at her home or school from some of his subordinates, usually female, and be invited to perform some special duty for the Colonel. She would be taken to Gaddafi's Bab Al-Aziziya compound, subjected to a medical examination by the Ukrainian nurses he employed, then delivered to Gaddafi who would usually rape her on the spot. Over the years, hundreds of girls as young as thirteen were subjected to this treatment, with many ending up in hospital with internal injuries after a session with the Colonel. Some were allowed to leave again after a day or two, but others were imprisoned in a humid basement in the compound for years. By comparison, Mao's compulsive deflowering of China's virgins looks almost innocent. Gaddafi, fuelled by Viagra in his later years, typically demanded four sexual partners a day. He would pore over photographs of weddings, looking for attractive girls, and sometimes order women to be brought to him on their wedding day. When he travelled to other countries, he invariably gave talks to women's groups, which added to his reputation as a champion of women while providing another source of sexual fodder. He routinely demanded that the wives of his soldiers and guards have sex with him (men who objected to this were executed), and he was obsessed with seducing the wives of other heads of state. It appears that quite a few of them acquiesced to his desires (for which they were rewarded with suitcases full of cash, gold and jewels). Gaddafi's chief procurer was an unsmiling Tuareg woman named Mabrouka who travelled the world with an unlimited expense account. She targeted singers, actresses and other celebrities, and a famous Lebanese singer is said to have agreed to have sex with Gaddafi for one million euros.

Gaddafi's sexual tastes were not confined to women, however. He was an enthusiastic seducer of young boys, and would even demand sex from his generals and ministers. His proclivities here were well known to the Libyan people. After his downfall, when the posters and images of Gaddafi which had covered almost every available surface in Libya were torn down and replaced with caricatures, many of them depicted him dressed as a woman.

Annick Cojean, a respected journalist for *Le Monde*, recorded some of the stories of Gaddafi's sexual victims in her 2013 book, *Gaddafi's Harem*. She found it very difficult to get people to talk about any of this, not just because the victims themselves were ashamed (and would have been shunned by their families had what happened to them become known), but because the whole of Libya was mortified by these events. Cojean's account was backed up by Gaddafi's former chief of protocol, Nuri Mismari. He gave a long interview to the *Al-Hayat* newspaper in which he recounted incidents he had witnessed where Gaddafi beat women so badly they required medical treatment. He also confirmed that the Colonel had a coterie of boys known as 'the services group'.

addafi had one son with his first wife, Fatiha (whom he divorced in 1970), and five sons and a daughter with his second, Safia. As the children of dictators are prone to do, they flaunted their immense wealth and power shamelessly, jetting off for holidays in exotic locations, drinking champagne and hanging out with celebrities. This caused great resentment among the naturally conservative Libyans. As Gaddafi continued to trade on his image as a pious Muslim and simple-living Bedouin, it is puzzling that he did not do more to curb their excesses.

The most interesting of his sons was the eldest from his second marriage, Saif al-Islam. As a young man, he had gone to Austria to study for an MBA (taking his two pet tigers with him, as you do). Saif was suave, articulate and sharply dressed, and when he began talking up the virtues

of democracy and free-market economics, Libyans could scarcely believe their ears. He founded a charity, and used it to mount campaigns against torture and negotiate the release of Islamists from prison. He encouraged his father to appoint a reformist economist as de facto prime minister, and under him some businesses were privatised. In Western countries, Saif was lauded as the face of a new Libya, but in truth he was more talk than action. Then again, he never had a chance of bringing about real reform. Gaddafi had invented the perfect political system with his Jamahiriyah, and there was no way he was going to change it.

n 17 December 2010, a Tunisian street vendor, Mohamed Bouazizi, frustrated by constant harassment from government officials, set himself on fire. His death was the trigger for the wave of protests against corrupt and

oppressive governments dubbed the 'Arab Spring'. Less than a month after Bouazizi's self-immolation, Tunisia's president, Zine El Abidine Ben Ali, fled the country, never to return. Gaddafi denounced the overthrow of Ben Ali in no uncertain terms, and made dire threats to the rebels and anyone who helped them. He also made a show of travelling around Libya, listening as people told him their problems and hinting at reform. But the ground was moving under his feet. There were large demonstrations in Benghazi, the main city in the eastern part of the country. The home to the Senussi and King Idris, whom Gaddafi had overthrown, and of many of the Islamists he had ruthlessly put down in the 90s, the east had always been his biggest headache. As payback for its Islamist tendencies, Gaddafi had punished Benghazi by withholding food and resources, adding to the seething resentment there. On 17 February, when its residents took to the streets in a 'Day of Rage', security forces fired on them, killing dozens.

The harder the regime cracked down on them the larger the demonstrations grew, spreading to other cities — even Tripoli. A rumour spread that Gaddafi had fled to Venezuela and his friend Hugo Chavez. In part to refute that, he made one of the strangest public appearances of his career. Sitting in a white golf cart and holding a large white umbrella over his head, unshaven and wearing an odd hat with side flaps, Gaddafi was filmed attacking the foreign media in a speech lasting less than twenty seconds. Then he folded his umbrella and took off.

With most of the east now under rebel control, Gaddafi decided to concentrate on securing Tripoli. He knew he could count on the loyalty of his security forces, which were mostly led by members of his family. But the regime was starting to disintegrate, with some high-ranking officials defecting to the West or the rebels. Then, on 20 February, Saif made an appearance on TV. He denounced the rebels as Islamists and

tools of the Western powers, and made threats that were as blood-curdling as his father had ever made. He did a lot of finger pointing. Saif had been the embodiment of the Libyan people's hopes of reform for years, and his speech staggered them. It seems that the rest of the Gaddafi clan blamed Saif and his reformist ideas for paving the way for revolution, and had forced him to toe the family line.

For all their successes, the rebels, who had now established a National Transition Council, were desperately short of weapons and ammunition. The regime began to retake some of the cities that had fallen to them, with particularly bitter fighting taking place over Misrata, and a major offensive was planned for Benghazi. On 17 March, Gaddafi was heard on the radio telling the people of Benghazi that they would be chased "street by street, house by house and wardrobe by wardrobe". With a massacre of potentially horrendous proportions in the offing, the U.N. Security Council acted with uncharacteristic decisiveness, imposing a no-fly zone over Libya and authorising Western military action on the ground. In the ultimate insult to Gaddafi, the great pan-Arabist, the Arab League supported the move. The U.S., Britain and France launched bombing raids on military targets, and the next few weeks saw fierce fighting as the regime managed to retake some cities then lose them again. In August, the rebel forces advanced on Tripoli, and to their surprise found little resistance — Gaddafi's vast, much-feared security machine had fallen apart. The people of Tripoli erupted with joy, tearing down Gaddafi's posters from the walls and setting fire to his tent at Bab Al-Aziziya. The white golf buggy from which he had made his ridiculous speech in February was driven triumphantly through the streets.

But where was Gaddafi? Many thought he was hiding in the Sahara desert, perhaps in a huge underground bunker he was rumoured to have built. In fact, he had fled back to Sirte, which he had transformed over the years into Libya's second biggest city and a luxurious enclave for the regime's elite. It had been his son Moutassim's idea — surely it was the last place they would think to look for him. He spent his last days making phone calls, reading the Koran, living on rice and pasta scrabbled from deserted flats, and raping young boys in front of his guards. The rebels who besieged Sirte were surprised by the fierce resistance they encountered and knew there must be senior regime figures in the city, but they still had no idea Gaddafi was among them.

On the morning of 20 October, with the rebels closing in, Gaddafi, Moutassim and his remaining followers climbed into about seventy-five cars and set off for the nearby village where Gaddafi had been born. The convoy was spotted by NATO, and an American drone and French planes fired missiles at it, one of them exploding in front of his car, blowing out the windscreen. After a brief gunfight with rebels from Misrata, Gaddafi and a few others managed to get away and hide in two concrete drain pipes under a road. The rebels found them by following a trail of blood, and more shots were fired. According to some accounts, one of Gaddafi's men, who was wounded, revealed that Gaddafi was in the drain. Hardly believing their luck, the rebels dragged out a bedraggled, blood-spattered and disoriented Gaddafi, who was muttering, "What's going on. What's wrong?" The rebels fired their machineguns into the air, shouted 'Allahu Akbar!' (God is great!) and 'Ya kalb!' ('You dog!') and recorded the chaotic scene on mobile phone cameras. One of the videos clearly shows a rebel attempting to ram a knife or stick up the dictator's backside as he was manhandled along a road. "What did I do to you?" Gaddafi asked as he was pushed onto the hood of a car which was briefly driven around, then he was dumped on the back of a pickup truck. Some rebels were shouting that he should be taken alive while others demanded he be killed.

Despite all the videos that were being taken at the scene, none of them captured the moment of his death. The National Transition Council later claimed he was killed in crossfire.

But the more likely scenario is that one of the rebels (often said to be a teenager) took matters into his own hands and shot Gaddafi at close range in the head and chest.

A video taken shortly afterwards shows his body on the ground and rebels tearing his shirt off. Someone spray-painted the words “This is the place where the rat Gaddafi was hiding” above the drains, and a young rebel was seen waving around the Colonel’s gold-plated pistol.

The National Transition Council demanded that Gaddafi’s body be handed over to them, but the Misratans weren’t going to give up their prize that easily. They took it to Misrata where it was paraded through the streets. Then the bodies of Gaddafi and Moutassim were placed side by side on mattresses in a meat freezer, and for days Libyans queued to view their stinking remains, some bringing their children. The Muslim injunction that a corpse be buried within twenty-four hours was cheerfully ignored.

t the end of World War II, Libya was left with its infrastructure wrecked, political institutions non-existent and people who had faced years of oppression. After Gaddafi’s fall, its situation was strikingly similar.

“I have created a Utopia here in Libya,” he once declared. “Not an imaginary one that people write about in books, but a concrete Utopia.” To understand Gaddafi, it is necessary to understand that this Utopia he had made was *real* to him. He was a man of the desert, born into a tribe which looked after its own, had no need of a government, and kept women on the other side of the tent. For Gaddafi, this was the ideal society, and it remained so until his downfall. If the Libyan people couldn’t always get all the consumer goods they wanted, or food, well, that was alright, character building in fact, for the Bedouin did not need all that.

While he was always paranoid about assassination, Gaddafi thought the threat was from foreigners or Libyan 'stray dogs'. Did he ever get an inkling of what his beloved masses really thought about him? A curious, self-pitying, allegorical story he wrote called 'Escape to Hell' (published in English in a collection of the same name) suggests he did. He wrote that "I both love and fear the masses, as I love and fear my father."

> *The masses can be so compassionate when they are happy, carrying their sons upon their shoulders. In this way, they carried Hannibal, Barclay, Savonarola, Danton, Robespierre, Mussolini and Nixon, yet how harsh they can be when they become angry. They conspired against Hannibal and poisoned him, burnt Savonarola at the stake, brought their hero Danton to the guillotine. Robespierre was destroyed by his beloved fiancee, while the masses dragged Mussolini's corpse through the streets, and spat in Nixon's face as he departed the White House for good having applauded his entrance years before…*
>
> *I feel that the masses, who would not even show mercy to their saviour, follow me around, burning me with their gaze. Even when they applaud me, it feels like they are pricking me...*

CHAPTER 9

IDI AMIN

IDI AMIN

Became president of Uganda in 1972
Died in comfortable exile in Saudi Arabia in 2003

The 1970s were a time of garish and vulgar display, of outrageous outfits, novelty songs and appalling taste all round. It was a decade into which the absurd figure of Idi Amin, his military uniform glittering with medals he had awarded himself, fitted perfectly. Field Marshall Doctor Idi Amin Dada, VC, DSO, MC, President-for-Life of Uganda and Conqueror of the British Empire, 'Big Daddy' for short, kept the world laughing for years with his ridiculous pronouncements and dictatorial hi-jinks.

The 300,000 to 500,000 Ugandans murdered during his regime weren't laughing as hard.

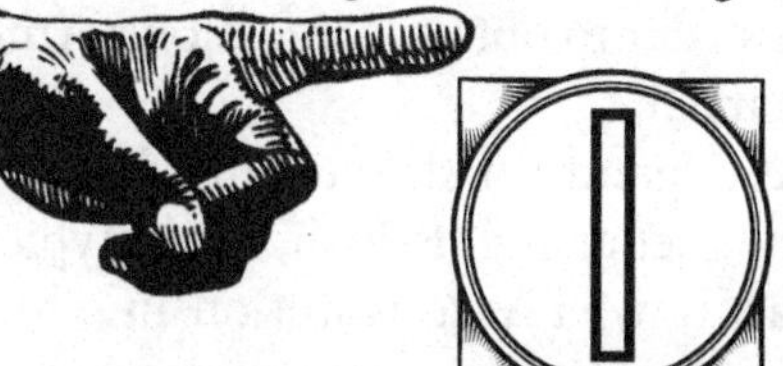

Idi Amin Dada was born in 1924 or 1925 in Koboko, north-western Uganda, just south of the Sudanese border. His father was a peasant farmer who abandoned mother and son soon after Idi's birth. His mother was, according to some sources, a witch who travelled around dispensing charms and curses. Amin was born into the small, mainly Muslim Kakwa tribe, and spent much of his formative years among Nubians, the collective name given to itinerant workers who had come to Uganda from the warrior tribes of Southern Sudan.

Uganda was still a British colony, and the young Amin

became a trainee cook in the King's African Rifles, then enlisted as a private in 1946. He was poorly educated, spoke no English and was, as one British officer put it, "virtually bone from the neck up, and needs things explained in words of one letter". But they loved him. He was tall (6 feet 4 inches or 193 cm), strong as an ox (he would be Uganda's heavyweight boxing champion from 1951 to 1960), fiercely loyal to his superiors, and funny. Amin in turn loved everything about the army — the parades, the uniforms, the titles. The KAR's pipe major taught him how to play the bagpipes, and after that he would often be seen wearing a kilt and a tartan forage cap.

Amin was made a corporal and sent to fight in Kenya during the 1952-1956 anti-British Mau Mau rebellion. He was eventually promoted to lieutenant, becoming one of only two Ugandans commissioned by the British prior to Uganda achieving independence in 1962. He also acquired a reputation for brutality, having headed a crackdown on cattle-rustling in north-eastern Uganda during which his men committed numerous atrocities, including the castration of eight Kangoli tribesmen in order to obtain confessions. Amin narrowly escaped court martial.

Prior to independence, Uganda had been divided into four tribal kingdoms. The departing British, with typical insouciance, left behind an unwieldy constitution in which power was shared by the prime minister and four kings. The most important of these was Mutesa II of the Baganda tribe, known as King Freddie, who was made president. Tensions soon mounted between him and the prime minister, the socialist Milton Obote. Meanwhile, there was civil war in the neighbouring Belgian Congo. Obote sympathised with the rebels and ordered Amin to help them. He did so by giving them arms in exchange for ivory and gold, and in the process deposited the equivalent of hundreds of thousands of dollars into his own bank account.

When details of this scheme were raised in Parliament, with Obote and Amin both implicated, Obote reacted by suspending Parliament and the constitution and declaring himself president. King Freddie, in turn, ordered the federal government out of his traditional lands (which included the capital, Kampala). Obote summoned Amin and ordered him to attack King Freddie's palace. He obeyed with gusto, shelling it. Hundreds of Baganda were killed. King Freddie managed to escape, and died in poverty in London three years later.

Over the next three years, Amin, now Army Chief of Staff, strengthened his power base by recruiting Nubians and Southern Sudanese into the army — men who owed their allegiance to him rather than the government. Obote began to nationalise the country's industry and the economy went into decline. Having survived two assassination attempts and fearing Amin's growing power, he made plans to arrest him. When Amin learned of this, he went into action. On 25 January 1972, while Obote was in Singapore for the Commonwealth conference, he mounted a coup. Despite the fact that there had apparently been no planning for this whatsoever, it quickly succeeded.

bote had turned Uganda into a virtual police state and there was much rejoicing at his overthrow. Amin travelled around the country and was treated as a hero by cheering crowds. He was feted in Israel and the U.K., where he lunched with Prime Minister Edward Heath, dined with the Queen at Buckingham Palace and visited his beloved Scotland.

Meanwhile, the killings had begun. Amin's first victims were members of the Langi and Acholi tribes in the armed forces (Obote was a Langi). Some four thousand of them were arrested, tortured and murdered over the next twelve months.

When Amin's troops were given carte blanche to shoot anyone suspected of a crime, the killings increased exponentially. Soon, truckloads of bodies were being dumped into the Nile every day, in the (often vain) hope that crocodiles would devour them. Some word of this leaked to the outside world, but it was generally put down to the normal score settling which followed a coup. In order to provide a cover for the killings, Amin claimed that Tanzania and the Sudan had been mounting raids across Uganda's borders.

Uganda's economy had already taken a battering under Obote. With Amin's increased military spending and illiterate soldiers in charge of whole ministries, it went into a steep decline. Amin knew that to retain power he would need to supply his troops with a steady supply of cash and goods. Where could he get it from?

In August 1972, Amin announced that he had dreamed that God had told him to expel all the Asians from Uganda.

There were around 50,000 Asians in the country at the time, many descended from the Indian coolies who had arrived in the 1890s to build the Kenya-Uganda railway. They were in control of most of its industry, as well as owning 80 per cent of small businesses. Many of the country's professionals — doctors, teachers, engineers — were Asian. They were told they had three months to get out.

At first, no-one could believe that Amin meant what he said. There were conflicting signals from the government — it was announced that Asians with Ugandan citizenship could stay, then those who were professionals. But eventually it sank in that Amin was serious. The Asians had come to build the railway, he said, and now that it was built they should go. As they had not generally mixed with the African population, who resented their wealth, Amin's 'Economic War', as he dubbed it, proved a popular move. It was applauded by some governments in neighbouring countries too. Amin gave assurances that the Asians would be compensated for their lost property, assurances which came to nothing. In fact, as they departed, they were often set upon by troops who beat them up — or worse — and stole whatever remaining cash or property they had with them.

Following this mass exodus, the Asian-owned businesses were distributed willy-nilly. Amin and officers took the richest pickings. Everything from grocery stores to dental practices to whole factories were given to people with no thought as to whether they would be able to run them. Typically, a soldier who had been given, say, an electronics store, would sell off all its stock, have no idea how to obtain more, and that was the end of it. The result was an economic catastrophe. Basic goods from salt to soap became scarce. According to Henry Kyemba, who was one of Amin's ministers before fleeing the country, and who went on to write a very good book about him, all of this came as a genuine surprise to Amin. He had believed that anyone could just walk into a business and run it.

Fortunately for the Ugandans, their country is one of the most fertile in Africa. As the economy tanked, people moved from the cities to the country, where they were able to live off the land. If not for this fact, Amin's dictatorship would never have survived for eight years.

Up to this point, Israel had been Amin's staunchest international supporter (he had undergone military training under the Israelis earlier in his career, and they had supported his coup). But while the Israelis, like the British, were willing to provide Uganda with financial aid, they insisted on having a say in how it was spent. And they refused to sell him fighter planes. (When the Israeli defence minister Moshe Dayan asked Amin what he wanted them for, he blithely replied, "I need them to bomb Tanzania.") He decided to switch sides. In February 1972, he visited Libya's Muammar Gaddafi, who offered him all sorts of goodies with no strings attached.

Amin suddenly came out against Israel. He professed admiration for Hitler's extermination of the Jews, called for Israel's destruction in a speech to the United Nations, and expelled all Israelis from Uganda.

min was now easing himself into his famous role as the biggest buffoon on the world stage. Many of his announcements and impromptu messages to other world leaders are the stuff of diplomatic folklore. To Tanzanian President Julius Nyerere, who had condemned the Asian expulsions, he wrote, "I love you very much and if you were a woman I would even consider marrying you although you have grey hairs on your head." On the Middle East situation he opined, "Arab victory in the war with Israel is inevitable and Prime Minister of Israel Mrs Golda Meir's only recourse is to tuck up her knickers and run away in the direction of New York and Washington." On the question of Scottish independence, he wrote to Queen Elizabeth, "Many of the Scottish people already consider me King of the Scots. I am the first man to ask the British government to end their oppression of Scotland. If the Scots want me to be their King, I will." He was, however, most solicitous about the industrial crisis his British friends were experiencing. He announced the formation of a Save Britain Fund, and at one point sent a cable to Prime Minister Heath urging him to send a plane to pick up some wheat and vegetables collected by farmers "before it goes bad". Over in the United States, President Nixon was having problems of his own, and Amin wrote wishing him a "speedy recovery" from Watergate.

Some of Big Daddy's pronouncements to his own people were just as idiosyncratic. There was, for example, his concerted campaign against women wearing wigs, which were, he claimed, often made from the hair of Vietnam War casualties, and other victims of colonialism. "I do not want Ugandans to wear the hair of dead imperialists or of Africans killed by imperialists," he declared. "No member of my own family is to wear a wig or she will cease to be a member of my family." Wigs could also be used "to conceal dangerous weapons". There were similar campaigns against mini-skirts and skin-whitening creams.

Amin's tomfoolery masked the worsening conditions in Uganda. Violence in the country escalated sharply when, in early 1973, a thousand Obote supporters crossed the border from Tanzania in a poorly planned coup attempt. They were dealt with ferociously by Amin's troops. The invasion gave Amin an excuse to postpone the elections he had promised on taking power, and also triggered reprisals against former officials of Obote's government who were rounded up, tortured and murdered.

The members of Amin's own government weren't much safer. Amin rarely attended cabinet meetings, never read government reports (being basically illiterate) and conducted most government business over the phone. Cabinet ministers found that the only way to keep up with his policy decisions was to listen to him on the radio (which was often how they found out that they themselves had been sacked). Amin had nothing but contempt for anyone educated, and regularly turned on his officials for little or no reason. Arrests were often made in public, a notable example being Uganda's Chief Justice, and a former prime minister, Benedicto Kiwanuka, who had made a judgment Amin disliked. Amin's men arrested him in the High Court in front of other judges, removed his shoes to increase his humiliation, bundled him into a car and took him away. His body was never found, but after suffering the usual tortures he is said to have been shot in the mouth, a common, symbolic end for those seen to have opposed the regime.

The activities of Amin's instruments of oppression, the

Public Safety Unit (secret police) and the State Research Bureau (Amin's 'bodyguards') were as ghastly as anything perpetrated under any dictatorship. Bodies regularly turned up horribly mutilated. In 1973, after fleeing the country, Edward Ragumayo, Amin's former minister of education, compiled a memorandum which he addressed to other African heads of state. After listing Amin's many failings as a leader, he went on to describe some of the tortures which had become commonplace.

> *The victims would line up, and the first one would be ordered to lie down while the prisoner next to him would be ordered to smash his head with a huge hammer... Then the third person would be ordered to demolish his brains and so on until the last man, who would either be shot by Towilli [the Nubian who headed the Public Safety Unit] himself or be killed in the same brutal manner by*

a police officer.

The victim's head would be smashed beyond recognition by one of the appointed executioners.

Slow killing is a common practice. Towilli would shoot into a man's arm, leg or chest and let him bleed to death.

Another method is to cut off any of the man's organs, such as an arm, leg, genitals, and let him die in agony. Sometimes these organs would be stuck into the victim's mouth…

The other despicable method is to cut a man's flesh, have it roasted and have him feed on it till he dies … There is a constant fire in which human flesh is roasted, and a man is fed on his own flesh until he dies of sepsis and bleeding.

Amin was widely believed to take part in blood rituals and cannibalism, and was said to have a fridge full of his victims' heads. Henry Kyemba gives credence to some of this. While Minister of Health, he learned of several occasions when Amin asked to be left alone in a mortuary with the body of an assassinated enemy. He notes that, among Amin's tribe, the Kakwa, it is customary for a man who has killed another man to taste his blood, thus making his victim's spirit harmless. He also heard Amin boast, on two occasions, that he had tasted human flesh. "It is very salty," he noted, "even more salty than leopard meat."

As for the scintillating subject of heads in fridges — which is what many people remember about Amin — hard evidence is somewhat thin on the ground. Joseph Kamau and Andrew Cameron, in *Lust to Kill*, quote two alleged witnesses. The first was Moses Aloga, who was a servant in Amin's house in Kampala, known as the Command Post. Aloga said that one of Amin's wives, Sarah, grew curious about the contents of two fridges in what was known as the Botanical Room, and prevailed on him to open them. The first contained beer, the second two heads, one of which belonged to her former boyfriend, a bandleader named Jesse Gitta. According to Aloga, when Amin came home and found Sarah crying in front of the still open fridge, he beat her so badly that she had to be hospitalised. The second witness was a nurse named Monica Nansamba, who worked in a Kampala military hospital. She says that on several occasions, hospital staff were ordered to remove the heads of victims, treat them, and send them to the Command Post. One day, six bodies came in for such treatment, and she recognised one of them as a girl named Jane, a schoolfriend of hers and the daughter of Peter Kabugo, an Information Ministry official. Nurse Nansamba says she was able to smuggle Jane's head away and take it to Kabugo who, in a state of shock, drove off with it, intending to present it to Amin himself. Kamau and Cameron write that Kabugo's body was found in his car the next day, minus its head. I find both of these tales a little too pat, and would have to say that the jury is still out on the whole heads-in-fridge business. Mind you, with Amin, you can't say it would have been out of character.

Big Daddy's sexual prowess was almost as legendary as his bloodthirstiness. He had three wives when he came to power, Malyame, Kay and Nora, who were soon joined by a fourth, Medina. He also had dozens of mistresses on the go at any one time. Officially he fathered some thirty children, although the real total was probably much greater. So occupied was he with his mistresses that his first three wives, feeling neglected, all took lovers. In March 1974, Amin found out that they had thrown a party for their lovers, and promptly divorced all three of them. While he didn't know it at the time, Kay was already pregnant to her lover, a doctor named Mbalu-Mukasa. In August, Kay's dismembered body was found in the boot of Mbalu-Mukasa's car, shortly after the doctor's body had been discovered — he had died from an overdose of sleeping pills. Amin was widely believed to have ordered Kay's death, but it seems that this was one murder in which he was not directly involved. Kay died during a botched abortion, almost certainly performed by Mbalu-Mukasa, who then panicked and killed himself. What is true, however, is that Amin ordered that Kay's arms and legs be sewn back onto her body (most accounts say in the wrong places, although Henry Kyemba does not back this up). He then had Kay's father and three children brought to the mortuary where, in front of TV cameras, he hurled abuse at the corpse and said to the children, "Your mother was a bad woman. See what has happened to her!"

Amin's love of Scotland was well in evidence at the celebrations for the fourth anniversary of his rule. Soldiers wearing kilts and plastic sporrans paraded around a football stadium as a pipe band cranked out 'Scotland the Brave'. They were joined by commandos in camouflage gear, infantrymen in khaki, frogmen in rubber suits, formations of businessmen and schoolchildren, tribal dancers and bare-breasted dancing girls. Amin gave a speech in which he summed up the achievements of his administration. Detention without trial was now a thing of the past, he said. The economic war had been won and all important posts were now occupied by Ugandans. Tribalism had been eliminated. Alas, corruption still existed, which was why he had not returned the country to civilian rule, but the future was bright. "My popularity is ever increasing, not only in Uganda, East Africa, Africa, but also in the whole world," he told the cheering crowd. "Fellow countrymen, what we have achieved during the four years we have been in power is indeed great."

The 1975 summit meeting of the Organisation of African Unity (OAU) was due to take place in Kampala, with Amin as chairman. With the excesses of his regime becoming increasingly widely known, some of its thirty-seven member states announced they would boycott the meeting. In the end it went ahead, although many heads of state did not attend, sending deputies in their place. Those who did go were treated to some priceless Amin moments. At one point, in a piece of theatre he dubbed 'The White Man's Burden', Amin appeared before delegates in a sedan chair carried by four white Ugandan businessmen. The spectacle had been arranged by 'Major' Bob Astles, a former British soldier who was the head of the 'Anti-Corruption Squad' and Amin's right-hand man. The President then descended from the sedan chair and serenaded the assembly with one of the two tunes he could play on the piano accordion. A few days later, delegates found themselves watching a wedding ceremony in which Amin married his fifth wife, Sarah Kyolaba, a nineteen-year-old soldier whom he had noticed as she performed with the jazz band of the Ugandan Army's 'Suicide Regiment'. (She's the one who is said to have later found the head of her former boyfriend, the bandleader, in Amin's fridge.)

Idi Amin, the comical black dictator, was a particular figure of mirth in Great Britain. Alan Coren wrote weekly 'bulletins' from the President for the humorous magazine *Punch*, which were later collected in two best-selling books. There was even a novelty song, 'Amazin' Man', which reached the charts, with Amin's voice provided by comedian John Bird, and a female chorus trilling:

Idi, Idi, Idi Amin
Most amazin' man
That's ever been
He's the general, the president, the king of the sea

Idi, Idi, Idi Amin.

All great fun, and as the real Big Daddy was such a walking caricature, perfectly understandable. I wonder, though, whether there was a little post-colonial guilt in all of this. Amin was, after all, inextricably linked to Britain. He had been trained by the British army, he had visited the Queen, and ever-present by his side was the sinister figure of Bob Astles. Even when Britain severed diplomatic ties with Uganda, as it later did, it continued to trade with it. (Twice weekly, a plane flew from Uganda to Stansted Airport in Britain. Known as the 'Stansted whisky run', it returned packed with luxury goods for distribution to Amin's cronies.) But if there was a trace of guilt in the media portrayal of Amin, there was also undeniably a lot of gloating. Defenders of colonialism could point to him and say, "Look at that. See what came after we left?"

part from exterminating his enemies, real or imagined, and pillaging the Ugandan economy, Idi Amin only ever had one consistent aim — to make the country a Muslim state. Soon after his rejection of Israel, he could be heard claiming that it already was one, with an 80 per cent Muslim population (the actual figure was under 10 per cent, with most of the remainder being Christian.) Over the years, he appointed increasing numbers of Muslims to important positions in the government and military. He also welcomed Palestinian militants into the country, and used them as bodyguards. It's almost certain he had prior knowledge of the plan when, on Monday, 28 June 1976, an Air France plane packed with Israelis was hijacked by members of the Popular Front for the Liberation of Palestine, who ordered that it be flown to Uganda's international airport in Entebbe.

Here was a perfect opportunity for Amin to stick it to the Israelis. He arrived at the airport, where the hostages had been gathered in a disused terminal, in full dress uniform. All smiles, he hugged the hijackers, and told the hostages that their best hope would be to tell their government to solve the Palestinian problem. He even helped draft the hijackers' ransom demand — that fifty-three terrorists held in prisons in Israel and other countries be released within forty-eight hours. The deadline was later extended to the following Sunday, which would give Amin time to fly to Mauritius, where he was to hand over the chairmanship of the OAU, and return.

He arrived back on Saturday. That evening, at 11.45 p.m., the Israelis landed a team of commandos at Entebbe. An hour later they were gone again, taking most of the hostages with them (two had been killed during the raid). They had also killed all seven hijackers and twenty Ugandans, and blown up eleven of Amin's Russian-built MiG fighter planes as they sat on the tarmac. Amin literally didn't know what had hit him. Like all the other officials in the area, he had gone into hiding as soon as the raid began.

Amin tried to put the best spin on this humiliating disaster, telling the Israelis, "you did not get the good MiGs — the planes your soldiers destroyed were waiting for repairs". Privately he was furious, and took what revenge he could. Only one hostage had not been rescued — an eighty-year-old British-Israeli woman named Dora Bloch, who was in hospital when the raid took place. State Research Bureau men arrived at the hospital, dragged her kicking and screaming from her room, and later dumped her body in a road outside Kampala in full public view. Despite this, the government maintained that she had been returned to the airport an hour before the raid. Amin also ordered attacks on Kenyans in Uganda, Kenya having provided aid to the Israelis during the raid. Hundreds of them were rounded up and murdered, and for a while it looked like the two countries might go to war, but as all of Uganda's oil and many of its other supplies had to come through Kenya, Big Daddy was eventually forced to back down. In the meantime, Britain had broken off diplomatic relations with Uganda, the first time this had happened to a Commonwealth country. "I am the conqueror of the British Empire," crowed Amin. "British just removed the union jacks from Uganda and ran away."

min had now acquired another title, President-for-Life of Uganda, but for the first time he was facing some organised opposition. Students at Makerere University demonstrated and there was unrest in the army, with soldiers disgruntled because they weren't being paid. A delegation of senior officers went to Amin and asked him to step down (he had them jailed). As a smokescreen, Amin made the usual noises about Obote supporters planning a coup and bringing arms into the country. He also suggested for the first time that the churches were involved.

In the early hours of 5 February 1977, soldiers arrived at the home of Janani Luwum, the Anglican Archbishop of Uganda, put the muzzle of a gun to his stomach and searched the house, saying they were looking for arms. The following night, a similar raid took place at the home of a bishop.

Luwum, incensed, composed a memorandum which described the raids, then went on to detail other crimes perpetrated by the army and security forces. It was all written in the most respectful terms, as if Amin was not responsible for, or even aware of, what was happening, but it was political dynamite. Signed by Luwum and eighteen clergymen, it was sent to government ministers.

A few days later, Amin summoned ministers, diplomats and various other officials, including Archbishop Luwum, to a meeting at the Nile Hotel in Kampala. They arrived to find two-thousand soldiers in the forecourt, surrounding piles of foreign-made weapons. While these looked suspiciously like the arms regularly issued to the army, the guests were told they had been brought into the country by Obote supporters. A number of fabricated statements were then read out, one of which implicated Archbishop Luwum in the plot. Amin asked the soldiers what should be done with such people. "Kill them!" they shouted back. The Archbishop and two cabinet ministers were arrested.

What happened in the next few hours is not entirely clear, but the bullet-riddled bodies of the three men arrived at a mortuary next day. Luwum, still dressed in his robes, had been shot in the face, and it is widely believed that Amin himself had done this after losing his temper. Ugandan radio, without missing a beat, announced that the three men had died in a car accident. This time, the State Research Bureau had actually gone to the trouble of staging a fake accident using two damaged government cars as props (one of them had been damaged by Amin, who used it for hunting). The killings prompted worldwide outrage. Even some of the African nations who had supported him were tiring of Idi Amin now.

Amin was again short of cash to pay his soldiers, and the quickest solution seemed to be a spot of pillage. He prepared the ground by claiming that Tanzanian troops, supported by Cubans, had begun to make raids into Ugandan territory. On October 1978, in retaliation for these fictitious attacks, Ugandan troops crossed the border into Tanzania, raping, killing and looting as they went, and occupied a large area known as the Kagera Salient. Amin claimed it as Ugandan territory, saying, "All Tanzanians in the area must know that they are under direct rule by the Conqueror of the British Empire."

Tanzania's president, Julius Nyerere, one of Amin's most vociferous critics from the beginning declared, "We are going to fight this snake until it is out of our house." Amin countered with a possible solution to the crisis. "I am keeping fit so that I can challenge President Nyerere in the boxing ring and fight it out there rather than the soldiers lose their lives on the field of battle." He suggested Muhammad Ali as referee, and even offered to fight with one arm tied behind his back. Nyerere declined the challenge.

The end came quickly. Tanzanian troops expelled the Ugandans from the Kagera Salient, and when they reached the Ugandan border, kept going. They were joined by many Ugandan exiles. Despite the heroic actions of Field Marshall Amin, as reported on Ugandan radio, his army offered little resistance. At the last moment, Colonel Gaddafi sent three thousand Libyan troops to help, to no avail. Tanzanian troops entered Kampala on 11 April. Amin fled, taking with him four wives, several mistresses and about twenty children.

He went first to Libya, then Iraq, before being given asylum in Saudi Arabia. King Fahd, in a spirit of Muslim solidarity, granted him a pension of $14,000 a month and provided him with servants, drivers and cars, on condition that he play no role in politics. He and his family lived in a house in Jeddah, where he occupied himself fishing, praying in mosques, hanging around gyms and hotel lobbies, and eating large amounts of oranges in an attempt to revive his flagging sexual stamina, a habit which earned him the nickname 'Dr Jaffa'. He occasionally made the headlines again — in 1989, for example, he was caught trying to sneak into Uganda and was sent back — but it was mostly a pleasant and uneventful retirement which lasted over two decades until his death in 2003 from kidney failure.

Rarely has a deposed dictator — especially such a bloodthirsty one — had such an idyllic end. It must be said, though, that this was entirely in keeping with Amin's character. Whatever his intellectual shortcomings, the man was cunning as a rat and a great survivor. During his rule, he kept constantly on the move, never spending two consecutive nights in the same place, and it was noted that he seemed to have a sixth sense when it came to surviving assassination attempts, of which there were over twenty.

It has often been speculated that Idi Amin was literally insane due to syphilis or some other illness, and his actions would seem to bear this out. I don't believe he was. I think the key to understanding Amin is to see the way he thought in magical terms. He had decided at some point, for whatever reason, that he was a man of destiny with a direct line to God, and believed if he said something was so, that made it so. A small example of this came when he was gearing up for his invasion of Tanzania, and announced that British troops were part of the forces massing on the Tanzanian border.

"Ugandans need not worry about this," he said, "because I have already conquered the British." Amin had first made this grandiose claim on the slender pretext that the British had cut diplomatic ties with Uganda, but once he had said he was the Conqueror of the British Empire, his words became a reality. In his mind, the British really could pose no further threat to him. The amazing thing is that this way of thinking got Amin so far.

On the announcement of Amin's death there was widespread mourning in Uganda, a fact which astonished many Western observers. It was no doubt partly due to events following his overthrow (Milton Obote was re-elected as president in 1980, and his second period in office, lasting until 1985, was every bit as bloody as Amin's). But at the end of the day, Idi Amin, for all his brutality and craziness, was remembered by many native Ugandans as a leader not afraid to give the finger to the world's superpowers.

CHAPTER 10

SADDAM HUSSEIN

SADDAM HUSSEIN

Became president of Iraq in 1979
Pulled from a hole in 2003, and hanged in 2006

One day in 1987, Saddam Hussein was being shown around the ruins of the ancient city of Babylon, which lay about an hour-and-a-half's drive south of Baghdad. Babylon had been the home of the mighty king Nebuchadnezzar, whose empire stretched across most of today's Middle East. He occupied Jerusalem in 587 BC, destroyed the Jewish Temple and deported the Jews. He was Saddam's hero. Saddam was a patriot, and his greatest dream was to restore to Iraq its ancient glory.

Centuries of neglect and looting had taken their toll on Babylon, and as Saddam walked around it, puffing on one of his ever-present Cuban cigars, he saw little more than some broken-down walls and piles of rubble. This wasn't good enough! So he made a snap decision — he would rebuild Babylon (despite the fact that no-one knew what it had looked like).

Work began immediately. As archaeologists around the world looked on aghast, the remains of ancient walls were levelled and tens of thousands of yellow bricks were brought in to build new structures. Many of these bricks were stamped with inscriptions like "The Babylon of Nebuchadnezzar was rebuilt in the era of the leader President Saddam Hussein."

The centrepiece of Saddam's new Babylon is a recreation of the royal palace. It's a vast, boxy, fortress-like structure, occupying an area equivalent to five football fields. It's shoddily built, and it's hideous. Alas for the Iraqi people, Saddam's goal of restoring Iraq's position as the pre-eminent Arab power went about as well as his recreation of Babylon.

addam (the name, appropriately enough, means 'the one who confronts') was born on 28 April 1937 in Al-Awja, a village by the Tigris River near the town of Tikrit. His father died three months before he was born. His mother, Sabha, who was inclined to mysticism and claimed to be psychic, afterwards married Saddam's father's brother, Ibrahim Hasan. Because his father was dead and his mother was considered weird, the other boys in the village bullied Saddam, and he took to walking around carrying an iron bar. He later said that his closest companion when he was young was his horse.

According to almost all the accounts of Saddam's life published in the West, his stepfather hated him, beat him, sent him off to work in the fields and refused to let him go to school. This is usually put forward as one of the explanations for Saddam's later brutality, but when the Americans interrogated him at length after his capture in 2003, he categorically denied it. "It's not true," he said. "Ibrahim Hasan — God bless him. If he had a secret, he would trust me with it. I was more dear to him than his son, Idam." Whatever the truth of all this, when he was ten, Saddam set off for Tikrit, a dusty town best known as the birthplace of Saladin, the famed warrior who had ejected the crusaders from Jerusalem in the twelfth century. Here he was taken in by his uncle, Khairallah Talfah, a former army officer, who arranged for him to attend school.

Saddam proved a good enough pupil despite his late start, but he hated the discipline and clashed with his teachers. He slipped a snake into the robes of one he didn't like, and at the age of fourteen is said to have tried to murder another one after receiving a beating. (He went to the teacher's home one night, armed with a gun, but fled after mistakenly shooting the teacher's brother in the leg.) As he learned to read and write, he received a different sort of education from his uncle, an ardent nationalist, who told him about the political situation in Iraq and the many iniquities of the British.

Prior to World War I, the region that became Iraq was known in the West as Mesopotamia, and was divided into three provinces, Baghdad, Basra and Mosul. Like other Arab homelands, it was a possession of the Ottoman Turkish Empire. In 1914, after the Ottoman Turks sided with Germany, Britain declared war on them, and sent troops to occupy Basra. The Emir of Mecca seized the opportunity to mount a revolt against the Turks, spurred on by the British government which assured him that the Arabs would be granted independence once the war was won. His son Faisal was put in charge of the Arab Revolt, with T.E Lawrence, AKA Lawrence of Arabia, acting as his military adviser. In March 1917, when British troops entered Baghdad, they were hailed by the locals as liberators.

Once the war was over, though, Britain was less inclined to let go of Mesopotamia — and its oil reserves. After two international conferences, it was decided to break up the Arab territories into several states. Britain was granted a 'mandate' over Mesopotamia, which meant that it would continue to control the country while supposedly paving the way for independence. That didn't go down too well with the Arabs, and a rebellion broke out that the British met with brute force (including the deployment of poison gas). It was eventually agreed to give in to Arab demands for independence, or at least appear to. Mesopotamia was renamed Iraq and declared a monarchy, with Faisal installed as its first king, despite the fact that he had never set foot there. Behind the scenes, the British continued to pull the strings, and Arab nationalism simmered.

In the late 1930s, with another war looming, many nationalists and officers in the Iraqi army were pro-German, and when the crunch came and Britain declared war on Germany, the Iraqi government failed to follow suit. Prime Minister Rashid Ali promised to honour Iraq's existing treaties with Britain, but the British didn't trust him and forced him out. This stirred the Iraqi army to action and Rashid Ali was reinstated, but he wouldn't last long. Churchill believed Basra and its port were vital for Britain's war effort, and when Rashid Ali refused to allow further troops on his soil, Britain declared war on Iraq and quickly crushed its meagre forces. The Iraqi colonels who had supported Rashid Ali were executed and other officers were imprisoned, including Saddam's uncle Khairallah, who was put away for five years. He hadn't been free for long when Saddam turned up in Tikrit, hungry for education, so the wounds of these events were still raw.

addam moved to Baghdad with Khairallah and his family in the 1950s, and enrolled in high school in 1955. Thanks to oil revenues, Baghdad was a booming city, and some Iraqis were becoming very rich indeed, but most remained very poor and this caused considerable resentment, with many people, especially students, turning to communism. There were riots and strikes throughout the decade and Saddam quit school so he could join in. He also joined the Ba'ath Party, which espoused secularism, socialism and pan-Arabism (the dream of uniting all Arab countries into one). The Ba'athists boycotted the 1957 election, and allied themselves with a dissident faction within the army known as the Free Officers.

The Free Officers made their move on the morning of 14 July 1958, sending a brigade into Baghdad. As demonstrators surged into the streets, soldiers surrounded the palace. King Faisal II and other members of the royal household who attempted to flee were cut down with machine gun fire. (Iraqis don't muck around.) The monarchy was abolished and a republic proclaimed. Abdul Karim Qasim, one of the leaders of the Free Officers, became prime minister, and appointed several Ba'athists to important posts. There followed a period of great political uncertainty as the country debated — often violently — its future. Iraqis were almost evenly divided between communists and Arab nationalists, the latter having been inspired by the Egyptian president Nasser's nationalisation of the Suez Canal in 1956. Since then, Nasser had formed the United Arab Republic, with Egypt and Syria its first two members, and invited Iraq to join, but Prime Minister Qasim declined. He was clearly veering toward communism, and began kicking Ba'athists out of his government. The Ba'ath Party decided that he needed to be assassinated without delay, and their enthusiastic young member Saddam Hussein was just the man to organise it.

After the revolution, Saddam had contributed to the ongoing national debate by killing a communist who was a political rival of his uncle. He spent six months in jail, and on his release thought it prudent to lay low in Tikrit. Summoned back to Baghdad, he put together an assassination plan with some of his colleagues. On 7 October 1959, as Qasim's car made its way along Rashid Street, Saddam and the others started firing. Qasim was hit in the arm and shoulder but survived. Saddam was wounded in the leg as he fled.

The story of the assassination attempt and Saddam's subsequent flight into exile would become the foundation myth of Saddam the great revolutionary hero. It was told and retold, becoming increasingly dramatic, in countless articles, books and a movie in 1980. According to the fully-formed version, after one of his colleagues dug a bullet out of his leg with a razor blade, Saddam rode through the desert on horseback pursued by military patrols, then, still in agony from his wound, embarked on a perilous swim across the Tigris River. After reaching Tikrit, he collected two comrades and they made an arduous desert crossing into Syria.

This is all good, exciting stuff, but according to an alternative account of the assassination attempt, it failed because Saddam panicked and started shooting too soon.

After a brief stay in Damascus, Saddam went to Cairo where he joined the Egyptian branch of the Ba'ath Party and resumed his high school studies. Back in Iraq, seventeen Ba'athists were executed for complicity in the assassination attempt, and Saddam was sentenced to death in absentia.

In February 1964, the Ba'athists struck again. A heavily armed group including Saddam's uncle Khairallah, the latter's cousin and close friend from Tikrit, Hasan al-Bakr, and several army officers surrounded the Ministry of Defence where Qasim was holed up. He was dragged out after a couple of days of fierce fighting, given a quick trial and shot, with his execution broadcast on television that night. A new Revolutionary Command Council (RCC) was formed, with Abdul Salam Arif as president, and Bakr as prime minister.

Some score settling followed as the Ba'athists turned on the communists. Thousands were hunted down and executed by the National Guard, and Saddam, back in the country, was reportedly heavily involved. The CIA also lent a hand. They were glad to see the back of Qasim, and provided the Ba'athists with the names of communists to kill. Then it was the Kurds' turn. They had been pushing for an independent state, and were dealt with ruthlessly, their villages attacked with napalm and poison gas.

President Arif then turned on Bakr, fearing he had leadership ambitions of his own. He had Bakr arrested and

Saddam went into hiding again. He began working on a new assassination attempt, with Arif the target, but the plot was uncovered and Saddam was arrested and thrown into prison. He spent most of his time there reading (including all of Hemingway's novels). Once a week he was visited by his wife, Sajida, the daughter of his uncle Khairallah, whom he had married soon after his return from Egypt. She brought along their son Uday, who had messages from Saddam's Ba'athist colleagues concealed in his baby clothes. After about two years of incarceration, much of it spent in solitary confinement, Saddam managed to escape.

The Ba'athists mounted another coup in 1968. President Arif had died in a helicopter crash two years earlier, and his brother had taken his place. On the morning of 17 July, a contingent of Ba'athists and soldiers entered the grounds of the Presidential Palace. According to the official account, Saddam was right in the thick of it, wearing a military uniform (although he wasn't in the army) and perched on a tank, but in fact he almost certainly wasn't there. This coup, the fourth in ten years, turned out to be an uncharacteristically bloodless affair, with the president quickly agreeing to surrender and go into exile. Bakr took his place.

While Saddam didn't have an official post in the new government, he was given an office next to the president's, and assigned a project — planning a new security apparatus for Iraq. This meant that he was intimately involved with the pursuit of those deemed to be enemies of the regime, chiefly communists and Jews. Many were publicly hanged in Baghdad's Liberation Square, leading to condemnation from many countries. And it seems that Saddam was a hands-on security chief who wasn't above carrying out executions himself, including, allegedly, throwing one prisoner into a vat of acid.

Saddam once remarked that he knew there were many

people who wanted him dead. "However," he said, "I am far cleverer than they are. I know they are conspiring to kill me long before they actually start planning to do it." One of his favourite ploys was to fabricate elaborate plots against the Ba'ath Party, usually said to be backed by the CIA, the Israelis or the Iranians, which became a pretext for arresting dozens of people at a time. He would eventually put together a security apparatus as efficient and all-encompassing as any country has ever seen, and it would never be short of enemies. On the slightest suggestion that a man harboured anti-government sentiments, he could be arrested, imprisoned and tortured, often without knowing exactly what he was supposed to have done wrong. If he was lucky, he might emerge again months or years later, after which he and his family would keep very quiet about what had happened.

The real turning point in Saddam's career came towards the end of 1969, when he was appointed to the RCC, the body that effectively ran Iraq, and became its vice chairman. Overnight, he went from having no official government post to being the second-highest-ranking official in Iraq.

After working in the background for years, he began to promote himself as the Ba'ath Party's chief ideologue. He made numerous speeches outlining his vision for Iraq, which he wanted to make one of the key players in the Arab world, and knew that this would depend on economic development. The Ba'athists achieved one of their major aims in 1972, nationalising the Iraq Petroleum Company and greatly enriching the government's coffers. Saddam was also pragmatic when it came to trade. He thought political differences shouldn't prevent countries from entering into mutually beneficial trade details, and helped engineer a host of such deals with the United States, the Soviet Union, Britain, France and other countries.

Saddam believed that Iraqis should be immersed in Ba'athist ideology from an early age, and education was vital if this was to happen. The country had very high rates of illiteracy, but during the early 1970s primary education was made compulsory and free. Then, in 1978, Saddam announced a massive new campaign, with all illiterate Iraqis between the ages of twenty-one and forty-five ordered to learn to read within twenty-one months or face severe punishments including imprisonment. The government employed thousands of new teachers and spent millions of dollars to make this happen. The emancipation of women was also on Saddam's agenda, for he believed his revolution could not succeed without their help. "Women make up one half of society," he said in a speech to a women's organisation in 1975. "Our society will remain backward and in chains unless its women are liberated, enlightened and educated."

Saddam, or 'the Deputy' as he was known, had become the public face of the Iraqi government, both within the country and in the outside world. He was certainly an impressive looking figure with his finely tailored suits and imported silk neckties. He was perceived internationally as a man you could do business with, and his campaigns for literacy and female emancipation won him favourable notices in the Western press and kudos from the United Nations. For a brief period, he was probably the world's favourite dictator, a veritable poster boy for authoritarianism, doing a tough job in a tough part of the world.

In July 1979, President Bakr announced he was retiring (after some arm-twisting from Saddam, it is said), and handed power to his deputy. Saddam began his rule with an extraordinary piece of political theatre. Summoning around a thousand members of the Ba'ath Party to a meeting, which was filmed, he announced that a Syrian plot to overthrow the Ba'athists in Iraq had been uncovered. A senior Ba'athist official named Muhyi Abdul Hussein Mashadi was brought on stage who was said to be the ringleader. Looking terrified, Mashadi proceeded to read out the names of sixty-six men, and as each name was called, security officers hustled the accused out of the auditorium. Saddam, smoking a cigar, looked rather bored by the whole thing. Towards the end, one man in the audience stood up and began shouting "Long Live Saddam!", and everyone else soon joined in enthusiastically.

About a third of the accused plotters were executed, including Mashadi, who had agreed to read out the names after Saddam had threatened to have his wife and daughter raped. (Saddam and other members of the RCC carried out some of the executions.) It was a purge worthy of Stalin, and he followed it by appointing many of his relatives to important posts.

While laying down the law to his Ba'athist colleagues in no uncertain fashion, Saddam was keen to present a softer side to the Iraqi people. He liked to be seen as a humble man, a servant to his people, and a loving husband and father. Newspapers and TV often ran stories about Saddam spending quality time with his sons Uday and Qusay, and daughters Raghad, Rana and Hallah, attending their birthday parties, going on picnics with them, or interrupting a cabinet meeting to sew a button on one of his daughter's dresses. "I can't imagine life without love," he said.

He liked to be driven around the country, stopping at random in the streets or at farms and factories, to greet people and give them a hug. In interviews he would dispense fatherly advice on matters such as personal hygiene. In one, he said, "It's not appropriate for someone to attend a gathering or to be with his children with his body odour trailing behind him, emitting a sweet or stinky smell mixed with perspiration. It's preferable to bathe twice a day, at least once a day." Another ploy was to adopt a rudimentary disguise (traditional Arab headdress, for example), and arrive at an ordinary family's house with a television crew in tow. The family members would pretend not to recognise the most recognisable man in Iraq, as he asked them what they thought about Saddam Hussein and his government. When their answers were sufficiently fulsome, he would dramatically reveal his identity, a look of delight on his face.

979, the year Saddam became president, also saw the overthrow of the Shah of Iran and Ayatollah Khomeini instituting an Islamic republic. This presented Saddam with a problem, but also, or so he thought, an opportunity.

Saddam belonged to the Sunni branch of Islam, but around 60 per cent of Iraqis are Shiites. (Iraq's other major ethnic group, the Kurds, are not Arabs but are mostly Sunni, and make up around 17 per cent of the population). Relations between Shiites and Sunnis had been fairly amicable in Iraq, but Saddam feared that the Ayatollah's victory could stir up Islamic fervour among Shiites that could threaten his regime. He also saw the Ayatollah as a threat to his goal of becoming the dominant player in the region, and tried to belittle him, saying his revolution wasn't really an Islamic one (Islam being an Arab creation and the Iranians being Persians). Saddam launched a crackdown on Shiite organisations, and expelled hundreds of Iraqis of Iranian descent, but this simply provoked the sort of street protests he had feared. As the situation deteriorated, he had many Shiites executed, including Iraq's senior Shiite cleric, Ayatollah Sadr, who was reportedly forced to watch his sister being raped, then had his beard set on fire before he was killed.

As Ayatollah Khomeini urged Iraq's Shiites to rise up, Saddam made a fateful decision. In September 1980, using a border dispute as a pretext, he ordered Iraqi troops to enter Iran. His goals seem to have been to cut Khomeini down to size and pick up a bit of oil-rich territory for Iraq, and with Iran still in post-revolution disarray, he calculated that his invasion would be a blitzkrieg-style affair lasting no more than two weeks. But the Iranians fought much more fiercely than he expected, and the Iraqi advance soon stalled.

The Iran-Iraq War would become one of the strangest, most pointless, most self-destructive (for both sides) wars in history. Saddam directed operations, and whatever his talents may have been, military strategy wasn't one of them. His army was far better trained and equipped than Iran's, but instead of attacking Iranian cities head on, the Iraqis laid siege to them and bombed them in the hope they would surrender. They didn't. Throughout the war, the Iraqis were keen to keep casualties on their side low, but this wasn't due to any regard for human life. Rather, Saddam knew that he had declared war for flimsy reasons, and feared that huge casualties could turn the Iraqi people against him. The Iraqis also failed to use their armoured divisions or air force in any sort of sensible way. Instead, once they became bogged down in Iran, they busied themselves building defensive structures on territory they held — trenches, bunkers and so on, all of dubious strategic value. Their most extraordinary endeavour was to construct a moat 15 miles (24 kilometres) long and up to 3 miles (5 kilometres) wide, at an estimated cost of over $1 billion. Iraqi commanders in the field were often baffled by the orders they received from Baghdad.

If Iraqi strategy was seriously flawed, Iran under the Ayatollah and the mullahs seemed to have no strategy at all other than launching waves of ill-equipped and untrained men at the heavily armed invaders. Many were just boys mad keen for martyrdom, and they were slaughtered in their hundreds of thousands. The extent of the carnage, and the stalemate that the war soon settled into, has led many to compare it to World War I.

Saddam imported vast quantities of arms and equipment from the Soviet Union and other countries during the war, and in 1985 began bombing civilian targets in Iranian cities. With both leaders still refusing to blink, the war entered a more deadly phase in 1988. The Iraqis launched a missile attack on Tehran lasting two months, and Iranian forces entered Kurdish territory in Iraq. This led to the worst atrocity of the war when Iraq deployed chemical weapons on Kurdish civilians, killing five thousand. The operation was overseen by Saddam's cousin, Ali Hassan Al-Majid, who earned himself the nickname 'Chemical Ali'.

The Iranians feared that Saddam was about to launch a chemical attack on Tehran, and in July 1988 the Ayatollah agreed to a U.N.-brokered cease-fire. The war had lasted almost eight years and resulted in the deaths of 1.5 million people, mostly Iranians. Saddam declared it "a spectacular Iraqi victory", despite the fact that he had gained no territory from it, or anything else really. He celebrated his achievement with the Victory Arches, erected at two entrances to Baghdad's Grand Festivities Square. Each consists of two enormous, outstretched hands emerging from the ground, holding crossed swords 459 feet (140 metres) long. The hands were based on casts of Saddam's hands — including thumbprints. The bases are decorated with hundreds of looted Iranian helmets.

uring the Iran-Iraq War, the United States was generally content to watch Iraq beat up on Iran. It condemned Iraq's use of chemical weapons, but renewed diplomatic relations with the country in 1984, and offered some military assistance. The Americans weren't above playing both sides, though. In 1981, they had begun selling arms to Iran, with the proceeds siphoned off to the Contra rebels opposing the left-wing Sandinista government in Nicaragua.

The U.S. was far less impressed by Saddam's next military venture — his invasion of Kuwait. Saddam's 'spectacular victory' over Iran had left Iraq with a debt of around $60 billion, most of it owed to Saudi Arabia and Kuwait. He had hoped that they would forgo the debts in a spirit of Arab solidarity, but was sorely disappointed. Kuwait had originally been part of Mesopotamia but was hived off when Iraq was created, and the Ba'athists had long wanted it back. Saddam now accused it of exceeding oil export quotas, thus making oil cheaper and hurting Iraq's economy.

Iraq began bombing Kuwait City on 2 August 1990. Iraqi troops rolled across the border, easily overcoming Kuwaiti forces, and the Emir of Kuwait fled. It was all over in twelve hours. The United Nations and the Arab League immediately condemned the invasion, with the former imposing economic sanctions on Iraq, and Saddam responded by taking Westerners in Iraq hostage. In one of the great PR fails of all time, Iraqi television broadcast footage of him meeting with a group of British hostages and their children. Singling out five-year-old Stuart Lockwood, he put his arm around the boy, asked him (through an interpreter) if he had been getting milk with his breakfast, and tried to sit him on his lap. The fatherly act that Saddam liked to put on in Iraq didn't play so well with an international audience.

Fearing that Iraq was about to invade Saudi Arabia, which

would have given Saddam control of most of the world's oil reserves, President George H.W. Bush began sending troops there, while his administration put together a coalition to free Kuwait. Thirty-four countries eventually joined it, including Arab countries, making it the largest coalition put together since World War II. Saddam was defiant, going on radio to declare that Iraq would inevitably triumph in what would be "the mother of all battles".

The campaign to liberate Kuwait, codenamed Operation Desert Storm, began in January 1991 with a massive aerial bombardment of Iraq that went on for weeks and destroyed much of its infrastructure. (The Presidential Palace, Ba'ath Party headquarters and the Ministry of Defence were all flattened on the first day.) Realising how badly he had miscalculated, Saddam tried to reframe his invasion of Kuwait as part of the ongoing struggle against Israel, which failed to convince anyone, then offered to withdraw his troops — but only after all other problems in the Middle East had been resolved. This offer was, not surprisingly, rejected. Coalition troops entered Iraq on 24 February, and several epic tank battles followed. Meanwhile, coalition forces in Kuwait were meeting little resistance from the Iraqis. Realising the game was up, Saddam ordered his troops to retreat from Kuwait City on 27 February. They set off along the main highway to the Iraqi city of Basra, only to be bombed mercilessly from the air. The 'Highway of Death', as it became known, was littered with hundreds of wrecked and smouldering vehicles, many containing charred corpses, and became the most enduring image of the Gulf War.

Saddam went on Iraqi radio to sum up his latest military adventure as only he could. "Applaud your victories, my dear citizens," he said. "You have faced thirty countries and the evil they have brought here. You have faced the whole world, great Iraqis. You have won. You are victorious. How sweet victory is."

The Bush administration had considered following the liberation of Kuwait by pushing on into Iraq and taking Saddam down, but decided that the cost in American lives would not be worth it, while there was no viable opposition that could take over. Instead, Bush gave a speech in which he urged the Iraqi people to "take matters into their own hands" and rise up against him. Naturally, some Iraqis took this to mean that the U.S. would actively support such actions. Shiites in the north, and Kurds in the south, duly launched uprisings, but with the U.S. failing to step in, Saddam was able to crush them.

The Gulf War left Iraq's economy close to ruin. Its electricity and telecommunications infrastructure had largely been destroyed, as had its ability to produce oil. In any case, the economic sanctions imposed after it invaded Kuwait remained in place, and Iraq was prevented from selling oil to other countries. Wages plummeted and many people were close to starvation. (A United Nations report in 1997 found that almost a third of Iraqi children under five were malnourished.) Most of the social progress that Saddam had achieved in the early years of his regime, including the emancipation of women, was wiped out. Meanwhile, he ensured that members of the Ba'ath Party were taken care of, while he and his family continued to enrich themselves.

Indeed, as his people starved, Saddam increasingly flaunted his wealth (estimated to total some seven billion dollars in 2000, most of it salted away in other countries). He thought wealth was a symbol of power, while he was also keen to demonstrate that sanctions weren't hurting *him*. He became addicted to building palaces, erecting up to fifty of them around the country. Many of these were vast structures, built in a mix of modernist and Islamic styles, with bunkers and escape tunnels beneath them, and surrounded by manicured

gardens, fountains and manmade lakes. Their interiors were dictator chic on steroids: lots of gold, crystal chandeliers, marble floors, porcelain figurines and fake antique furniture, including an elaborate throne for Saddam to sit on. But by far the most bizarre features of the palaces were the artworks that hung on their walls. Unbeknownst to the Iraqi people (who rarely saw a painting without Saddam in it), he had developed a love for fantasy art with a notably erotic bent. Think long-haired, bare-chested, sword-wielding warriors and naked, pneumatic women locked in fierce combat with dragons, serpents and other fantastical monsters. They were the sort of works to be found on the covers of sword-and-sorcery paperbacks, and after his downfall, two original works by the American artist Rowena Morrill, one of the most celebrated practitioners of the genre, were found on his walls. When told about this, Morrill was understandably bemused.

Saddam instituted a personality cult almost as elaborate

and all-encompassing as that of the Kims in North Korea. As soon as Iraqis got out of bed in the morning, they were likely to be confronted by their president's face. It was on banknotes and stamps, the front pages of newspapers, and posters plastered virtually everywhere you looked. There was a statue of Saddam in every town square, while it became almost compulsory for buildings housing government ministries and other organisations to feature on an external wall a huge, hand-painted, appropriately-themed mural of Saddam. (The Ministry of Health, for example, had one of Saddam patting the head of a sick man, while the Ministry of Justice had him in a judge's robes, holding a scale of justice.) Some Iraqi artists had full-time careers creating images of Saddam, and in the mid-1990s, he was listed in the *Guinness Book of Records* as the most painted head of state in the world. In the evening, Iraqi television broadcast video montages of Saddam going about the business of being father of his nation, accompanied by tacky pop songs extolling his praises. On news broadcasts, he was inevitably the lead story.

addam's eldest son, Uday, was almost a caricature of a spoilt dictator's son. He liked sports cars, cigars, scotch whisky, gold jewellery, flashy clothes, cowboy hats and young women in great numbers. When drunk, as he often was, he was prone to acts of psychotic violence, and was notorious for raping and beating up women. He was the head of Iraq's Olympic Committee and Football Association, and had players who underperformed tortured, ordering them to be flogged with electrical cables or thrown into vats of raw sewage. He also kept pet lions, and is said to have once had two nineteen-year-old students who had offended him thrown into their cage where they were eaten. Behind the scenes, Uday ran an elaborate smuggling operation designed to circumvent the sanctions, which brought in a huge amount of money for Saddam and his family.

Saddam was close friends with his chief food taster, Hanna Jajo. In the late 1980s, Jajo introduced him to Samira Shabander, an air stewardess who was married to the head of Iraqi Airways. Saddam immediately fell in love with her, and made her his second wife after she had divorced. His first wife, Sajida, and the rest of his family were outraged by this, none more so than Uday. One night in 1988, he turned up drunk at a party where Jajo was present and beat him to death with a club. Saddam went ballistic. He threw Uday into prison where he languished for weeks, then packed him off to Switzerland. He eventually cooled down and let Uday return.

Uday was racking up quite a few enemies, and there was little surprise when, as he was being driven to a party a year later, his Porsche was sprayed with bullets. He was hit eight times, and his chauffeur was killed. He never completely recovered from his injuries, which left him in constant pain, partially crippled (as well as impotent, some said), and more sadistic than ever.

As Saddam's eldest son, Uday had originally been seen as his heir apparent, but as his behaviour grew increasingly unhinged, Saddam turned to his younger son, Qusay, who was certainly a more level-headed man than his brother. Unlike Uday, he looked like Saddam and modelled himself on him. He was married with four children, worked hard and drank moderately, although he could be as brutal as anyone when the occasion required it.

Saddam's daughters Rana and Raghad married two brothers who were cousins of their father — Saddam and Hussein Kamel. Like most of Saddam's relatives, they were given plum government posts. Saddam Kamel worked in Iraq's secret service, while Hussein Kamel became Minister of Defence and was instrumental in establishing the elite Republican Guards, until Uday, jealous of his power and influence on Saddam, forced him out. Uday harboured another grudge against Saddam's half-brother, Watban Ibrahim, who was minister of the interior, and also managed to have him removed from office, but he still wasn't happy. In 1995, he arrived at a party at Saddam Kamel's house where Watban was present. Uday was carrying a sub-machine gun, and after getting into a fist-fight with Saddam Kamel, who knocked him down, he started firing. He killed six young women, but only managed to hit Watban in the leg.

The Kamel brothers decided they had had enough and made the drastic decision to defect from Iraq, taking their wives and children with them. One night in August 1995, they boarded a fleet of Mercedes and drove to Jordan, where they asked King Hussein for asylum. While he had originally been an ally of Saddam's, relations between their respective countries had cooled significantly since then, and after consulting President Clinton (who promised U.S. protection for Jordan), he welcomed the defectors. A few days later, Hussein Kamel gave a press conference where he denounced Saddam and called on the Iraqi army to overthrow him. He also gave information to the U.S. about Iraq's chemical weapons program, with which he had been heavily involved. Saddam, needless to say, was furious. He had dozens of the brothers' associates arrested, and sent Uday to Jordan to try to get them back, but King Hussein proved immune to his charms.

Hussein Kamel's call for revolution was a flop. The brothers had been far too enmeshed in the regime to be welcomed by Iraq's fragmented opposition, and the U.S. lost interest in them once they had given up all their secrets. After a few months living in relative seclusion in Jordan, they became bored and homesick. Then, one day, Hussein Kamel's phone rang. It was Saddam, and he assured him that if they all returned, all would be forgiven. Incredibly, Hussein believed him. Shortly after this, the brothers and their families got back into their Mercedes and returned to Iraq. On crossing the border, they were greeted by Uday who managed to whisk away Saddam's daughters and their children. The brothers returned to their home town of Tikrit, and their house was soon surrounded by Republican Guards. After a gun battle lasting thirteen hours, they were dead.

addam grew increasingly disengaged from the day-to-day running of Iraq during the last years of his rule. Paranoid about assassination attempts, he rarely appeared in public, and moved around the country constantly, spending each night in a different house or palace. He delegated foreign and internal affairs to subordinates for the first time, and concentrated on projects designed to secure his name for posterity, such as the rebuilding of Babylon. (Sadly, Iraq's poverty meant plans to recreate the Hanging Gardens and the Tower of Babel had to be shelved.) Saddam also became much more religious, and prayed diligently every day. In 1997, he commissioned a unique copy of the Koran, written in his own blood, as a lasting testimony to his piety. It took a calligrapher two years to complete. Some have questioned how Saddam could have provided enough blood for this in just two years, but it seems his blood was mixed with chemicals. (What to do with this book would pose something of a quandary for Iraqi clerics after Saddam's downfall — it's apparently heretical to render the Koran in blood, but it's also forbidden to destroy a Koran.) Perhaps the strangest development during Saddam's last years, though, was his sudden transformation into a novelist.

Saddam was a lifelong reader (his favourite book was

Hemingway's *The Old Man and the Sea*). His first novel, *Zabiba and the King*, appeared in 2000, and although it was published anonymously, no-one in Iraq was in any doubt about who wrote it. Set in the seventh century, it tells the story of a king who falls in love with a young girl named Zabiba who is married to a man who mistreats her. Most of the novel consists of long conversations about statecraft between the king and Zabiba, who urges him to leave his palace with few windows, get out among the people and become one with them. One night, on her way home from the palace, Zabiba is accosted by three masked men armed with swords. Their leader knocks Zabiba down, beats her and rapes her. She resists fiercely and manages to bite her attacker on the neck. Arriving home, she sees her husband wrapping a bandage around his neck, and rushes back to the palace to tell the king what has happened. Zabiba's husband turns out to be one of a group of rebels who have been plotting against the king. The rebellion is crushed by the king with the help of Zabiba, who dies during the fighting and is hailed as a martyr.

On one level, the book is an allegory. The king represents Saddam of course, Zabiba represents the Iraqi people, and Zabiba's husband represents America, the country that raped Iran by bombing it during the Gulf War. (After she has been raped, Zabiba muses that the gang that attacked her could not attack the king directly. "So why not throw shame on the king by attacking his beloved? By taking her and destroying her from the inside, by making her an outcast among the surrounding peoples.") The book also clearly had a personal meaning for Saddam. Zabiba was based on Sa'adoon al Zubaydi, a twenty-four-year-old girl who became his fourth wife in 2000. She apparently encouraged him to write the book, in which Saddam clearly expresses his frustration at being so isolated from other people, a prisoner in safe houses and his own palaces.

Zabiba and the King may be a dreadful novel, but it does give some insight into the sometimes peculiar recesses of its author's mind. By far its strangest passage comes after Zabiba has been raped. She's lying on the ground, being comforted by her horse, and pondering the fact that human beings can be much worse than beasts.

> *Even an animal respects a man's desire, if it wants to copulate with him. Doesn't a female bear try to please a herdsman when she drags him into the mountains as it happens in the North of Iraq? She drags him into her den, so that he, obeying her desire, would copulate with her. Doesn't she bring him nuts, gathering them from the trees or picking them from the bushes? Doesn't she climb into the houses of farmers in order to steal some cheese, nuts, and even raisins, so that she can feed the man and awake in him the desire to have her?*

Zabiba and the King was published in an edition of a million copies, relentlessly publicised on television and radio, and made into a hit play. It was followed by three more novels: *The Fortified Castle*, *Men and the City* (a fictionalised account of the rise of the Ba'athist Party) and *Be Gone Demons!* Some have doubted whether Saddam actually wrote these books, but this is to underestimate how seriously he took his writing career. (Later, after he had been captured by the Americans, his biggest complaint was that they wouldn't allow him to have writing materials — they feared he might try to commit suicide with a pen — so he could finish a book he had started while on the run.) Indeed, towards the end, Saddam seems to have been so consumed by his writing that he withdrew almost completely from politics. In 2003, as the American-led coalition geared up to invade Iraq, all he could think about were the proofs of his last novel.

After the Gulf War ended in 1991, the United Nations established a commission to ensure that Saddam no longer had weapons of mass destruction (chemical, biological and nuclear). It toured the country for years, inspecting facilities and destroying stockpiles of banned weapons. The commission's presence enraged Saddam. He expelled all its American members from Iraq in 1997, and the following year, announced that he would no longer co-operate with the weapons inspectors at all. President Clinton and his administration had been hoping that the economic sanctions, combined with U.S. support for Iraqi opposition groups, would lead to Saddam's downfall. As this clearly wasn't happening any time soon, they resorted to military action. Over four days in December 1998, American and British forces rained bombs and missiles on a hundred Iraqi military installations.

While President Clinton loathed Saddam, he resisted

calls to deal with him decisively by invading Iraq. George W. Bush, elected in in 2000, was more open to the idea (while he clearly thought he had some unfinished business of his father's to attend to). He brought a number of prominent 'neocons' into his administration, including his secretary of defence, Donald Rumsfeld, who believed that the U.S. had a duty to impose democracy on totalitarian regimes. After the September 11 attacks in 2001 and the U.S. invasion of Afghanistan, the neocons argued that Iraq should be next, claiming that Saddam had given aid to al-Qaeda. Cooler heads in the administration pointed out that a secular regime like the Ba'athist one in Iraq was unlikely to have any truck with the religious fanatics of al-Qaeda, and that the evidence that Saddam still had WMDs was ambiguous at best (while even if he did, he posed no direct threat to the U.S.). Nevertheless, Bush's rhetoric on Iraq grew more bellicose as the months went by, while Saddam reaffirmed his position as Iraq's leader by holding an election in October 2002. His motto during the campaign was "Everyone loves Saddam", and its theme song was Whitney Houston's 'I Will Always Love You', which was on high rotation on radio and television. In the end, Saddam, the sole candidate, received 100 per cent of the vote, an even better result than the previous election where he had scored only 99.96 per cent. He also tried to mollify the U.N. by allowing weapons inspectors back into Iraq.

The U.S. hoped to put together a broad coalition for the invasion of Iraq, as it had earlier done for the liberation of Kuwait. Bush found a firm ally in British prime minister Tony Blair, but most other governments were opposed to the war, and in February 2003 there were anti-war demonstrations in sixty countries (the one in Rome attracted three million people and is considered to have been the largest anti-war demonstration in history). In the end, only British, Australian and Polish troops would join the invasion. Meanwhile, as forces were gathering against him, Saddam reacted with all the crazed bravado you would expect from a man who had hailed the bloody debacle of the Iran-Iraq War a victory. "Our chests are filled with the great conviction in our victory," he declared, "whose fruit will be in our hands and whose banners will be all over our heads as a great people in a glorious nation..." As the invasion got under way, he would be equalled in bombast by his chief government spokesman, Mohammed Saeed al-Sahhaf, whose daily press conferences and ridiculous pronouncements earned him the nickname 'Comical Ali' (a play on 'Chemical Ali', the nickname of Saddam's gas-happy cousin). His finest moment would be to deny that American tanks had entered Baghdad when they could actually be heard rumbling in the distance.

The Presidential Palace in Baghdad was bombed on 20 March, and coalition troops entered Iraq the following day. They encountered little resistance from the Iraqi army, and reached Baghdad on 7 April. Television reports showed American soldiers wandering around one of Saddam's garish palaces by the Tigris River, staring in amazement at the fantasy paintings and atrocious furniture. Two days later, Baghdad fell, and the occasion was marked by the pulling down of a large bronze statue of Saddam in Firdos Square which was broadcast live around the world.

Saddam had gone into hiding, and his whereabouts would be unknown for nine months. During this time he released a number of audio and video tapes, urging the Iraqi people to fight on. In July, his sons Uday and Qusay were killed in a gun battle in Mosul. Photos of their bullet-riddled bodies were released to prove to Iraqis they were dead.

In December, the U.S. forces received a tip-off that Saddam was hiding at a farmhouse near Al-Dawr, a village south of Tikrit. The man who had owned fifty palaces was found in a hole eight feet by six feet (2.4 metres by 1.8 metres) wide,

equipped with one lightbulb and a fan. He was heavily bearded, dressed in a white T-shirt, black shirt and black pants, and carried a pistol. Dragged out of the hole by American soldiers, he announced, "I am Saddam Hussein. I'm the president of Iraq and I want to negotiate." The fact that he surrendered so meekly, rather than going out in a hail of bullets — as the script demanded — caused great consternation and disappointment throughout the Arab world.

Shortly after the war's conclusion, the U.S. Senate issued a report saying that the intelligence assessments regarding Saddam's links to al-Qaeda and his continued possession of weapons of mass destruction were wrong. And yet, on the latter point at least, the failure of the intelligence services could to some extent be forgiven. Saddam had indeed complied with U.N. demands to destroy his WMDs, but, believing that his prestige and power in the region depended on having them, he could never bring himself to admit this.

fter his capture, Saddam was taken to the American 'Green Zone' in Baghdad where he was interrogated by CIA analysts including John Nixon, who later wrote a book about the experience called *Debriefing the President*. It's a fascinating account, not least because it's so rare for former dictators to be asked to account for themselves. Saddam, who was brought into the interrogation room every day with a hood over his head, still considered himself president of Iraq, and found the whole process impertinent, but he was also a man who liked to talk. While clearly evasive in some of his answers, at other times he seems to have been quite frank, and he only blew his top once — when questioned about the gassing of Iraqi Kurds (a people he had professed to love and respect earlier in the interrogation). The only mistake he admitted to making was failing to co-operate more fully with the U.N. weapons inspectors, saying, "I don't exclude myself from the blame." As for America's prospects in Iraq, he was scathing. "You will fail. You are going to find that it is not so easy to govern Iraq." Given the chaos that enveloped the country and the wider Arab world after the invasion, this was, if anything, an understatement.

"You are going to fail in Iraq," Saddam continued, "because you do not know the language, the history, and you do not understand the Arab mind." This was a problem that went both ways, however, for it's abundantly clear that Saddam understood little about the world outside the Middle East, and the United States in particular. (Saddam was once interviewed for American television by the journalist Diane Sawyer, who asked him about the death penalty that applied in Iraq for anyone who criticised the president. Saddam was incredulous when Sawyer told him that the same did not apply in the U.S.) Perhaps the most astonishing thing to emerge during the interrogation is how little planning, or war-gaming, or consideration of possible consequences took place before Saddam ordered the invasions of Iran and Kuwait. And when things started going wrong, there was never any Plan B.

Saddam was charged with crimes against humanity, and his trial commenced in October 2005. He remained defiant throughout, refusing to recognise the legitimacy of the court (while many international observers agreed that it was a show trial). Saddam was found guilty and sentenced to death by hanging on 5 November 2006 — his request to be executed by firing squad was denied. A Shiite government under President Nuri al-Maliki was now in power, and he wanted Saddam executed as quickly as possible. With the Islamic holiday of Eid al-Adha approaching, the American government thought it would be prudent to have the execution delayed, but the U.S. military in Iraq wanted to be rid of Saddam as much as al-Maliki, and persuaded the acting U.S. ambassador to authorise a handover. This took place after midnight on 30 December, after which the Iraqis took Saddam to an army base in Baghdad.

A grainy video showing what happened next was soon released and screened on Iraqi TV, then around the world. Saddam, wearing a long black overcoat and looking about as calm and resigned as you could in such circumstances, is seen being led up a set of metal steps. A masked man puts a noose around his neck as other men present shout things like "Go to hell" at him. Saddam is in mid-prayer when the trapdoor opens.

CHAPTER 11

KIM JONG-IL

KIM JONG-IL

Attained power in the 1980s
Died from a probable heart attack in 2011

The working people of socialist North Korea normally work eight hours, rest eight hours, and spend the remaining eight hours studying or in cultural activities.

However, there is a great leader possessed of a revolutionary fighting spirit, inexhaustible energy, extraordinary ability and vigour. He solves any problem, however difficult, purposely, gives directions and deals with a number of work-items simultaneously; but he knows no rest. It is none other than Secretary Kim Jong Il, the indomitable revolutionary fighter. I could say many other laudatory things about him, but even if I did, I cannot help feeling that they would fail to do justice to him.

—From *A Paean of Great Love: Kim Jong Il and the People*

im Jong-il was indeed a remarkable man. He was a child prodigy who could speak at the age of three weeks, and while a university student wrote fifteen hundred books. He was an artist, a poet, an architect, a musician, a clothes designer, a composer of operas, a genius of cinema. The first time he set foot on a golf course, he scored eleven holes in one.

Whatever you think about these claims and even wilder ones (did I mention he invented the hamburger?), Kim did have one remarkable achievement to his name: coming to power in the first place. It's often assumed that, as the son of North Korea's founder and 'Great Leader', Kim Il-sung, he had his job handed to him on a plate. In fact, the younger Kim wheedled and intrigued his way into power with as much rat cunning as any dictator.

Goebbels wrote, "If you tell a lie big enough and keep repeating it, people will eventually come to believe it", and few nations have been based on bigger lies than North Korea. It all began with Kim Il-sung, who wasn't really Kim Il-sung. He was an impostor.

His real name Kim Song-ju, and he was born in a village near Pyongyang in 1912. The Japanese had annexed Korea two years earlier, and when Kim was seven, he and his family crossed the Chinese border into Manchuria, where economic conditions were somewhat better. Kim was educated in a Chinese school, and joined the Chinese Communist Party in 1931, the year that Japan invaded Manchuria. From the mid-1930s, Kim was the leader of a guerrilla unit fighting the Japanese, but contrary to his later myth, he never fought them on Korean soil. By 1941, the Japanese Imperial Army had cut such a swathe through the resistance that Kim and his remaining fighters were forced to seek refuge in the Soviet Union, where he became the captain of a battalion in the Red Army.

Following Japan's surrender, Korea was divided, with the North controlled by the Soviets, and the South by the United States. (Nobody thought to ask the Koreans what they thought about this, which was a bit rough given they had been victims of the Japanese during the war, not aggressors.) The Soviets needed someone to lead a puppet government in the North, and Kim, whose leadership qualities had been noticed, was placed on a shortlist, with Stalin making the final decision. Kim was unknown in Korea though, and at some point it was decided to pass him off as Kim Il-sung, a

legendary guerrilla leader who had been born in 1905 and *had* fought the Japanese in Korea.

When Kim arrived in North Korea in September 1945, people were baffled — the boyish thirty-three-year-old looked nothing like the famous guerrilla leader, and many saw through the ruse immediately. (Kim, who hadn't been in the country since he was seven, also spoke Korean so poorly he had to have lessons.) To bolster his image, the Soviet propaganda machine went into action, embellishing Kim's wartime record, presenting him as a tactical genius with almost superhuman qualities. It was the beginning of the Kim Il-sung personality cult.

Kim set about reorganising North Korea on Stalinist lines. Industry was nationalised, land was seized from wealthy landowners and distributed to peasants, and programs to tackle the country's chronic levels of illiteracy were introduced. The early results were very promising, making Kim Il-sung an immensely popular leader.

With the help of the Soviets, Kim also built up the North Korean Army into a formidable force. He was intent on reunifying Korea — under his rule of course. Stalin was wary, but Kim argued that the U.S. wouldn't come to South Korea's aid if the North Koreans attacked, and that communists in the south would rise up to support them. Neither assumption would prove correct but Stalin allowed himself to be persuaded, and on 25 June 1950, the North Korean Army, equipped with a hundred and fifty Soviet tanks, crossed the border. (Kim always claimed — and North Koreans still believe — they were retaliating after an attack from the South.) In four days they had overtaken the South Korean capital, Seoul, but President Truman was also quick off the mark. The first U.S. troops arrived in July, and although they too were initially overwhelmed by the North Koreans, a ferocious U.S. bombing campaign stopped them in their tracks. The Americans were eventually joined by troops from Britain, Canada, Australia and other countries, fighting under the banner of the United Nations for the first time. They recaptured Seoul in September, then pushed into North Korea and took its capital, Pyongyang in October. In desperation, Kim appealed to Mao Zedong for help, and he agreed to send Chinese forces.

When the Korean War ground to a halt after three years, 3.5 million people were dead (including 2.5 million North Koreans, a quarter of the population), and most of North Korea had been reduced to rubble. And it had all been for nothing — the border between North and South remained virtually unchanged, although it was transformed into a 4-kilometre-wide 'Demilitarized Zone'. This didn't prevent Kim Il-sung from proclaiming the campaign a magnificent victory (while having many army officers and others he blamed for its failure imprisoned or executed).

Kim never gave up his ambition to reunite Korea, but after the war concentrated on making his case by building up the North Korean economy. In this, he was initially successful, with economic growth in the North outstripping the South until the end of the 1960s. However, as most of this was concentrated in heavy industry — the first love of all Stalinists — few of the benefits flowed down to ordinary people. Kim had promised them they would "live in tile-roofed houses, clothed in silk, eating rice and meat soup". As it happened, most of them ended up living in shoddy concrete apartment blocks, clothed in a synthetic fabric called vinalon, eating more corn than rice and dreaming of meat soup.

Life for Kim Il-sung and his family was different. Their principle residence was a huge estate in Pyongyang surrounded by high walls, while Kim had dozens of villas, often described as palaces, dotted around the country. And while most North Koreans survived on the barely adequate

rations supplied by the state, all of Kim's food came from special farms, orchards and greenhouses. Grains of rice for the Great Leader's table were individually polished to ensure that every last one of them was perfect.

ccording to the official accounts, Kim Jong-il was born in a log cabin on the slopes of Mount Paektu in northern Korea, the tallest mountain in the country and a place of great spiritual significance for Koreans, in 1942. At the moment of his birth, a thunderstorm abated and the clouds parted to reveal a brilliantly-coloured double rainbow and a new star twinkling in the sky. The cabin where he was born is now a regular place of pilgrimage for North Koreans.

In fact, Kim was born in Vyatskoye, a village in Siberia, in 1941. His mother, Kim Jong-suk, was Kim Il-sung's first wife and a former member of his guerrilla unit (she had been its seamstress), and had accompanied him when he fled to the Soviet Union. As a child, and for many years afterwards, Kim Jong-il was known by the Russian name 'Yura'.

After Kim Il-sung's triumphant return to Korea, Kim Jong-il grew up in luxury, surrounded by people who fawned on him as he stomped around in a miniature army uniform, issuing orders to the servants. His childhood was not a happy one, though. When he was six, his younger brother Shura drowned in the family pool, and his mother, whom he adored, died in 1949. When the Korean War broke out the following year, he was evacuated from Pyongyang and didn't see his father again for several years.

Few North Koreans were aware of Kim Jong-il's existence until the 1970s, when he became his father's heir apparent. At that point, North Korea's propaganda machine, with a lot of input from Kim himself, began creating a backstory for him, but they had their work cut out. Kim was chubby and short,

standing around 5 feet 2 inches (1.58 metres) tall. (Later, his height would be augmented by his trademark bouffant hairdo and high heels.) He lacked his father's good looks and charisma, and there were no wartime exploits that could be embellished endlessly. Instead, the propagandists emphasised the younger Kim's genius. According to the official biographies that now began to appear, he had been a brilliant school student who wrote a commentary on Lenin's treatise *The State and Revolution* at the age of eight. Recognising his young son's gifts, Kim Il-sung had taken him along as he travelled around the country delivering his 'on the spot' guidance at farms and factories, pointing out ways to improve conditions which had escaped other mere mortals. Later, when he attended Kim Il-sung University, lecturers had kept a close eye on him when they spoke in case his expression indicated they had made an error, and a few words of criticism from his lips would lead to the curriculum being instantly changed. Of course, he had won every academic honour going.

Those who actually knew him at the time remembered a different Kim — one who had little time for studying. He preferred watching foreign movies (which would become a lifelong obsession), hosting wild parties, chasing girls and tearing around the otherwise empty streets of Pyongyang on an imported motorbike.

Kim Il-sung began a massive build-up of North Korea's armed forces during the 1960s. It became, and remains, the most militarised nation on earth, with almost all young men expected to spend ten years in the army. The ostensible reason for this was the threat of imminent invasion by the U.S. and South Korea. Meanwhile, South Koreans were terrified by the prospect of imminent invasion by the North, and their fears weren't allayed when it was reported the North

Koreans were digging huge tunnels beneath the Demilitarized Zone. Then there were the random acts of aggression Kim delighted in. For example, in 1968 he despatched thirty-one commandos across the border — their mission, to assassinate South Korea's President Park Chung-hee. They almost did it, too, with most of them killed as they neared the presidential residence. (However, one commando defected as soon as he saw that South Korea was nothing like the war-ravaged, impoverished American colony depicted in North Korean propaganda.)

North Korea was drawing even further into itself. Kim Il-sung had adopted a new economic policy known as *juche* or 'self-reliance', which virtually ended trade — and indeed all contact — between North Korea and the rest of the world. The policy had been conceived after Kim fell out with his most important allies, the Soviet Union and China, but it soon became an end in itself. The idea of *juche* struck a chord with Koreans, a fiercely proud and nationalistic people — Korea was known as the 'Hermit Kingdom' long before the Kims came along. It also served to differentiate Kim from other communist leaders, and is considered one of the reasons why North Korea has survived when almost all the other communist regimes have collapsed.

Kim Il-sung was also thinking about a successor, and by the late 1960s it was clear it would be a member of his own family, probably one of his sons. This was an idea that defied all the tenets of Marxism-Leninism, but in the North Korean context made a kind of sense. Kim had been appalled to see Stalin's reputation trashed by his successor Khrushchev, and didn't want the same thing happening to him. The concept of a dynastic succession also conformed to Confucianist principles, including the importance of filial loyalty, and the idea that the eldest son should inherit the family's wealth. From this perspective, Kim Jong-il was the obvious choice to succeed his father, but the situation wasn't that simple.

In 1963, Kim Il-sung had taken another wife, his former secretary, Kim Sung-ae. Kim Jong-il hated her and refused to call her mother, and his resentment increased when she had two sons whom his father clearly liked more than him. As the first lady of North Korea, Kim Sung-ae gained considerable power, occupying a similar position to Mao's wife Jiang Qing in China. Her eldest son, Kim Pong-Il, was considered to be the most likely successor, while another contender was Kim Il-sung's younger brother, Kim Yong-ju. No-one thought that Kim Jong-il was in the running.

Faced with these obstacles, Kim Jong-il adopted a simple strategy. He would prove himself to be the most loyal follower of his father in the country, and the foremost interpreter of his thought. If Kim Il-sung's legacy was to be preserved, he was the man to do it.

After graduating from university in 1964, Kim went to work for the Central Committee of the Korean Worker's Party, and became one of the main players in North Korea's version of Mao's Cultural Revolution. This essentially involved raising the personality cult of Kim Il-sung to dizzying new heights. The roles that other Korean partisans and the Chinese played in defeating Japan were written out of history, so that Kim appeared to have done it virtually single handed. As one official biographer put it, Kim was "a legendary hero…capable of commanding heavens and earth, an unrivalled brilliant commander who, as it were, can shrink a long range of steep mountains at a stroke and smash the swarming hordes of enemies with one blow." Another wrote that he "turned pine cones into bullets and grains of sand into rice, and crossed a large river riding on fallen leaves". The official ideology of North Korea would henceforth be known as 'Kimilsungism', with all cultural products including books, movies and plays focusing on the 'Sun of Mankind'.

Kim Jong-il threw himself into the job with enthusiasm. He arranged for statues of Kim Il-sung to be erected in town squares, and designed the first badges bearing his face. It became compulsory to wear these badges, and to hang a portrait of the Great Leader in your living room. (Failing to dust it properly — and there were regular inspections — could lead to a hefty prison sentence.) For his father's sixtieth birthday, Kim had a huge bronze statue of him, 66 feet (20 metres) high, erected in Kim Il-sung Square in Pyongyang. It was originally covered with gold leaf worth an astonishing $850 million, until China's Deng Xiaoping, shown the statue on a visit, pointed out this was a bit ridiculous for a communist country.

Kim Jong-il was zealous in purging officials who had, in his eyes, deviated from the party line. Thousands were banished to the country's extensive gulag system where they were horribly tortured, then worked to death. In furthering his leadership ambitions, he had to tread very carefully, though. On one occasion, when a Party official suggested he would be a worthy successor to his father, he had the man shot for being disloyal to Kim Il-sung.

One of Kim's last memories of his mother was watching with her the very first North Korean film, *My Home Village* (which helped to create the myth that Kim Il-sung's guerrillas had defeated the Japanese), and his obsession with cinema has often been traced to this event. As a teenager, he had North Korean embassies around the world working overtime making illegal copies of films and sending them to Pyongyang where they were dubbed so he could watch them — and he is said to have watched *all of them*. Kim rarely left North Korea in his lifetime, and his perception of the outside world largely derived from movies. He eventually amassed a collection of over fifteen thousand titles which were kept in a heavily-fortified three-storey building. His favourites were James Bond films and anything with Elizabeth Taylor.

Kim was able to marry his political ambitions and his love of movies when he was appointed director of the Propaganda and Agitation Department. He set about reshaping North Korea's primitive film industry, criticising film-makers for favouring aesthetics over ideology, involving himself in all aspects of production from scriptwriting to editing, and even writing a handbook for directors. The first film he supervised, *Sea of Blood*, about a brave female partisan fighting the Japanese, was released in 1969 and greeted with enthusiasm. It was followed by many others, including the film considered Kim's masterpiece, *The Flower Girl* (1974), in which the heroine suffers countless indignities at the hands of the Japanese until saved by Kim Il-sung's glorious (and fictitious) liberating army. It had North Korean audiences bawling their eyes out, and was even a hit in China. Kim also worked closely on operas, and his operatic version of *Sea of Blood* had another rapturous reception. It was, in fact, these cultural achievements that first brought him to the attention of the North Korean public. Kim Il-sung loved them, too, which wasn't surprising as they all portrayed him as the greatest man who ever lived.

The party's Central Committee endorsed Kim Jong-il as Kim Il-sung's successor in 1974. The decision wasn't made public though, and while his portrait began to be seen next to those of his father in public places, he was initially referred to in newspapers by the oblique title of 'the Party Centre' or, later, 'the Glorious Party Centre'. It seems there was some trepidation on the regime's part about announcing the Communist world's first hereditary succession plan, as well there might have been. Certainly, many of North Korea's old guard did not like or trust Kim Jong-il and were appalled by the idea. At one point, it appeared that their opposition to him had succeeded, for in October 1976 all his official portraits suddenly disappeared, and the 'Glorious Party Centre' was no longer heard from. Kim fought back, though, side-lining or purging his enemies, and arranging it so that all communications directed to his father had to first go through him. While Kim Il-sung was still officially the leader, and worshipped throughout the country as a god, Kim Jong-il was firmly in control of the party and the government. It seems that Kim Il-sung did not actually realise the extent to

which he had been usurped by his son.

While every bit as ruthless as his father, Kim Jong-il was a very different sort of leader. The elder Kim was a showman who liked to be seen by his people, and travelled around the country constantly delivering that famous 'on the spot' guidance. Kim Jong-il was, by contrast, almost a recluse. He rarely made public appearances, and when he did he never spoke (so that a rumour spread that he had some sort of speech impediment). Indeed, the North Korean public did not hear his voice until a ceremony in 1992 when he uttered a single sentence: "Glory to the People's Heroic Military."

Kim's managerial style was also different. Kim Il-sung conducted official business in a harmonious fashion, but Kim Jong-il seemed to thrive on conflict. When chairing meetings, he liked to see people at each other's throats, with everyone criticising everyone else and striving to demonstrate their superior loyalty.

Kim might have been difficult to work for, but those who pleased him were awarded handsomely. He was an inveterate gift giver, handing out Mercedes Benz cars, Omega watches,

Japanese television sets and other sought-after consumer items to those in his good books. He also had notoriously expensive tastes. He loved French wines, and had a cellar stocked with ten thousand bottles. He was the world's greatest consumer of Hennessy's Paradis cognac, importing up to $700,000 worth of it a year, and after ordering his embassies to send him samples of every brand of cigarette in the world, settled on Rothman's as his favourite. He had a team of chefs who could reproduce the signature dishes of many countries, with two brought in from Italy just to make him pizza. Like his father, Kim had palaces scattered around the country. They were equipped with swimming pools, golf courses, stables for his imported thoroughbred horses, fun fair rides and hunting grounds where Kim could shoot ducks and wild deer.

Then there were the infamous drinking parties that he held once a week. The venue was usually a large and featureless building in Pyongyang which served as a combined banquet hall, disco and cinema, and was known as the 'Fish House' because of its floor-to-ceiling aquarium. He liked to arrive at the parties late, when the other guests — mostly high-ranking government officials and military men — were already drunk. As he sipped cognac, he directed proceedings, requesting the band to play his favourite South Korean songs (which the rest of the population would be arrested for listening to). There were always dancing girls present, and Kim would sometimes tell them to strip naked, then order his embarrassed guests to dance with them. He thought that observing people drunk was an excellent way to judge their characters, and it was understood that guests at the parties could say whatever they wanted to each other. Kim also liked to conduct official business during the parties, issuing orders which were written down and quickly actioned, despite the fact that he might have no memory of them when he sobered up.

Guests at the drinking parties were sworn to the strictest secrecy, and Kim Il-sung knew nothing about them. One of Kim Jong-il's secretaries made the mistake of telling his wife about them, and she was so shocked she wrote to Kim Il-sung. Kim Jong-il, of course, intercepted her letter, and the woman and her husband were invited to the next party where she was arrested. Kim announced to the other guests that she was to be shot there and then. Her husband, stepping up to the plate, begged Kim for the honour of shooting her himself, and Kim handed him a gun.

Much of the money to pay for Kim's lavish lifestyle came from an enterprise called Division 39 which, despite being set up within the party, was essentially a private company with Kim as its CEO. Although some of its activities, such as banking, were legal, Division 39 was primarily involved in arms dealing, counterfeiting (of both currency and products) and drug running on a massive scale. It brought in billions.

Kim Il-sung and Kim Jong-il may have differed in many ways, but they were in complete agreement on one subject — girls. Like Mao, both men thought it was their right and privilege to deflower the prettiest girls in the land, but Mao never organised his trysts on such an industrial scale.

Kim Il-sung had a reputation as a womaniser going back to his days in the 1930s fighting the Japanese. In addition to his official wives, he had numerous mistresses who gave birth to children over the years. (Some of his illegitimate sons, while never officially acknowledged, were given important posts in the regime.) After the end of the Korean War, a special unit was established within the Central Committee whose job was to scour schools across the country looking for girls who met the required standards — they had to be pretty, no more than 5 feet 4 inches (165 centimetres) tall, and have soft voices and no scars. Inducted into the so-called 'Joy Brigade' from the age of thirteen, they were given two years of extensive training in singing, dancing and satisfying the sexual preferences of the Great Leader, and later his son. They were then installed in the numerous villas that dotted the country, ready to provide their services should one of the Kims turn up. Families considered it a great honour if one of their daughters was chosen for the Joy Brigade, for it brought many material benefits (although few would have realised that sexual services were involved). After the girls had spent a few years in the Joy Brigade, marriages were arranged for them with up-and-coming young men within the Party who knew nothing of their pasts.

The Joy Brigade played an important part in the regime's efforts to prolong Kim Il-sung's life (following the Chinese belief that a man could live longer by sleeping with young girls). Easily the strangest task they are said to have performed was the so-called 'human bed', which involved a number of girls lying with their legs interlocked in a certain way, allowing the Great Leader to sleep on them.

Kim Jong-il also founded the Kim Il-sung Institute of Health and Longevity, the sole purpose of which was to keep the Great Leader alive. One of its recommendations was that he regularly eat dog penises at least 2.8 inches (7 centimetres) long.

For all his cinematic achievements, Kim Jong-il was painfully aware that North Korean films were still laughed at in other countries. What was to be done? The answer, when it came to him, must have seemed obvious: kidnap the most famous director and most famous actress in South Korea, and put them to work.

The director was Shin Sang-ok, the actress Choi Eun-hee.

Shin directed and produced over a hundred and fifty films during the 1950s and '60s, from black-and-white melodramas to Technicolor blockbusters, with many starring Choi, his wife and muse. By the late '70s, though, his career was in disarray. Shin and Choi had divorced after he had an affair with another actress, and he had fallen out of favour with the increasingly repressive South Korean government of General Park Chung-hee. In 1977, he abruptly lost his licence to make films, which left him devastated. Kim read about this and saw an opening.

In January 1978, Choi travelled to Hong Kong after being offered a business deal connected to the acting school she ran. Lured to a beach on Repulse Bay, she was bundled into a boat by men wearing long wigs and taken to a freighter which took her to North Korea. Still in a state of shock, she was met at the dock by a smiling Kim Jong-il who had a photographer ready to record the momentous event. Shin was initially suspected of being involved in her disappearance. Then, while searching for her in Hong Kong a few months later, he too was kidnapped.

Having obtained his prizes, Kim seemed in no hurry to put them to work. Choi was deposited in a luxurious but tacky mansion and subjected to endless hours of political indoctrination. She was also invited to his parties, and they developed an odd sort of bond, with Kim treating her like a mother figure. Shin, on the other hand, was kept at a distance, while undergoing the same mind-numbing schedule of indoctrination. While they had heard rumours, neither knew for certain that the other was in North Korea.

After making two escape attempts, Shin was taken to Prison Number 6, also known as the 'enlightenment centre'. It held six thousand prisoners who were given meagre rations and forced to sit in the 'torture position', cross-legged with heads bowed, in tiny cells for sixteen hours a day. If they moved a muscle they were beaten savagely. Shin was there for almost two-and-a-half years. Then, in 1983, he was suddenly told he was forgiven. Ten days later, five years after he had been kidnapped, he found himself at a lavish party in Pyongyang, reunited with Choi, as a beaming Kim announced to a cheering crowd that they would be put in charge of North Korean film production, and (to their surprise) they would be married again.

Shin went on to direct seven movies for Kim, with Choi appearing in most of them. Surprisingly, they were allowed to depart from the rigid propaganda that had characterised all the country's cinematic output until then, and the films included a thriller, a romance and a martial arts flick. When they were screened, North Korean audiences couldn't believe their eyes. Never before had they seen a realistic depiction of the world outside North Korea, or of love between a man and a woman, and the films were incredibly popular. They even won some international awards (albeit in communist countries). Kim's plan seemed to have worked perfectly, but the truth is that it backfired on him. In later years, many defectors from North Korea said that it had been Shin's films which first opened their eyes.

Despite the bizarre situation he was in, Shin found it exhilarating to be directing again. He and his crew were allowed to travel to Eastern Bloc countries for location shooting, and his budget had no limits. (When he told Kim he wanted a shot of a train blowing up, Kim gave him an actual train to blow up.) Yet he and Choi, who had quickly fallen in love again, never ceased to plan their escape. The fact that Kim allowed them out of the country provided them with their best chance, although they were always accompanied by bodyguards.

The last and certainly unlikeliest film Shin directed in North Korea was a Godzilla imitation called *Pulgasari*. Kim

was so keen for this to be a success that he imported the Japanese film crew that had worked on the latest Godzilla film, including the actor who wore the Godzilla suit. The result is a wonderful piece of schlock which has attained cult status among connoisseurs of bad films. Set in the middle ages, it tells the story of a village ruled by an evil governor who seizes the villagers' farming tools and cooking utensils to forge into weapons, threatening them with starvation. They find salvation in the form of Pulgasari, a tubby, dragon-like monster who eats iron and grows bigger the more he eats. After many epic battle scenes and Pulgasari rampaging around tearing down buildings, the governor is vanquished. But Pulgasari is still hungry and the villagers are forced to feed him their farming tools, putting them back where they started. On one level, it's a typical socialist fable about poor people rising up against an oppressor, but Shin's subversive streak is evident here. Pulgasari can be seen as representing the Kim dynasty which has supposedly saved North Korea from the evils of capitalism, only to offer it starvation.

Kim certainly didn't notice that, though, and was so pleased with the film he agreed to Shin's suggestion that they open up a production office in Vienna. Once there, Shin and Choi were able to give their bodyguards the slip and get to the American Embassy where they defected.

he North Korean regime had watched with annoyance and frustration as South Korea became an economic powerhouse. The last straw came when Seoul was awarded the 1988 summer Olympics. In 1987, two North Korean agents boarded a Korean Airlines passenger jet bound for Seoul and planted explosive devices in an overhead locker before disembarking at a stopover in Abu Dhabi. The plane exploded over the Andaman Sea, and all 115 people on board were killed. The agents were about to be arrested in Bahrain when they swallowed cyanide capsules, but one of them, Kim Hyon-hui, survived. She later confessed to the bombing, saying that Kim Jong-il had ordered it.

Kim had been hoping to dissuade people from travelling to Seoul for the Olympics, but the plan failed and they were a huge success. Determined not to be bested, he ordered that the World Festival of Youth, a sort of Communist version of the Olympics which Pyongyang was hosting in 1989, would be even more spectacular. In preparation for it, residents of the city who were deformed, disabled or simply too short were expelled. In a memoir published in 2008, Kim Hyun-sik, a former North Korean university professor who had taught Kim Jong-il, wrote that one of his friends, a doctor, had been responsible for getting rid of the short people. The operation began with party workers distributing leaflets claiming that the state had devised a new drug to boost people's height, and asking for volunteers to test it. Thousands of people turned up on the appointed day, and the doctor's task was to go among them, picking out the shortest. Told they would be taken somewhere with a clean environment where the drug would be more effective, they eagerly boarded two ships, one for the men, the other for the women. The ships set off, dropping the volunteers on various uninhabited islands where they were left to fend for themselves. Most were never seen again.

The handover of power from the elder Kim to the younger initially seemed to have positive results for ordinary North Koreans. There was a certain degree of cultural liberalisation, with classic works of Western literature being published in translation for the first time, and cassettes of foreign music for sale in the markets. Men were permitted to grow their hair longer, and women were encouraged to wear make-up and nice dresses. Even dancing was allowed! Foreign visitors to the country noted that the population seemed much less guarded, less glum than they had a decade earlier.

But much of this apparent change was illusory. Foreigners were generally restricted to Pyongyang, the country's well-scrubbed showpiece city. Kim had been reshaping it since the mid-'70s, ordering the demolition of whole neighbourhoods to make way for vast boulevards and motorways that would rarely see cars. Then there were the huge, mostly useless building projects that Kim always wanted completed at

super-fast speed, including an Arch of Triumph larger than the one in Paris, the Juche Tower topped by an illuminated metal flame, and a 105-storey pyramid-shaped hotel which has never hosted a single guest. In the rest of the country, however, the food shortages that had been a feature of life since the 1970s were becoming much worse. By the mid-1990s, the government rations that sustained the population began arriving later and later, then ceased altogether. Even the soldiers were starving. The regime tried to blame the famine on flooding (and there are still many accounts which accept this as a fact), but the truth is that Kim Il-sung's *juche* policy, the focus on military spending and the country's grossly inefficient command economy had all made the famine inevitable.

When Kim Il-sung belatedly became aware of the situation, he decided that funds should to be diverted from the military to pay for food and consumer goods. Kim Jong-il, who was now in charge of the military (despite having never been a soldier), resisted the idea. The two Kims were said to be in the middle of a heated argument about this when, despite the best efforts of the Institute of Health and Longevity and a steady stream of young women and dog penises, Kim Il-sung died from a heart attack in June 1994. Expertly embalmed by Soviet technicians, his corpse — which is still, by the way, officially North Korea's president — lies in state in a huge mausoleum on the outskirts of Pyongyang.

Meanwhile, the famine continued. It was a severe embarrassment for Kim Jong-il that it coincided with the death of his father and his own official assumption of power, for he knew that he did not command the loyalty among ordinary people that his father had. He tried to blame the food shortages on corrupt officials, and had the agriculture minister publicly executed. (To emphasise the point, he also ordered the previous agriculture minister, who had died in

1984, dug up from the Revolutionary Martyrs' Cemetery and shot as well.) But he remained unwilling to dilute the purity of the communist system. In a speech in 1994, he said that any move to private ownership or individualism would lead to "the exploitation and oppression of the popular masses by a small ruling class". (How did he keep a straight face?) Even Mao had been flexible enough to allow people to grow their own food and sell what they didn't need when he had to deal with his own mass famine following the Great Leap Forward. Instead, the North Korean government promoted recipes for the tasty and nutritious 'substitute foods' that could be made from bark, leaves, grass, corn cobs… In desperation, hundreds of thousands of people crossed the border into China, while others resorted to cannibalism. With civil disobedience breaking out across the country, and even members of the elite beginning to starve, the North Korean government was forced to swallow its pride and appeal for foreign aid.

At this point, with his regime at its most vulnerable, Kim was handed an unexpected lifeline by South Korea. A new left-wing government came to power there in 1998, and under President Kim Dae-jung introduced a 'Sunshine policy' of reconciliation with North Korea. Kim reacted cannily to this. He agreed to a few minor concessions, such as allowing some South Koreans to travel north for family reunions, and easing up a little on the military provocations. In return, he received large amounts of aid, while South Korean companies like Hyundai were encouraged to invest in the North. This was enough to stabilise the economy. Nevertheless, the famine continued for several years. It's estimated that up to three million people starved to death, while two-thirds of the children who survived it were stunted for life. In terms of the percentage of a country's population killed, it is considered the worst manmade famine in history.

Kim Jong-il did eventually oversee some liberalisation of the economy. People were allowed to open market stalls, and start companies that could trade with other countries, bringing in some much needed foreign currency. The regime also claimed (dubiously) to have made improvements in human rights. North Korea continued to be a pariah state, though, chiefly because of its nuclear weapons program, which dated back to the 1980s. Kim had agreed to abandon the program in 1994 in return for U.S. help in building two nuclear power plants, but evidence emerged in 2002 that it was on again. Kim, in a rare moment of candour for a dictator, told his officials to admit everything.

2002 was also the year that President George W. Bush, who never concealed his visceral hatred of Kim, made a State of the Union address in which he lumped North Korea, Iran and Iraq together in his 'Axis of Evil'. Some in the Bush administration argued that Kim should be assassinated, or a military coup against him encouraged. Others warned that the military men who would replace him would likely be even more aggressive. In the end, the decision was to wait and see, with many predicting that the North Korean regime would surely collapse in a few years anyway. This assumption was reinforced by the fact that Kim Jong-il had become an international figure of fun, a megalomaniac in a khaki jumpsuit who quaffed expensive French wines as his people starved — when he wasn't planning to turn Seoul into a "sea of fire", that is. The popular conception of Kim was captured in Trey Parker and Matt Stone's 2004 satirical puppet film *Team America: World Police*, in which Kim is seen in his Bond-villain-style lair, singing "I'm so ronery" and planning to blow up the world. There's no way that Kim, the movie fanatic, would not have seen this.

s Kim approached his sixtieth birthday, he naturally thought about the issue of succession, and few doubted that there would be a third generation of the Kim dynasty. Indeed, it seems that Kim may have been more interested in preserving the dynasty than his father's communist ideals. In 2000, the U.S. Secretary of State, Madeline Albright, travelled to Pyongyang to meet with Kim ("I was wearing heels, but so was he," she later wrote). Over dinner, he told her about the various political systems he had been studying, including that of Thailand, which he said he admired because it combined a strong monarchy with a market economy.

Kim's eldest son, Kim Jong-nam, was initially the favourite to succeed him. His mother was a movie actress who had become Kim's mistress in the 1960s, and he was considered intelligent, if somewhat dreamy. He faced embarrassment when he was detained with two women and a boy as they tried to enter Japan in 2001 — they were travelling on fake Dominican Republic passports and reportedly wanted to visit Tokyo Disneyland. The Japanese eventually released them, but after that Kim Jong-nam spent much of his time in Moscow and China and was rarely heard of.

The other two candidates for heir were the sons Kim had with his third wife, Kim Yong-suk, a former dancer whom he met when she performed at one of his parties in the 1970s. Little was known about Kim Chong-jol and his younger brother Kim Jong-un, apart from the fact that the former was an ardent fan of American baseball. In an interview on Japanese TV in 2003, Kim Jong-il's former sushi chef, Kenji Fujimoto, said that Chong-jol was a pleasant young man, but his father thought he was 'girly'. Jong-un, on the other hand, was mean, and Fujimoto confidently predicted that he would be the successor, a view shared by few North Korea

watchers at the time.

Kim Jong-il failed to make an appearance at celebrations for North Korea's sixtieth anniversary in September 2008, and rumours spread that he was either seriously ill or dead. It was eventually confirmed that he had suffered a stroke in August, and this was followed by a second, possibly more serious one in October. He appeared to make a full recovery though, and in April 2009 turned up at the Supreme People's Assembly, where he was unanimously re-elected president. Two months later came the first reports that Kim Jong-un had been anointed his successor.

Little changed during Kim Jong-il's last years. Huge numbers of people (the figure of 200,000 is often suggested) continued to languish in political prisons. North Korea continued to develop nuclear weapons and long-range missiles that could deliver them to mainland America. Kim also maintained the policy pioneered by his father of launching ad hoc, often baffling attacks on the South. In April 2010, for example, a 'suicide squad' in a submarine armed with torpedoes sank the South Korean frigate *Cheonan*, killing forty-six seamen. A few months later, a North Korean artillery unit shelled the South Korean island of Yeonpyeong, killing four. Why? No-one really knows.

Kim made official visits to China and Russia in 2011, travelling as usual in an armoured train (he had a fear of flying). He seemed to be firmly back in charge, but on 19 December, a tearful presenter on North Korean television announced that he had died of a heart attack two days earlier, while travelling on a train outside Pyongyang.

As with his birth, nature had something to say about his death. The North Korean news agency KCNA reported a strange red glow in the sky over Mount Paektu, while the ice on nearby Lake Chon cracked with a noise "so loud, it seemed to shake the Heavens and the Earth".

Kim Jong-il was a man of many contradictions. While he was often dismissed as a madman, others have seen him as a canny operator who consistently outfoxed his opponents. He spoke in a rapid, disjointed manner, the words tumbling over each other, and he was prone to mood swings and temper tantrums (he is said to have shot his barber when he messed up the famous bouffant hairdo). Yet foreign visitors who met him almost always spoke about how charming and solicitous he was — the perfect host. He was even capable of self-deprecating humour. Choi Eun-hee, the South Korean actress he had kidnapped, recalled Kim making fun of his image in the rest of the world. Striking a pose, he said, "Come on, Madame Choi, what do you think: How do I look? I'm small as a midget's turd, aren't I?" It's impossible to imagine any other dictator saying anything like that. On another occasion, Choi's husband, the film director Shin, was at one of Kim's drinking parties when members of the Joy Brigade became hysterical as they shouted "Long live the Comrade Dear Leader!" over and over again. Kim turned to Shin and said, "Don't believe any of it. It's all bogus, it's just pretence."

Kim's most interesting characteristic was his perception of himself as an artist. "I rule through music and literature," he liked to say. Such pretensions are not unusual among dictators, but this belief, and in particular his obsession with movies, seems to me to go to the core of his being. In his handbook on cinema, Kim wrote that, "in the socialist system, the director is not a mere worker but the Commander, the Chief who assumes full responsibility for everything, ranging from the film itself to the political and ideological life of those who take part". Kim wanted to control every aspect of life in North Korea in the same way.

First came the script. The Soviets worked on the first draft of it when they created the myth of Kim Il-sung as the

man who defeated the Japanese. Kim Il-sung added to it by proclaiming the appalling disaster of the Korean War a great victory. But it was Kim Jong-il who wrote the final draft, providing the cult of Kim Il-sung with all the trappings of a religion, including iconography, scriptures and rituals, and proclaiming North Korea the world's only perfect society.

North Koreans begin to learn the script almost from the moment they are born — indeed, the first words a baby is likely to utter are 'Kim Il-sung'. Children grow up reading books about the Kims as children, and for the rest of their lives, virtually every book they read, film they watch or song they hear will add a little more to the script.

All that is needed, then, is a stage on which the script can be performed, and that is of course Pyongyang, virtually the only part of North Korea that the rest of the world is allowed to see. Kim's model capital, full of empty streets and buildings, department stores stocking fake goods, and a carefully screened population capped at two million, is more a set than a real city. And it's the setting for Kim Jong-il's grandest and most enduring production, which you may see at least a few seconds of every year on the news. This is the Arirang Mass Games, originally conceived by Kim as a celebration for his father's sixtieth birthday in 1972, They are an annual, month-long extravaganza involving parades of military hardware and goose-stepping soldiers, spectacular displays of gymnastics, and tens of thousands of people creating vast murals of the Kims, missiles, slogans and other images by flipping cards with amazing, almost eerie precision. The people who perform in the games are chosen when they are as young as five, and spend virtually every day of the rest of their lives practising for them. What would happen to anyone who held up a card incorrectly doesn't bear thinking about.

NOTES AND SOURCES

Introduction

Atkinson, Michael, 'Hitler, Cineast', *The Believer*, issue 96, February 2013.

Kalder, Daniel, *Dictator Literature*, Oneworld: London, 2018.

Ullrich, Volker, *Hitler: Ascent 1889-1939*, Knopf: New York, 2016.

York, Peter, *Dictators' Homes*, Atlantic Books: London, 2005.

Daniel Kalder's *Dictator Literature* deserves a special mention here. Kalder took upon himself the unenviable task of reading a comprehensive selection of the writings of twentieth century tyrants, from Lenin's interminable theoretical diatribes to Saparmurat Niyazov's much sillier but equally interminable *Ruhnama.* It took him eight years and I'm surprised he was still alive by the end of it. His analysis of the books, and their authors, is unfailingly incisive and illuminating.

Benito Mussolini

Bosworth, R.J.B., *Mussolini*, Arnold: London, 2002.

Hibbert, Christopher, *Benito Mussolini*, Penguin: Harmondsworth, 1975.

Mussolini, Benito, *The Cardinal's Mistress*, Albert & Charles Boni: New York, 1928.

Mussolini, Rachele, *My Life with Mussolini*, Robert Hale: London, 1959.

Olla, Roberto, *Il Duce and his Women*, Alma Books: Richmond, 2011.

Smith, Dennis Mack, *Mussolini*, Weidenfeld: London, 1993.

I thought researching a figure as famous as Mussolini would be a doddle, but this turned out not to be the case. He was, and continues to be, such a controversial figure in Italy that the various accounts of his life are often driven by hidden agendas and wildly contradictory. The events leading up to his death are particularly murky. (Apparently ten or so men came forward over the years, claiming to be the partisan who had discovered Mussolini in the back of the van, dressed as a German soldier.) My account of these events is whittled down to the bare facts which his biographers agree on.

Bosworth's book is a dispassionate and detailed political biography which dispels many myths about the Duce. Hibbert's is rather perfunctory on the years of Fascist rule, but becomes more detailed as it goes on until it becomes an almost hour-by-hour account of Mussolini's end (although, as noted above, other biographers disagree with the details). As its title suggests, Olla's study focuses on the dictator's busy sex life.

Rachele Mussolini's ghost-written memoir predictably whitewashes its subject but is good for incidental deal.

Enver Hoxha

Fevziu, Blendi, *Enver Hoxha: The Iron Fist of Albania*, I.B. Taurus: London, 2016.

O'Donnell, James S, *A Coming of Age: Albania Under Enver Hoxha*, East European Monographs: Boulder, 1999.

Orizio, Riccardo, *Talk of the Devil*, Secker & Warburg: London, 2003.

Ruchala, Cali, 'Comrade Lulu and the Fun Factory', *Degenerate* No. 5, 2002.

Sweeney, John, 'Albania: spies and whispers', *GH*, September 1990.

Information on Hoxha in English was very scarce for many years. This was to some extent rectified with the publication of Fevziu's book, a very thorough political biography. Ruchala's sardonic article is also worth tracking down (it can be found on various websites) although it contains a number of factual errors.

Tony Hawks is a British musician and comedian whose books include *Round Ireland with a Fridge* (which is about him going round Ireland with a fridge). *One Hit Wonderland* (Ebury Press: London, 2003) tells the story of another bet he made — that he would have a top twenty hit in some country — any country — within two years. After various false starts he remembered the cult status Norman Wisdom has in Albania and wrote a song (with Sir Tim Rice, no less) for him to sing there. Hawks describes their trip to the country, where the eighty-seven-year-old Wisdom was mobbed like a member of a boy band wherever he went, and their song 'Big in Albania' reached number 18 on the charts.

When Wisdom died at the age of ninety-five, the then Albanian president, Sali Berisha, sent a letter of condolence to his family.

Mao Zedong

Benton, Gregor and Lin Chun, *Was Mao Really a Monster?*, Routledge: London, 2010.

Chang, Jung and John Halliday, *Mao: The Unknown Story*,

Jonathan Cape: London, 2005.
Dikötter, Frank, *The Cultural Revolution*, Bloomsbury: London, 2016.
— *Mao's Great Famine*, Bloomsbury: London, 2010.
— *The Tragedy of Liberation*, Bloomsbury: London, 2013.
Li, Zhisui, *The Private Life of Chairman Mao*, Arrow: London, 1996.
Marrin, Albert, *Mao Tse-Tung and his China*, Viking: New York, 1989.
Tsetung, Mao, *Quotations from Chairman Mao Tsetung*, Foreign Languages Press: Peking, 1976.
— Selected *Readings From the Works of Mao Tsetung*, Foreign Languages Press, Peking, 1971.
Terrill, Ross, *Mao*, Stanford University Press: Stanford, 1999.

Mao received a ridiculously positive press in the West for decades, starting with Edgar Snow's fawning *Red Star Over China* (1937). This was partly due to a lack of reliable information about conditions inside China, and partly due to the bias of biographers.

This began to change with the publication of *Mao: The Unknown Story*. Its co-author Jung Chang, who had been a Red Guard, had written the best-selling memoir *Wild Swans* (1992), and her *Mao* was a bestseller, too. It portrays its subject as essentially a monster from a young age, an amoral egotist who only ever acted in his own self-interest, schemed his way to the top of the Communist Party by betraying his colleagues, and relished the millions of deaths he caused. Running to over 650 pages, with some 150 pages of notes, it looks authoritative, but it actually succeeds in being something I would have thought impossible — it's too hard on Mao. At every point, his actions are interpreted in the worst possible light, and many of its assumptions are highly contentious. The book received overwhelmingly positive reviews in mainstream publications, but was roundly attacked by historians who noted that it played so fast and loose with its sources that it was impossible to check many of its claims. *Was Mao Really a Monster?* is a collection of academic responses to the book.

In recent years, archives in China have increasingly been opened up to foreign historians, and Frank Dikötter has made full use of them in his remarkable trilogy. Each of these books, which focus on the experiences of ordinary people, is a staggering catalogue of meticulously documented horrors. (The details I give about the outbreak of cannibalism in Wuxuan during the Cultural Revolution come from Dikötter.) If you want to know what it was like to live in Mao's China, these are the books you should read.

And if it's the more disgusting details of Mao's life you're after, Zhisui Li's remarkable memoir is the place to go.

François Duvalier

Abbott, Elizabeth, *Haiti: The Duvaliers and Their Legacy*, McGraw Hill: New York, 1988.

Buselle, Rebeca (ed), *Haiti, Feeding the Spirit*, Aperture: New Jersey, 1992.

Cussans, John, *Undead Uprising: Haiti, Horror and the Zombie Complex*, Strange Attractor Press: London, 2017.

Diederich, Bernard and Al Burt, *Papa Doc: The Truth About Haiti Today*, McGraw Hill: New York, 1969.

Ferguson, James, *Papa Doc, Baby Doc*, Blackwell: Oxford, 1988.

Haiti, it's like nowhere else! Official Visitors Guide, National Office of Tourism and Public Relations: Haiti, 1974.

Marquis, John, *Papa Doc: Portrait of a Haitian Tyrant*, LMH Publishing: Kingston, 2007.

Métraux, Alfred, *Voodoo in Haiti*, Andre Deutsch: London, 1959.

Whicker, Alan, *Within Whicker's World*, Coronet: London, 1983.

apa Doc is probably the most mythologised dictator in this book, by which I mean that there are a great many lurid tales told about him which are impossible to verify. Abbott's book is a case in point. It's billed on the cover as 'the first inside account', because Abbott was married to a hotelier in Haiti, and was the sister-in-law of Henri Namphy, who headed an interim Haitian government after Baby Doc fled to France. It's packed with details about Papa Doc's alleged voodoo practices, but most of this is hearsay.

Marquis's book is chaotically organised and appallingly edited, but is very good for local Haitian colour. Marquis was a journalist who spent time in the country, and even scored a rare interview with Papa Doc.

Cussans's book is a superb exegesis of the way that vodou (the preferred spelling among academics) and its tropes — in particular the figure of the zombie — have been appropriated in Western popular culture.

Graham Greene's novel *The Comedians* (1967) gives a vivid and grimly comic picture of life in Haiti under Papa Doc, and is highly recommended. Papa Doc tried to blame it for the collapse of the Haitian tourist industry.

Nicolae Ceaușescu

Almond, Mark, *The Rise and Fall of Nicolae & Elena Ceaușescu,* Chapmans: London, 1992.
Behr, Edward, *'Kiss the Hand You Cannot Bite'*, Penguin: London, 1992.
Sweeney, John, *The Life and Evil Times of Nicolae Ceausescu,* Hutchinson: London, 1991.
Pacepa, Ion Mihai, *Red Horizons,* Regnery: Washington, 2014.

The books by Almond, Behr and Sweeney were all written soon after Ceaușescu's fall, and benefit from the authors speaking to many of the players involved. There was a lot of arse-covering being done in the post-Ceaușescu era, however, so the accounts of certain events in these books don't always tally exactly. Behr's is the most detailed account, Sweeney's the most comprehensive on Ceaușescu's geopolitical scheming.

Pacepa's book is another proposition altogether. Written in the form of a diary of Pacepa's last few months in Romania before defecting, it's a thoroughly absorbing page-turner. Some questioned its veracity when it was published, suspecting an overenthusiastic American ghost writer, and it's true that it contains many pages of transcribed conversations which Pacepa could not have remembered in such detail, but the basic facts that he lays out have never really been disproven. John Sweeney, rather bizarrely, wrote that it is "a good contender for the title of sleaziest book ever written" (which suggests to me he needs to read more sleazy books). Presumably this was because of the tawdry details Pacepa revealed about the Ceaușescus, and it's true that his descriptions of a sexually-needy Elena, her bathrobe partially open, urging 'Nick' to come to bed, can make the reader's gorge rise. But this material fills only a few pages of a long book — and there are a lot worse things that could be said about Elena.

Jean-Bédel Bokassa

Decarlo, Samuel, *Psychoses of Power*, Florida Academic Press Inc.: Gainesville, 1996.

'Nostalgia for a Nightmare', *The Economist*, 25 August, 2016.

Orizio, Riccardo, *Talk of the Devil*, Secker & Warburg: London, 2003.

Titley, Brian, *Dark Age: The Political Odyssey of Emperor Bokassa*, McGill-Queens University Press: Quebec, 1997.

itley's book will probably remain the definitive account of Bokassa's rule. He tries to be scrupulously fair to the dictator, noting that the most lurid claims about him first appeared in French newspapers at a time when the French government was attempting to justify overthrowing him.

Ferdinand Marcos

Dent, Jackie, 'A Dynasty on Steroids', *Sydney Morning Herald*, 24 November 2012.

Fineman, Mark, 'Government Spares Huge Marcos Bust', *LA Times*, 8 March 1986.

Mijares, Primitivo, *The Conjugal Dictatorship of Ferdinand and Imelda Marcos*, Union Publications: San

Francisco, 1976.

Oliver, Amy, 'Imelda Marcos' famous collection of 3,000 shoes partly destroyed by termites and floods after lying in storage in the Philippines for 26 years since she exiled', *The Daily Mail*, 23 September 2012.

'Philippine blast wrecks Marcos bust', *BBC News*, 29 December 2002.

Rempel, William C., *Delusions of a Dictator*, Little Brown & Company: Boston, 1993.

Rotea, Hermie, *Marcos' Lovie Dovie*, Liberty Publishing: Los Angeles, 1984.

Seagrave, Sterling, *The Marcos Dynasty*, Harper & Row: New York, 1988.

Seagrave's book is a detailed examination of the rise and fall of the Marcoses. An American journalist, he is scathing about U.S. involvement in the Philippines. He also runs very hard with the idea that Marcos found Yamashita's Gold (he wrote another book entirely devoted to the subject). As I've noted, though, others dismiss the idea. My feeling is that Marcos probably did find some Japanese loot, but not nearly as much as Seagrave and others claim. Incidentally, on several occasions Imelda has said that Marcos found Yamashita's Gold (which is hardly surprising as it suggests their wealth wasn't entirely stolen from the Philippine people).

Mijares's dual biography is an impassioned denunciation of the Marcos regime, focusing on the martial law years. A year after Mijares's disappearance and probable murder, his sixteen-year-old son Luis received a phone call from a man who said his father was alive, and invited him to a meeting. He went. His body was found outside Manila horribly mutilated, his eyeballs hanging out, his hands, feet and genitals crushed.

Rotea was a Filipino journalist, and his book is based on

extensive interviews with Dovie Beams. It's a slapdash affair which appears to have been self-published, and gives more information about her affair with Marcos than anyone could probably want.

Rempel's book is built around extracts from Marcos's diary. As dictators rarely keep diaries, it is interesting to read these, though what they leave out is more instructive than what they contain.

Muammar Gaddafi

Blundy, David and Andrew Lycett, *Qaddafi and the Libyan Revolution*, Weidenfeld & Nicholson: London, 1987.

Cojean, Annick, *Gaddafi's Harem*, Grove Press: New York, 20013.

David, Moses, *The Basic Mo Letters*, Gold Lion: Hong Kong, 1976.

Gaddafi, Muammar, *Escape to Hell and Other Stories*, Blake Publishing: London, 1999.

Kawczynski, Daniel, *Seeking Gaddafi*, Biteback Publishing: London, 2011.

Oakes, John, *Libya: the History of Gaddafi's Pariah State*, The History Press: Stroud, 2011.

Pargeter, Alison, *Libya: the Rise and Fall of Gaddafi*, Yale University Press: London and New Haven, 2012.

scape to Hell and Other Stories gathers twelve 'stories' (which range from fables to rants) initially published in 1993, and four political essays. In some of them, Gaddafi damns the hollowness of the city while extolling the virtues of the village and the desert. He launches sarcastic attacks on Islamists, while in other pieces he is clearly

attempting to burnish his credentials as a great Islamic thinker. The writing is chaotic, disjointed and often baffling, which probably makes it one of the best insights you can get into Gaddafi's mind. An example of the style:

> *Muslims, without exception, are called to prayer, light and heavy armed. The full prayer will be given later on in this article. It was discovered only recently by means of cobalt rays, and helps the one who learns, teaches, or recites it to do away with all types of modern science, and especially applied sciences. How ridiculous we were when we caused schools, institutes, vocational training centres, and universities to spread through the country, and this also includes prefabricated and travelling schools...*

Idi Amin

Kamau, Joseph and Andrew Cameron, *Lust to Kill*, Corgi: London, 1979.
Kyemba, Henry, *A State of Blood*, Ace: New York, 1977.
Meladey, Thomas and Margaret Melady, *Idi Amin Dada: Hitler in Africa*, Sheed, Andrews and McMeel: Kansas City, 1977.

The Confessions of Idi Amin (Universal: London, 1978) by someone using the pseudonym 'Trevor Donald', consists of transcripts of interviews and taped conversations with Amin, plus diary extracts and even poems by him, which are all obvious fabrications. Some of it is quite amusing though. A sample Amin diary extract:

> *We need more entertainment here. This place needs a bit*

> *more life. I'll talk to David Frost and his people in England. They know how to put on stage shows and bring artists from all over the world to perform here. Perhaps a few singing shows, with pop stars like that Abba group from Sweden. They'd be real swingers, coming from Sweden. And that Rod Stewart with his beautiful white girl, Britt Eggland, or Eklund, or however she spells it.*

'Trevor Donald' went on to write *Idi Amin's Women* (Gazelle Books: Melbourne, 1978), which is equally ludicrous. ("Beautiful. Passionate, untamed…they gave their bodies to Africa's most evil man!")

Alan Coren's parody books are *The Bulletins of Idi Amin* (Robson Books: London, 1974) and *The Further Bulletins of Idi Amin* (Robson Books: London, 1975).

Saddam Hussein

Balaghi, Shiva, *Saddam Hussein: A Biography*, Greenwood Press: Westport, 2006.

Bennett, Brian and Michael Wieskopf, 'The Sum of Two Evils', *Time*, 25 May 2003.

Fineman, Mark and Sebastian Rotella, 'Bound by Blood and Torn by Rivalry', *The Times*, 23 July 2003.

Franchetti, Mark, 'Sadistic torture and murder just "a job" in Uday's regime', *The Australian*, 12 April 2013.

Goldenberg, Suzanne, 'Footballers who paid the penalty for failure', *The Guardian*, 19 April 2003.

Hussein, Saddam, *Zabiba and the King*, Virtualbookworm.com Publishing: College Station, 2004.

Karsh, Ephraim, *Saddam Hussein: A Political Biography*, Futura: London, 1991.

MacFarquhar, Neil, 'Saddam's Babylon: A Beloved

Atrocity', *New York Times*, 19 August 2003.

Makaya, Kanan, *Republic of Fear*, University of California Press: Berkeley, 1998.

McGeough, Paul, 'Storm over tyrant's unholy blood', *Sydney Morning Herald*, 18 December 2003.

Nixon, John, *Debriefing the President: The Interrogation of Saddam Hussein*, Corgi: London, 2017.

Sharrock, David, 'Saddam does battle with Nebuchadnezzer', *The Guardian*, 5 January 1999.

Scott, Shane, 'For dictator, a ravenous rise to rule', *Baltimore Sun*, 19 March 2003.

Wilkinson, Marian, 'Not mad, just bad and dangerous to know', *Sydney Morning Herald*, 16-17 November 2002.

There is still no definitive biography of Saddam Hussein in English. Of the works I have relied on, Karsh and Rautsi's is a solid study which ends with the Gulf War, and Balaghi's is a short but lively affair that takes the story up to Saddam's capture. Makiya's book is predominately a political study of the Ba'ath Party, but contains an interesting dissection of Saddam's strange handling of the Iran-Iraq War.

Nixon's *Debriefing the President* provides a marvellously up-close-and-personal account of Saddam after his downfall which shows that the old tyrant could turn on the charm when he wanted to. After weeks spent interrogating Saddam, Nixon returned to the U.S. and was invited to the Oval Office to give a report on him to President George W. Bush and Vice-President Dick Cheney. In Nixon's account of this, Bush comes across as every bit as clueless when it came to Saddam and Iraq as Saddam was clueless about America. He then goes further, spending almost two pages listing the similarities he perceived between the two leaders, e.g. they both lacked meaningful military experience, made military decisions based on political objectives, considered themselves great men, described themselves as "gut players"… The list goes on.

Kim Jong-il

Becker, Jasper, *Rogue Regime: Kim Jong Il and the Looming Threat of Nuclear War*, Oxford University Press: Oxford, 2005.

Breen, Michael, *Kim Jong-il: North Korea's Dear Leader*, John Wiley & Sons: Singapore, 2012.

Broinowski, Anna, *The Director is the Commander*, Penguin (Australia), 2015.

Jang Jin-sung, *Dear Leader*, Rider: London, 2014.

Fischer, Paul, *A Kim Jong-Il Production*, Viking: Great Britain, 2015.

Kim Hyn Sik, 'The Secret History of Kim Jong Il', *Foreign Policy*, September-October 2008.

'Kim Jong-il death: "Nature mourns" N Korea leader', BBC, 22 December 2011.

Maass, Peter, 'Dear Leader', *The Weekend Australian Magazine*, 29 November 2003.

Martin, Bradley K,. *Under the Loving Care of the Fatherly Leader: North Korea and the Kim Dynasty*, Thomas Dunne Books: New York, 2004.

Ryall, Julian, 'South Korean ship sunk by crack squad of "human tornadoes"', *The Telegraph*, 22 April 2010.

Takashi, Nada, *A Paean of Great Love: Kim Jong Il and the People*, Foreign Language Publishing House, Pyongyang, 1984.

NOTES AND SOURCES

For a country long considered the world's most enigmatic and opaque, there is now quite a lot of information about North Korea and the Kim Dynasty out there. Of the various books by defectors, perhaps the most interesting is Jang Jin-sung's *Dear Leader*. Jang was a writer who worked in Office 101 (yes, really) of the United Front Department, which advised on relations between the North and South. After writing a poem that Kim Jong-il admired, Jang had the rare privilege of meeting him. Later, he worked on an official biography of Kim, and was able to read many documents, and meet many key players, from the years when Kim was scheming to attain power.

Paul Fisher's *A Kim Jong-Il Production* is an engaging and very thorough account of the kidnapping of Shin Sang-ok and Choi Eun-hee. This is the closest you'll get to knowing what it was like to hang out with Kim Jong-il.

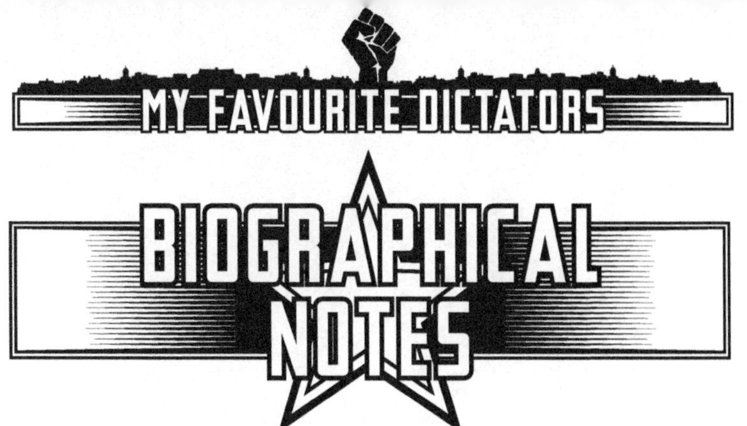

HRIS MIKUL has been clipping weird stories out of newspapers for as long as he can remember. He's been writing and publishing *Bizarrism*, Australia's longest-running zine, since 1986, and also produces *Biblio-Curiosa*, a zine devoted to strange fiction. His other books include *The Cult Files*, *Tales of the Macabre and Ordinary*, *The Eccentropedia* and *Bizarrism Vols 1* and *2.* He lives in the Sydney suburb of Newtown, home of many an eccentric, with his partner Cath.

LENN "GLENNO" SMITH is an art mercenary, paying the rent in Sydney with his wonderful wife Gina and the beginnings of an army of vengeful cats. He spends most of his time drawing wizards for doom bands and spikey lettering for bands that don't care if the text is legible or not. He teaches illustration, plays in a band called Chinese Burns Unit and can be found in a sitting position at his desk most hours of the day. Glenno is also making inroads into the dysfunctional world of fine art, curating and exhibiting in a vain hope to seem legit and adult… not to mention gathering cult-sized numbers of followers via Instagram. Consider his refreshing Kool-Aid at #glennoart.

HEADPRESS.COM